The Message is Murder

The Message is Murder

Substrates of Computational Capital

Jonathan Beller

PLUTO PRESS

First published 2018 by Pluto Press
345 Archway Road, London N6 5AA

www.plutobooks.com

Copyright © Jonathan Beller 2018

The right of Jonathan Beller to be identified as the author of this work
has been asserted by him in accordance with the Copyright, Designs
and Patents Act 1988.

The interview in the appendix is republished with thanks to *Kulturpunkt*
and their aim "to create an online and offline base of documentation
available to everyone and free for further use."

British Library Cataloguing in Publication Data
A catalogue record for this book is available from the British Library

ISBN   978 0 7453 3731 9   Hardback
ISBN   978 0 7453 3730 2   Paperback
ISBN   978 1 7868 0178 4   PDF eBook
ISBN   978 1 7868 0180 7   Kindle eBook
ISBN   978 1 7868 0179 1   EPUB eBook

Typeset by Stanford DTP Services, Northampton, England

Simultaneously printed in the United Kingdom and United States of America

For my students,
who so generously engaged

Racism, specifically, is the state-sanctioned or extralegal production and exploitation of group-differentiated vulnerability to premature death.

—Ruth Wilson Gilmore

Statistics is the science of distribution.

—Norbert Weiner

Contents[1]

Introduction

"A labyrinth of symbols," he corrected. "An invisible labyrinth of time."
—Borges

It's not information that wants to be free; it's us. *The Message is Murder* deduces from the informatic flux that informs the screen-mediated misrecognition endemic to the phrase "information wants to be free," the concept computational capital in order to track the background calculus of capitalized power as it restructures representation, finance, identity and sociality from the mid-twentieth century forward. Engaging in discrepant readings of Jorge Luis Borges, Alan Turing, Claude Shannon, Alfred Hitchcock and Karl Marx in a first section on discourse, informatics and the value-form, and in studies of photography, cinema and computation as deployments of a logistics of racialized and gendered domination in a second section, *The Message is Murder* analyzes the unthought formations of violence presupposed by and consequent upon the everyday functions of communication's media, media that are increasingly programmed and programmable—informatic.

It's not the brand that wants to free itself from the slave. To register the violence endemic to everyday transmissions, this book argues—and in its own way demonstrates—that the rise of information itself is an extension of the ongoing quantification and instrumentalization of the life-world imposed by early capitalism, and further that the abstraction of "information" and its mechanization as "computation" take place in the footprint of the calculus of the value-form and the leveraged value-expropriation of labor by capitalized industry.

The decline of the Fordist factory and the rise of post-Fordism make ambient computation the mise en scène of new types of work and new types of exploitation. This situation is most familiar today—if also poorly understood—as "digital culture." The fact that the worldwide generation of inequalities relies on the generation and intensification of discursive, visual and screen-mediated social difference resultant from its processing by "digital culture" is not an incidental factor in the rise of computational capital and its metrics of quantification but a key feature of its formation. Built on an axiomatics of racial inequality and gender inequality, today's codifications, abstractions and machines, far from being value-neutral emergences intelligible in some degree-zero history of technology, are rather racial formations, sex-gender formations, and national formations—in short, formations of violence. As we shall see, digital culture is built on and out of the material and epistemological forms of racial capitalism, colonialism, imperialism and permanent war. This violence is literally inscribed in machine architectures and on the bodies and lives of all who are other, particularly those of the Global South, and increasingly the rest. It is recapitulated and re-inscribed by the normal functioning of informatic machines under the protocols of computational capital—an assemblage that as with the name "digital culture," is once again indexed while being conceptually reduced when rendered in the vernacular as "the media."

Brief introduction to the study

The Message is Murder offers a sustained riposte to Marshall McLuhan's oft-repeated formulation "the medium is the message" which locates the primary significance of a new medium in its far-reaching transformation of the sense ratios and its secondary significance in the new practices its mediation of another (prior) medium's content makes possible. Here we see that the world-media system is a means to securitize violence. The book is written in a dissident relation to the burgeoning field of media studies and the deracinated technocratic imaginaries that too often inform its practices. It views the generalized stupidity, ignorance and psychosis as well as the criminal avarice and securitization of countries like the United States of America as screen products—direct results of cinema, television and computation functioning as media of capitalism. Both content fetishism and platform fetishism obscure the geo-political implantation of these media formations—an implantation that is inseparable from both political economy and coloniality. The forces that not only shape our intellect and imagination, but also have in fact become inseparable from what these are, create and indeed *are* the media infrastructure of capitalization. This text then, as a work of writing, of media theory, and necessarily, of financial counter-speculation, must go to some lengths to argue that informatic media formations neither emerge nor function in spaces without qualities, histories, or, for that matter, inequalities. This re-mediation means to say that math, science and information are not as is usually presumed value-neutral, degree zero conditions of emergence. To take the measure of today's machines and their constitutive operations, to understand the message that is our media, we must do more than focus on *technics*; we must attend to the surround.

In doing so, that is, in paying attention in one way or another to the colonized, the variously embodied and enminded, the possessed and the dispossessed, and, in general to the incorporation and erasure of what from the dominant standpoint appears as external to machines and to fixed capital today, I hope to demonstrate convincingly that most of what we currently think of as technologies, computing machines, and modes of abstraction are imbricated with social practices to such an extent that they themselves cannot properly be said to be stand-alone entities or platforms. Dominant technologies must therefore be seen as racial formations and gender formations as well as programs of capitalization. By this somewhat shocking claim (shocking, at least, to purists of all stripes—for what I am saying here suggests racist *machines* and not just racist academics, racist programmers and racist electorates) I do not mean to assert and do not assert anything ontological about race and gender. Rather, aim is taken at various forms of platform fetishism that draw artificial boundaries between the abstract or technical and everything else. This approach shows—*is designed to show*—that race, gender, media are co-constituents and co-constituted—in short, co-emergent historical formations. Unavoidably today, this co-emergence takes place within and indeed *as* the matrix of capital. Media theory cannot do without critical race theory or critique of political economy. In the current conjuncture, arguably no communiqué is exempt from a decisive relation to what Cedric Robinson rightly termed racial capitalism—or in the formulation I use almost synonomously, computational capital.[1]

The over-arching argument of *Message* is that "the media" as we now call them, are in large part developmental outgrowths of racial capitalism. As such, they (and in a rigorous sense, "we") are not only means of representation or communication, but means of production. To put this point even more directly, what go under the sign "media" today are in addition to whatever else they are, almost always means for value extraction and for the production and reproduction of inequality. It seems obvious, but inequality is neither just about income nor is it not about income; it is organized and enforced in a matrix of valuation that tracks and weights factors of whiteness, masculinity, geo-location, citizenship and much more. As this book endeavors to make clear utilizing a variety of attacks on traditional forms of understanding, dominant media formations—including, for example Claude Shannon's landmark mathematical theory of communication that underpins the capacity to assign numbers to linguistic signs, or, to give another example, the rise of photography—emerge directly out of formations of violence *already presupposed* and thus firmly rooted and re-incorporated in the social and in the imaginary. In their function these and other machines, abstract, concrete, cybernetic, with roots in the plantation, the factory, the colony, the patriarchal household, the university and the jail, reproduce and exacerbate inequality, oftentimes under the guise of a value-neutrality that tends to render their exploitative operations unconscious even if many of the resultant effects do not remain in the unthought, or the unfelt. As we shall see, chemistry, as in the case of photography, and statistics, as in the case of the mathematical theory of communication, cannot be separated from their social basis in racial violence. Suffering (the suffering of others) can never be fully separated from the fact of "Westernized" consciousness and thus logically from capitalizing mediation. Critical race media theory must make these connections.

It is in many ways remarkable that Marx's labor theory of value has not been widely recognized as being as important as Newton's theory of gravity. But then again, the orthodoxy of the church was less entrenched than that of capital. Indeed, as 1492 makes abundantly clear, Christian ideology was commandeered by capital as a platform. Ultimately, we must conclude, capital goes deeper than Christ. Consequently, just as Marx set out to reveal the dirty secret of the value form as dissymmetrical exchange between capital and labor, we find ourselves in the position of having to once again investigate that relation as it has mutated or evolved in relation to new machines of value extraction—those that operate on discourse or images by means of number—from within a context that does not perceive the universality of capitalist exploitation. Time and again it seems we must reinvent the wheel. Understanding the historicity of media formations and their (or, again, "our") current instrumental-ization of the *bios* is a matter not merely of intellectual history, or the history of technology; it is, in view of the argument made here, a matter of liberation, and, in the long view, of revolution. It is for this reason— the deferral of revolutionary justice—that I believe that *The Message is Murder* is particularly suited to the current conjuncture characterized by what, politically at least, looks like fascism. The revanchist return of the phallic pig as leader, this time, as leader of the "free world," with its racist and sexist id-grunts causing so much pain, is a systemic iteration—the output of an alien calculus capable of capturing and/or bypassing everyday intelligence. One is reminded here of the AI prosthetic composed of the old white man/corpse with a cable plugged into his open skull in China Miéville's *Perdido Street Station*. In response to the inter-facialization of power in such ghoulish form (and leaving aside for the moment the tremendous aesthetic repulsion generated by the mere faces of the white monsters in White Houses everywhere), this book is in dialogue with and is to some extent written by the long-standing protests and movements organized against inequality from multiple quarters on the left. Here, but polemically stated, not just here, race, gender, mediation, financialization, and exploitation are of a piece and must be thought together if a radical left is to reinvent itself in the rising geopolitical con-catenation of the many fascisms—what I think of as a new geopolitical form: fractal fascism interfacing what has become a kind of platform totalitarianism. This thinking of the separated (and indeed segregated) together, in terms suggested by the notion of an historical or planetary totality organized by computational media working as the fixed capital of the distributed social factory is a disturbingly difficult task given its profound importance. What is at stake in a critical race media theory is the very question of radical comprehensive transformation. The inertial structures of understanding, perception and semiosis inveigh against a concerted revolutionary praxis of theory, in part because of institutional pressures and conventions of "disciplines," and in larger part because these resources of the senses, the intellect, and the will are subsumed and automated in the operations and renderings of "technology" itself.

This latter issue of cognitive sumbsumption by ambient technology poses the problem of so-called common sense—particularly as technologies and the thoughts they script are increasingly vectors of capitalization. With media convergence and the rise of what I call Digital Culture 2 (DC 2) all prior media platforms: books, films, videos, photographs and even language itself, are being subsumed by computation. I say DC 2 because I argue in this book that what passes today for "digital culture" (and therefore as a kind of radical break) is actually digital culture 2.0. Global commodification, settler colonialism, the mercantile system, the middle passage, slavery, plantations, and industrial capitalism instantiated a first order digital culture (Digital

Culture 1 or DC 1) with universalizing aspirations through the globally expansive assignation of quantity to qualities from the early modern period forward. This earlier period of digitization had many names, most tellingly if also disavowingly perhaps, "Humanism," but its overarching operation was the (uneven) commodification of life. "Man," the new trump card that legitimated historically unprecedented forms of violence and genocide, was the measure of all things, but few thought to ask, what, was the measure of "man?" We no longer really have to wonder about the answer to that question since financial relations have so thoroughly and humiliatingly taken even *his* measure as a matter of practice. Those dispossessed of wealth cannot claim humanity and indeed "humanity" constitutes itself in and through the very dispossession of those who are denied communion in its sweetness and light. The legitimation of these relations of exploitation by which certain minority populations lord their humanity over the very people and peoples from whom they have procured it—precisely the peoples whom they have reduced in their own self-serving narcissism and psychosis to sub- and in-human status—are among the many pyrotechnics of the value form—one if its messages, you might say. Today media recreates Lords of humankind, as lords of the various media pathways to devaluation and dispossession. One technical effect among many, one message that inheres in the operations of "the media."

But even this ruse of humane sovereignty is collapsing from its internal contradictions. From airline accommodations to state proclamations, the civil veneer peels off, leaving only aggression, crass vindictive behaviour and bad manners. From a decolonizing perspective, the movement of "Humanism" (DC 1) to "Posthumanism" (DC 2), along with the rise of digital machines represents not a break but a shift in the granularity and scale of exploitation and struggle. Colonialism merely gives way to Computational Colonialism. "Man," formerly the subjective presentation of the universal value form of capital is an antiquated technology slated for replacement by a new order of colonization. Where for the subject "Man" the colonial world was perceived as populated by a sea of infantile sub-humans, in the post-human world, machine-dividuals perceive a matrix of images to be managed. Those of us who perceive that vital aspects of our extended being are enslaved, othered, black, see the master, whether embodied, machinic, affective, spatial, proprietary, algorithmic or whatever, as an alien presence, a body-snatcher. We strain ourselves to warn each other, "Get out!"

With that warning in mind, another of the fundamental theses informing this book is that discrete-state machines, that is, "computers," emerge in the footprint of problems scripted by the value-form. One could indeed argue this thesis by tracing the modern computer back to the brilliance of Charles Babbage and Lady Lovelace and their early nineteenth century efforts on "the analytic engine" and "the difference engine" to industrialize mathematical calculations via steam in order to save human labor in calculation. Or one could look to Marx's fragments on the machine that describe the fixed capital of industrialization as a "vast automaton." We might see clearly from these texts that the blueprint for modern computation already lay in the routinizing and bureaucratizing functions of the industrial machine as it applied not only to labor but to thinking, and as consequent from the suddenly apparent God-like power and range of machinic calculus following upon capital's "liberation of the productive forces;" their liberation, that is, from the producers. The "conscious organ" of the industrial machine, namely the worker, gives rise to the conscious organ of the post-industrial machine—you.

The expropriation of the worker's product meant and always means not just expropriated labor in a deracinated sense, but expropriated subjectivity—the early Marx's "sensuous labor." The mechanization of routine mental processes was a dream of both industry and computation. For capital, even in the industrial period, there was and remains a use-value for the development of metrics, the sytematicization of most efficient means, and the development of systems of account: the factory code, the streamlining of work-flow charts, the "one best way," Taylorization, and elsewhere "Fordism" or "Americanism," shows us that. "The one best way" set its sights on not just corporeal but on the cognitive function of the "trained gorilla." The expanding footprint of industrial capital required the mechanization and automation of the development not simply of machines of value extraction and disciplinary regimes of work through the by now traditional methods of wage-labor, but of the very methods and techniques of capital expansion: banking, management and communications infrastructure, monitoring of work-flow, inventory tracking, and the increasing integration of all human processes with methods of account: in short, cybernetics and information management. The overtaking of the icon "man" as the privileged point of subjectification by the new and astonishing agency of financialized intelligent machines reveals man for what it was—a now obsolescent platform of the operating system of heteropatriarchy and racial capitalism during DC 1.

Additionally, when bureaucratic (scientific) management becomes an industry in its own right, information becomes the general name for its product, its medium. The stuff we call "information," though ostensibly ahistorical, has a history—we are only beginning to discover how important that history is. For this book however, in order to expose certain aspects of information that are generally unacknowledged, I will rely not on industrial history, nor strictly speaking on the history of information theory, but upon various mid-twentieth century accounts of information that show it to function homologously to valuation. In historical hindsight the glimmers of an emergent informatics can be quite clearly apprehended as the direct and necessary elaboration of aspects of the operation of the value form in domains from which it was historically excluded but nonetheless needed to be colonized if the algorithm of profit was to continue its do or die expansive course. As will be indicated, the story of information is the story of the financialization of the formerly extra-economic domains including culture, communication and cognition. Information becomes the privileged medium of capital's message.

As with the argument that contemporary media are media of racial capitalism, I will be less invested here in offering a historical proof that information evolves in the footprint of the value form and more interested in deploying the argument as a heuristic device. If these two arguments: 1) that contemporary media are media of racial capitalism and 2) that information evolves in the footprint of the value-form, explain multiple phenomena better than other schemas, if they offer unexpected connections and provide new possibilities for thought, research and action, I will consider the arguments made.

Informatics implies the generalization of a quantifiable environment, an environment quantifiable in principle and one that opens everything in its purview not only to mathematical analysis but to a computable calculus of risk/reward, that is, to statistical analysis and to capitalist exploitation. It opens, in short, a new territory extending to all scales of space and time. It penetrates and surveys the colonial surround while inventing new forms of employ. As we shall see, "information" is not just "a difference that makes a difference" as Gregory Bateson famously suggested, it is a dialectical advance of the calculus of the value-form as historically worked up in the organization of the life-world by the system of abstractions short-handed as "capital," innovated in order that the financialization of all that appears, has appeared or could ever appear becomes historically possible, historically probable. The difference that information makes is in the first and last instance a social difference: revising Bateson, information is the difference that makes a social difference.

The development of digital metrics of account—discrete state machines and their many affordances—are in fact new ways of pricing what are effectively the productive and reproductive metabolic activities of socio-historical life. Along with that comes the invention of new forms of work and new modes of valorization. One could hope for more from critical theory than simply finding out that as a new condensation of social logic the Facebook "like" is a pinnacle of human achievement—and it would be overhasty to conclude that the present regime of financialization exhausted the possibilities that inhere in the paradigm of information, just as it would be overhasty (or at least pointless) to conclude that there was no hope for a planet playing host to the virulent, material intelligence of computational capital. But, for there to be some new, salient hope, we must clearly mark the transformation of labor (attention economies, neuro-power), of the value-form (derivatives, web-based "likes," crypto-currencies), of fixed capital (social-media, computers, codifications of race and gender through encoding skin, fashion, bodies, minds, religions and regions) and of accumulation strategies (media companies, sovereign debt, border walls, spectacle, clouds)—as symptoms of DC2 and its far reaching liquidation of tradition … and of traditions, and we must solemnly note, of many of the people who had and still have them. "We" must begin to reckon with historical tragedies and crimes, as well as with ongoing tragedies and crimes as precisely the racial, gendered, nationalist formations of violence that inhere in what we think of simply as "technologies."

Though it may be as obvious as it is troubling to point this situation out, in some circles it is still necessary to underscore as significant that there are those whose chances of liquidation are for programmatic, but nonetheless historical reasons, proportionally higher. Witness the brilliantly statistical ring to Ruthie Gilmore's widely cited definition of racism: "Racism, specifically, is the state-sanctioned or extralegal production and exploitation of group-differentiated vulnerability to premature death."[2] What are the media of this calculus and what are their histories of formation? In this text we will find that racism, in addition to being state-sanctioned, extra-judicial, institutionalized and otherwise legitimated is machine-sanctioned, data-visualization-sanctioned, and financialization-sanctioned as well. As statistically mediated, racism is part of what became "the science of distribution."[3]

From this description of a relationship between financialized machine-media and "group-differentiated vulnerability to premature death," the reader may perceive in outline the overarching media theoretical claim that informs this book: Racial Capitalism plus the notion of informatics as an extension and intensification of the dynamics of the value form diagrams a rudimentary notion of what I call Computational Capital. This term means not just capitalism as a computer, nor simply capitalism with or by means of the digital computer, it means capitalism as a digitally enabled program of accumulation and dispossession; capitalism as the deployment and intensive development of algorithms of inequality.

Digitization as we know it and live it is inseparable from financialization, informationalization and statistical analysis, and inseparable again from the imposition of standards of normativity and deviance that encode and thus over-determine the semiotic parameters of bodily phenotype, geo-location, gender and sexuality, among many other variables. As Robin Kelley explains in "Thug Nation: On State Violence and Disposability," and as Katherine Mckittrick, drawing on Simone Browne shows in "Mathematics Black Life," archives, metrics, words, and mass media representations, are the result of and repository of racial violence, and they reproduce racial violence.[4] If digitization results in what Matteo Pasquinelli has called "algorithmic governance" and what Benjamin Bratton terms "platform sovereignty,"[5] then the rise of DC 2 means a new stage of colonization. These descriptors, it must be emphasized, are ways of talking not about information in the abstract, but about the current form of *capitalist* society, where "control," as Sebastian Franklin calls it, has been submerged into the material operations of apparatuses, without any necessary alleviation of inequality. Rather than seeing an abatement of racism in the play of "color-blind" technologies, we experience its automation. What I am calling computational colonialism means an extractive and violent mediation at scales ranging from the sub-atomic to the planetary that result in the devaluation and dispossession of people(s). It is presided over by in/post-humans (though for the satisfaction of some "humans"). "Platform totalitarianism" more accurately reflects my own view of a systemic aspiration that must be fought at every turn; it flags the degree of capture and the multiple foreclosures organized by statistical analysis and confronted by what we used to call, in its most general term, life.

The "financialization of everyday life," the emergence of what Randy Martin terms "the society of risk," the submitting of all possible acts to a cost-benefit analysis (do I dare eat a peach?), all emerge by means of digitization—a digitization that has a long history of recursivity in relation to social practice. Real needs are addressed, but at a price, and as the mesh of valuation expands and becomes finer, neither the rewards nor the costs are evenly distributed. Norbert Weiner's definition, "statistics is the science of distribution," fails to mention that this science is a social science, or that it is directly relevant to political economy, though Weiner was acutely aware that this science would have consequences on both. The incessant development of digital technologies from monetary instruments to quantum computing has meant the intensification, along with the miniaturization and macro-expansion not just of machinic or computational apparatuses, but of financializing logics. In their shattering of the traditional notions and indeed categories of subjects and objects these developments, when taken together, appear as a kind of culmination of post-structuralism and postmodernity—bringing about by material means the disappearance of the referent by simulation in an economy of "likes." From the perspective of information, there are no subjects or objects left, only strategically constituted networks and virtual realms. The computational calculi of capital, already operative in the accounting systems of the industrial factory (the calculus of the commodity) or the cinema (the calculus of the image), have scaled up and scaled down several orders of magnitude and have co-evolved with the dynamism of geopolitical history (of domination and of struggle) organized in strict accord with the law of profit to create crowdsourcing, swarms, programmable images, augmented and virtual "realities," neurological, affective and libidinal strip mines. The metrics of valuation now accompany nano-shifts in affect and perception—each new attentional-communicative possibility is also a financial exploit. These social practices of production and consumption (both as domination and as struggle) that have for a long time now been part of the passion play of the dialectic have, over the course of this history, been sedimented into ideologies, institutions, perceptions and machines such that the resolution of financialized metrics are increasingly fine grained. Today dialectically advanced systems of control lay heavy upon the planetary *bios*. Capital: You want to talk to your fellow humans? It's going to cost you. You want to tweet your revolution? That's fine so long as your neuronal function helps the platform make money for my shareholders. You want to get rid of "man?" No problem, welcome to networked computing! With the colonization of communication, the means to an end logic imposed on work by mandatory wage labor has become the means to a means to an end imposed on discourse and images by mandatory unwaged labor (paid in informatic-social currencies such as likes). We work to communicate to commune but must do so in a circuit of graduated expropriation. The abstract end that was living recedes even as the concrete end of living approaches. Hope is giving way to Armageddon. For many the latter is fast approaching; and for many it is already here.

There is a logic here, a media logic to this semio-material system, and it is operative in the materiality of societies and their machines. Simply put, the logic is to use meaning for the purposes of accumulation and dispossession beyond all possible meaning. The abstractions of capital and indeed what now appears quite clearly as its algorithmic character emerge historically through the very concreteness and materiality of its history—its globally distributed productions and reproductions. This history, resultant in the planetary crisis for environments, migrants, the impoverished, the colonized, the enslaved, people of color, women, people who are gender non-conforming, those who are prisoners of men, of machines and of states, is all one with the full-blown realization of computational capital. What remains and/or exceeds all this digitality also happens to be "our" history—or at least what is left of it.

The book

The first part of *The Message is Murder* is effectively a long, improbable essay on different aspects of information. It is divided into five sections. The focus is the relationship between information and linguistic function and the attendant shattering of language-based ideas about humanism, philosophy and value. I endeavor to show that the conversion of difference (social difference, but then, what difference that makes a difference isn't social?) into information recapitulates historical forms of racialized and gendered violence and makes the world over in a form—puts it "in-formation" as Laurie Anderson might say—functionalized for a new order of capital. In brief, the informationalization of life and nature was an extension of the violence of its instrumentalization under the rationality of capitalism: Information appears as a formalization and encoding of practices of violence and violation, an ever more granular extension of the violence of abstraction under capitalism into the cosmos.

The second part of *Message* is a re-viewing of the seeming mess of visuality and visual technologies pre- and post-discrete state machine, undertaken with an understanding that the visual field can be retrospectively understood as being prepared as a domain of data-visualization. Visual and semiotic infrastructures for attentional production and the metrics thereof were being built by pre-Digital 2 images and apparatuses. Many of the structures and conventions of visuality developed and in some respects "perfected" by the still camera and the cinema will be imported wholesale and to a large extent unconsciously into machinic digitization and data visualization—a fact that implies that psycho-dynamics associated with visuality and the scopic are increasingly incorporated into a cybernetic system. Cinema is discussed in relation to the emergence of what I describe as pathologistics of perception and the photographic camera is analyzed as a machine of racialization. The final section positions the contemporary visual interface, or data-visualization, as a decisive worksite of computational capital running on informatic labor.

Part I of *The Message is Murder* understands the rise of informatics by considering its effects on aspects of linguistic operation. The dynamic play introduced by the incipient coupling of semiotics and informatics is surfaced through a consideration of Antonio Gramsci and Marshall McLuhan in Chapter 1, and detailed through analysis of the following: In Chapter 2, narrative structure and the codification of race in Borges; Chapter 3, thinking in drag in Alan Turing; Chapter 4, mathematical transcoding of discourse in Shannon and a related algorithmic repression and psychosis with respect to the qualitative life-world in Hitchcock; and in Chapter 5, the value-form as proto-informatic communication in Marx, particularly as computed in the function known as "price." The readings offered here are by necessity limited, and as emphasized, not those that a historian of technology might choose, however, they have been selected to underscore key aspects of the generalization of information and computation as they overcode the *socius*, transform the quotidian, and ostensibly separate process (and processing) from historical violence. Atypically given these fairly canonical materials and media-theory-type concerns, the analysis is attendant to race, gender and class—indeed these forms of social difference that will be encoded such that they make a difference are shown to be inseparable from the emergence and ultimate hegemony of computational capitalism. It will be shown that though information is a difference that makes a difference, this difference is, in any and all instances, social after all. Social differences are understood as co-evolving informatic vectors that, as historical results of prior regimes, are abstracted, encoded, recoded and re-inscribed on bodies in various ways: social, structural, military, carceral, epistemic, cybernetic, biometric, ideational computational etc. Information striates the field dominated by computational capital and exploits all domains through the creation, intensification and measurement of differences. The analysis here allies itself with the fact of struggle generally speaking, as well as to specific moments and modes of struggle against a virulent informational enclosure of peoples' futurity, aspiration, happiness, and living. In other words, the analysis is informed by an insurrectionary and subaltern relation to the hegemony of the capitalist overcode and its prolix forms of capture. This subaltern perspective allows us to glimpse something of extreme importance: *information emerges in the footprint of the value-form and is an extension of its functionality.* Computation, it will be shown, turns out to be financialization by other means. Communication, or what Charles Sanders Peirce calls "joint-acting," is the raw material of both.[6] This linking of communication to computation by means of information and financialization poses an urgent question for these times: If everyday communication results in the everyday murder of subalterns, how do we send a different message?

Part II of *The Message is Murder* makes the link between visuality and information by exploring the organization of the visual field in terms of social difference and the dialectics of attention vis-à-vis the machinic organization of the gaze. Chapter 6 considers photography as fundamentally a technique of graphing and fixing skin, and locates its antecedent form in slavery and the optics of racism ("the color line") of the early nineteenth century. It reads Barthes' *Camera Lucida* and the inquiry into "the essence of photography" offered there, as an elaborate utilization of a tropology of race deployed as a basis to make presumably value-neutral technical claims about the unique features of a medium. Chapter 7 takes the rise of the attention economy and cinema's productive organization of attention for capital as axiomatic, and then explores several of the paradigmatic consequences of the extraction of attention by visual machines. Historically speaking this absorption of human sensual capacities by mechanization results in the loss of gesture (Chaplin), the loss of sensibility (Wells) and psychosis (Hitchcock). Chapter 8 shows that cinema, like photography, profitably fixes agents as objects and then as targets by means of machine-mediated attention to strategically confer scripted forms of agency on spectators. This agency is built atop a deadly disavowal and oftentimes denial of black life and the life of numerous (and fungible) others. In a subsequent moment (analytically considered), spectators identified with the value-form (white, patriarchal, capitalist) are themselves dispossessed of much of the product of their attention. The loss of the power of thought and decision automate historical racism and psychosis in and as the drone. The drone-subject is at once prosthetic extension of the white-supremacist, capitalist gaze and paradigmatic symptom of what Donna Haraway called "the informatics of domination." Taken together, these pathologistics of cinemated looking reveal important aspects of the optics, psycho-dynamics, economics and informatics of speculative value extraction in the visual domain alongside their murderous and extractive consequences. At bottom, we confront an extractive cybernetic system of representation, floating atop the negation of racialized and gendered others, particularly, but not exclusively the Black, the Native, the Woman, the other. Chapter 9 analyzes the formalization of these specular and discursive relations as means to extract informatic labor and proposes a modification of the labor theory of value adequate to the age of computational capital. This new formulation rewrites the general formula for capital, M-C-M', as M-I-C-I'-M', where I is image and C is code. This, it turns out, can be rewritten more concisely as M-I-M', where I is information.

PART I

Informatics of Inscription/Inscription of Informatics

Gramsci's Press: Why We Game

Anyone who makes a prediction has in fact a "programme" for whose victory he is working, and his prediction is precisely an element contributing to that victory ... because reality is the product of the operation of human will to the society of things (the machine operator's to his machine).

—Antonio Gramsci[1]

An injunction to game

Communicative acts are directly or indirectly inscribed on desubjectified bodies. The extent of this desubjectification varies, but it follows racial, gendered, financial and national logics, among others; and in many cases approaches or achieves radical exclusion, extreme dis-mediation and social death. Surprisingly perhaps, computation, understood now in accord with the logic of media convergence to be the ultimate medium of communication, is not simply ancillary to this process of inscribing the messages of others on living bodies, but the very means by which this process has achieved a new level of efficiency, inexorability and hegemony.

Simply put, global communication and information processing utilizes planetary dispossession as its substrate. All of our high-tech communiqués are written on the backs of modern slaves. This book included.

How did this situation, in which it is statistically likely that your very utterance (whatever you might say) not only depends upon radical dispossession but also reinforces impoverishment and environmental degradation, come to pass? *The Message is Murder* endeavors to sketch an answer.

The strategy of *The Message is Murder* is a selective decoding of various moments of encoding: a consideration of the tips of various icebergs in what is very loosely a field called media studies that when considered together begin to tell a different history of four seemingly separate domains: capitalism, racialization, gender formation and information.

Western Marxism's poor record in relation to decolonization, blackness, critical race studies and queer activism, and the seemingly autonomous emergence of cybernetics and computation make these ostensibly separate sectors of social transformation known as capital, race, gender and informatics unlikely bedfellows at first glance. Capital, race, gender and information have been most often considered separately and in relative if not complete isolation from one another. But a second look informed by anti-racist, feminist, queer, postcolonial and indigenous struggles to understand that what is called "convergence" indicates not just media convergence (the fact that audio, video and text can all be digitized), but rather a total informatic convergence in which financial, biometric, and computational operations are increasingly unified. This convergence has a brutal history as well as dire implications.

A near total and becoming totalitarian convergence comes about because what we currently call digital culture is actually the second digital culture built atop a first order digitization by a racial capitalism that included colonialism, slavery, hetero-patriarchy and industrialization. The commodity form, which imposed an exchange value on every use-value, was already the incipient digitization of the *bios*. In dictating the exact dimensions of the slave ship cargo hold during the Middle Passage and in pricing the slave on the Mississippi auction block, this digitization of living persons and their qualities lay its representational code upon bodies. Price, it turns out, was a digital message, though not the only one. The horrifying example of the slave ship's hold, designed for maximum profits reveals the imposition of digital metrics on bodies, and here specifically on African bodies, on black bodies, with flagrant disregard for their person. It shows the convergence of a digital calculus on space, on movement, and on bodies and the ability of this calculus to marginalize or eliminate any sympathetic relation. This convergence results in an impossible-to-apprehend unmaking of black bodies, their reduction, as Hortense Spillers writes to "flesh," and their reconstitution by an unimaginable history of violence that gets reified as "race."[2] The media of commodification was also a message. Yes, money clearly, but so much else too that we are still at pains to decode.

What happens in the digital ether is not, as we have been sold, immaterial, fully abstract, or free, but rather ineluctably linked to the material conditions of the info-sphere's emergence and sustenance, and that in a way that includes all those externalities known (and indeed, unknown) as "the environment." This "environment," an externality from the standpoint of capitalism (Sean Cubitt, as we shall see shortly, has taught us to understand "the environment" as itself the symptom of a colonial logic), may and does take the form of forests, rivers, animals and people. Logically then, the included excluded of computational capital process may include not only forests and peoples but sectors of your mind that very possibly you thought were somehow exempt from finan-cialized digitization. The breaking news is that they're not. Vast swathes of our outsides and of our insides are within the enclosure of computa-tional capital's number crunch. That capture too is part of the message of *The Message is Murder*. In the domains traversed by messages, we play the odds or we get played.

The discrete laws of chance

Metrics are developed in relation to concrete practices with concrete goals in mind. The continuous amortization of consciousness through its sedimented encryption in the very techniques and instruments of rationality, not only as commodities for direct sale but as factories, machines, archives, the digital computer, data profiles, likes is the condition by which subjective practices are converted into fixed capital and their measure taken. If the factory floor, the slave ship's manifest, the spread sheet, the stock exchange and also the book, the cinema, television and electronic computation testify that the last seven centuries have approached a state in which, the medium is (the media are), in the most general sense capital, then so too is the message. Generally speaking then, messages are determinations of capital.

McLuhan's pithy phraseological condensation gave us a premonition that from a systems point of view, the hard distinction between medium and message was fast evaporating. A growing awareness of mediation suggested that beyond any particular affordance of an instance of com-munication, a systemic shift in the sense ratios and in the organization of society was brought about by any new transmission process—and that such ecological changes were ultimately more significant than any message in particular. "The medium is the message," sounded mysterious because it flew in the face of hermeneutics, referentiality and common sense. It heralded a new ontology from a future profoundly organized by media. The phrase was not just a historical insight into print and the epistemic and sensual instantiations of print culture suddenly made analytically available by the waning of print with the rise of electronic culture. It was also a prediction and therefore a program. Media platform shifts and the proliferation of new media suddenly made it apparent that human societies were, in Regis Debray's significant term, "mediological," and that as had been noticed with increasing frequency by philosophers, psychoanalysts and language theorists, there was no im-mediate access to anything like reality or truth. McLuhan's brilliant intuition at the dawn of the electronic age was that the long dominant and now disappearing print-media and, more particularly, the segmentation of language by moveable type lay the groundwork for shifts in perception, literary form, industrialization, finance, subjectivity and the scientific revolution. This insight into the consequences of breaking continuous flow into differentiable segments insisted upon and convincingly demonstrated the widespread collateral effects of a medium precisely at a moment when print was becoming one medium among many. This constellation of socio-cultural shifts identified by McLuhan's sudden awareness of the specificity of print is undeniable, but was it really print, as McLuhan gloriously argues in his consideration of "the Gutenberg Galaxy" that got linear history steaming forward? Or was print already an emergent medium of capital?

We are sympathetic with McLuhan's effort to give a non-capitalist accounting, but we also recognize that one must account for capitalism to do this well. Thus attention must be directed to capitalist mediation. The summation of subjective activity (sensuous labor) that produced the commodity (any commodity) became a medium not only for capital, but also for the development of capital. Labor merged with communication and workers' energy was absorbed wholesale. But from the standpoint of capital expansion, the particulars could be damned. Like Claude Shannon's mathematical theory of communication, capital's exchange-value was "content indifferent" so long as it increased. This relationship of indifference to content, shared between base 2 communication and capital as they shattered and fragmented traditional social media is no mere analogy. In considering the general formula for capital, $M-C-M'$ (where $M'>M$), we will see that McLuhan's most famous phrase, "the medium is the message," was made precisely of and for *that* medium, namely capital, even if he did not recognize it.

In a society organized and indeed governed by profit algorithms, lived social formations and technologies also lose their hard distinction. If it be granted that boundaries between media and message along with those between technology and social form blur, then this dissolution of objects and agents also applies to genre problems of theory and narrative. For if, as argued here, the medium is at once capital and the message, then logically the message as capital poses a real dilemma for revolutionary consciousness and revolution. Theory must seek to outmaneuver the programmed logistics of the sign aware, as it must be, that its principle affordances have been subsumed by capitalist production. With this problem made explicit, the reader of *Message* should consider themself hereby warned that some odd passages await them—indiscrete passages at odds with the laws of chance.

The general shift in the modality of the dispensation of sensuous labor time—its emerging combinations with semiotics, informatics and computation that colonize language and thought—requires a poetico-theoretical exploration of social-media (written with a hyphen) and of the new world-historical situation of the global organization of production and value extraction. The anti-capitalist account considers distributed production, the re-organization of space, time, bodies, senses and consciousness, new modes of exploitation and new strategies of accumulation, layered, it must be said on top of the old modes and strategies, some of which have been conveniently brought up to date. Brought up to date, at least, from the perspective of "The Lords of Things as They Are"—as "the father of cybernetics," Norbert Wiener, designated the ruling class in 1948. The persistent forms of domination that underlie new media and its cybernetics include settler colonialism, plantations, factory work, military and prison industrial complexes, migrant labor, forced migration, detention centers, camps, contemporary forms of enslavement, genocides. What type of poetry can disrupt all that?

Among the foundational insights of early cybernetics and information theory was the understanding of historical social relations in terms of systems of communication. In his search for insights into feedback and recursivity, Wiener observed numerous natural and social phenomena including among his observations of nature the mongoose and its battle with the rattler. From his social observations he clearly grasped the necessity of the control of communication as a means of governance:

Thus small, closely knit communities have a very considerable measure of homeostasis; and this whether they are highly literate communities in a civilized country or villages of primitive savages.

Strange and even repugnant as the customs of many barbarians may seem to us, they generally have a very definite homeostatic value, which is part of the function of anthropologists to interpret. It is only in the large community, where the Lords of Things as They Are protect themselves from hunger by wealth, from public opinion by privacy and anonymity, from private criticism by laws of libel and the possession of the means of communication, that ruthlessness can reach its most sublime levels. Of all of the anti-homeostatic factors in society, the control of communication is the most effective and important.[3]

Ruthlessness, then, is a means to volatility, and volatility (anti-homeostatic opportunity) is to be correlated with the centralized control of communication. The Lords of Things as They Are do not leave chance to chance. We will see this ruthlessness again in Borges, and it goes a long way to explaining anti-poetic phenomena such as ISIS, POTUS and derivative finance. Necessarily, then, this text before you, entering, as it must into nothing less than a regime of communication, is also a negotiation of practices of inscription. Ye olde poético is upon us, like it or not, for the discursive field is increasingly organized by algorithms of chance management. Utterance, positioned as standing reserve by ambient computation (the electronic replacement of homogenous segmentation in print culture), scripted in advance, generative like much of metabolism itself of swathes of data and meta-data for capture, is largely programmed for capitalist harvest. The book worth reading, sentenced to serve as an advertisement for itself, must seek to do more than merely to accomplish its own turnover.

The processes of inscription, description, prescription, subscription, ascription, conscription, layered and intercalated with the older techniques of expropriation and control and common to all forms of textualization, were for much of the twentieth century, generally understood as more or less connected to institutionalized practices of writing (pedagogy, the canon, the press, ideology, the law), but are today to be seen as at once informatic and directly related to digital technologies. Digitization, and more explicitly capitalist digitization, already begun by means of the commodity form and double entry bookkeeping, explodes to subsume all prior analogue mediations. We are still living through this mathematical and indeed political process and any analytic endeavor to take the measure of this result must also take the measure of its own strategy of engagement with the informatic field. "In every from of society there is a particular [branch of] production which determines the position and importance of all the others, and the relations obtaining in this branch accordingly determine those in all other branches."[4] Concisely and in accord with their own financial interests, the business pages of today's "newspapers" identify as ascendant that "particular [branch of] production," that is definitive in Marx's sense, as "Tech." Of "Tech" we may observe that "the relations obtaining in this branch accordingly determine those in all other branches." The tech industry is in fact the media industry and looking at the business pages with this in mind reveals that almost every story in the typical business section of the *New York Times* is in one way or another about media. Increasingly this is true of almost every story in the *New York Times*. As if in unconscious confirmation of McLuhan, media is constantly reporting on itself in order to say the message is the media. This fact underscores that computational media have become the command and control platform for all other industries and indeed for social life. We remind ourselves that this medium of information management inexorably functions through the writing and unwriting of 1s and 0s: through the production and reproduction of writing and of other writing machines—very possibly including ourselves. Weiner's prescient comparison between machinery that could learn and self-reproduce and "a virus [that] guides into its own form other molecules of the same virus out of the tissues and juices of the host"[5] in 1961 meant that the writing of 1's and 0s, implied the production of machinery that could both learn and reproduce itself out of what chanced by. Because we know that computation has saturated life in all its pores, and because we know that computation is the sine qua non of contemporary financialization—a financialization that has also colonized life—we observe that such viral machinery, with a capacity to learn through accumulation, storage and retrieval of knowledge has expanded to absorb writing and all other social practice. Who or what wrote that program?

Where the machine operator struggles to avoid being posited as chicken

Gramsci's machine operator who applies their will to the machine to produce reality is, in addition to an image of the factory worker on the assembly line, also an image of the prisoner/writer Gramsci himself. Negotiating political history, industrialization, fascism, and the miserable living conditions that included deprivation of freedom, health, and the constant oversight of the prison censor, Gramsci worked his machine to bring "the philosophy of praxis" or, in a word he could not write, "communism," into the world. The machine operator at his machine is both the assembly-line worker putting their subjective labor-time into the commodified factory object and the intellectual encoding predictions with a language-machine. It is writing—at once—as part of a program and as programming. The revolutionary programmer required what Gramsci called "the dual perspective," half animal and half human like the centaur, bound at once to an individual moment and a universal moment: "the more an individual is compelled to defend his own immediate physical existence, the more will he uphold and identify with the highest values of civilisation and of humanity, in all their complexity."[6] Nearly foreclosed by the accidents of history, the imprisoned intellectual, programming on a machinified language, seizes history's highest aspirations—as a weapon.

Gramsci, the machine-operator's image of the machine operator, speaks to the sedimentation of inequality in modern modes of creativity and thought, a sedimentation that is increasingly manifest in the vectors of force and manufactured consent mediated by our machines. The prison intellectual confronts the social mechanism, and the odds weigh heavily against them. Inequality sediments into and indeed informs machine-mediated thought, writing as always already cybernetics, as word processing, as organizing language function, navigating mass and computational media—manifesting the embattled AI that is us. The writer-machine is part of the structure of governance (and what is now algorithmic governance). We must take seriously Marx's insight that the sedimentation of dead labor as the machinery of fixed capital is also the sedimentation of alienated subjectivity and history directly utilized to further exploit the living labor of the worker. We must consider the writer—the writer whose language has been all but subsumed by the operating system of the machine.

In seeing the extensivity of technical processes, Adorno and Horkheimer account for the rationale/rationality of industrialization as follows:

> The technical process, to which the subject has been reified after the eradication of that process from consciousness, is as free from the ambiguous meanings of mythical thought as from meaning altogether,

since reason itself has become merely an aid to the all-encompassing economic apparatus. Reason serves as a universal tool for the fabrication of all other tools, rigidly purpose-directed and as calamitous as the precisely calculated operations of material production, the results of which for human beings escape all calculation. Reason's old ambition to be purely an instrument of purposes has finally been fulfilled.[7]

"Fulfilled." Yes, what price reason's "old ambition," its degree zero, its Cartesian (0,0,0) at the origin of modern subjectivity and mathematics, and literally the *original* subject?[8] Ironically perhaps, if not also accurately, the subject of rationality is also a conduit to the almighty, since the fulfillment of reason is at once the emptying out of the subjective perceptions and proof of the divine. *Cogito ergo sum.* Ergo God. The path to the sublime of God for the modern subject, the subjectivity of zero, was also the path paved by instrumental rationality. Language became subject to a calculus that it could not calculate and surrendered its power of fabulation to generalized skepticism as a condition of its own continued operation. What price (what sum) the divine ideology of no ideology manifest in both radical skepticism and the oh-so practical activity of the cogito, the cogitation, the emergent scientific calculus that is materialized as our written symbolic concepts, our mathematical formulations and as our machines of metal and glass—the apparatuses that Vilém Flusser characterizes as a thinking in numbers extended into matter?[9] One of Turing's great achievements was the demonstration in 1936 that numbers, be they computable or incomputable, could be treated in the absence of the human brain—calculation could be made machinic and automated in accord with very simple rules.[10] With Adorno and Horkheimer we see that the mechanics of industrialization feed forward and back into the conceptual mechanics of physics and math: these rational mechanics generate a media ecology of the subject, who is at once sovereign, ineffable, and disappeared into the rational material processes of his presencing. The subject's linear inscription of meaning and time, organized by and as writing, drawn from the very letters and numbers, that at once express him and designed both the machines—and their operations—that are his disavowed support, his infrastructure, and the world-historical accumulation resulting from his metabolism.

With the clean separation between science and poetry the division of labor which science had helped to establish was extended to language.

For science the word is first of all a sign; it is then distributed among the various arts as sound, image, or word proper, but its unity can never be restored by the addition of these arts, by synaesthesia or total art. As sign, language must resign itself to being calculation and, to know nature, must renounce the claim to resemble it. As image it must resign itself to being a likeness and, to be entirely nature, must renounce the claim to know it.[11]

Language becomes alienated intelligence while images become unintelligible likenesses. These functions and effects on representation are among the techniques and indeed technics of the epic expansion of mediation, its accumulation of amortized sensual labor. The consequences of rationality "for human beings escapes all calculation," while imposing calculation all the more.

McLuhan nonetheless endeavors to provide a rational account for the textual rationalization of discourse (by print) and its consequences:

Whitehead does not elaborate on the great nineteenth century discovery of the method of invention. But it is, quite simply, the technique of beginning at the end of any operation whatever and of working backwards from that point to the beginning. It is the method inherent in the Gutenberg technique of homogeneous segmentation, but not until the nineteenth century was the method extended from production to consumption.[12]

For McLuhan, it was the homogeneous segmentation that moveable type introduced into the flow of signs that gave rise not only to modern literature, with the novel's "equitone prose," but also Poe's ingenious method of working backwards from the desired result of a narrative to the events of the story. Homogeneous segmentation presides over a generalized shift in the sense ratios in which eye-man overtakes ear-man or tactile-man, but also redounds to the Industrial Revolution, the autonomization of the economy relative to society (as McLuhan explains through the work of Karl Polyani) and, of course, the scientific method. Whether the sequence is print, science, industrialization and economy, or segmentation, grammatization, manipulation and distribution, it ends in programming. "Got a problem?" says science. Start with the future and work your way back to the present. Want to write a scary story?" say literature. Start with the desired effect and design the objective correlative to create it. Here capital might say, "Want to make a profit?" Reverse engineer M' back to M. For McLuhan, the Gutenbergian segmentation into the discrete units of a string of symbols, that could, in a few short centuries and a hundred million murders later, be thought of as "the code," also brought about the scientific method, industrialization, shifts in the sense ratios, capitalist economy, and, almost incidentally, the great formal migrations in literary history. As importantly, print, and the ignorance with regard to its effects as a medium, oversaw a generalized misidentification of the agents of history since, as McLuhan says, the nation and the subject were instantiated by print in the sixteenth century. Woe to historians and all peoples who have a stake in history if they misidentify its primary agents!

It's the medium…. We can quibble about the details, particularly about what came first—capital or the Gutenberg press. But as McLuhan remarks about the chicken and the egg question post-electrification, "Instead of asking which came first, the chicken or the egg, it suddenly seemed that a chicken was an egg's idea for getting more eggs."[13] *Yeah … that's it!* The chicken seems like an egg's idea to get more eggs: another case of M-C-M', where this time, in a slightly expanded frame, C stands for chicken (or any other medium) and M, the thinking money, is the capitalist's nest egg, with M', the profit (more eggs), ready for the next cycle of chicken-driven expansion.

The capitalized egg dreamt the printed chicken to make more eggs. *Post hoc ergo proctor hoc.* Thus, from the protocol that calls for the commodification of chickens by eggs in order to increase the quantity of eggs, or for the production of readers by books to get more books we encounter once again the outlines of the argument I sketched with respect to computational capital, one that states that the germ of capital inaugurated the first universalizing digital culture and that history has been the multiply contested working out of this, its digital program. Like eggs, like books, like money: all things that were formerly con-stellations of qualities were now and seemingly forever commodities, unified by exchange value, for sale on the market. Suddenly all things had a digital under-chassis. Digital culture 1.0, that is, capitalism was, as Nick Dyer-Witheford tells us, already a computer, running the program for the egg to get more eggs, the book to get more books.[14] Let us not forget the (oftentimes migrant) farm labor that gets encrypted into this chicken and egg story, the Mexican and Latinx farm workers seeking reparations for having suffered colonial history and the innumerable deaths caused by the colonial calculus, endeavoring to free themselves by crossing the border, fighting *la migra*, and working in some egg-identified white man's agri-chicken business in the tireless pursuit to increase his egg-count. Nor should we lose sight of the design and manufacture of those little iron cages (of reason) or the use for heating of what is, for McLuhan perhaps the ur-medium of the electronic age, light bulbs. Famously without content—McLuhan regards the light bulb that allowed with equal facility study, surgery and late-night baseball, and loudly proclaims, "the medium is the message."

What then *is* the message transmitted to the chickens in the agri-hen house? What can the chicken read? Let there be light? Perhaps that in the span from invisible hand to calculating egg we find the computational unconscious at work. The intensification of the logistics of commodi-fication means the increasing capture of all aspects of life as a medium for quantum profit. I will have more to say about the computational unconscious in another book (*Computational Capital*) but this capitalizing capture of language, living, imagination, and the whole animal in turn means the incipient digitization of the life-world. The commodity form is precisely the instantiation of the protocol use-value/exchange-value, where exchange-value is at once the common denominator of all things of account, and, importantly, a de-qualification, that, via an implicit or explicit contract to exchange ownership rights removes said object, in this case a chicken, from its web of living connections, and renders it, in short, a number. This enclosure precedes most chicken's lives today, and exceeds their conscious knowing. With this digitization comes abstraction and programmability and the transposition of chicken lives to another domain. Modern media history then is also about the production and organization of what computational physics calls the digiverse—a place where capital has your number—all your numbers. These are the numbers of everything within capital's perceptual purview: from your presence (if not your "being"), to the universe, to all the multiverses posited by computational astrophysics and quantum theory: the digiverse would contain all.

When chicken development is commandeered by an unforeseen fork in the evolutionary road, and all the birds are bred for containeriza-tion as a medium of money, so much for the Garden of Eden. From a systemic point of view it seems to matter little what the chicken thinks. Rather, in a world in which all things are enumerated and organized by alpha-numeric codes, contingencies are to be understood as operative in a Borgesian garden, the Garden of Forking Paths, to be exact—a garden that is labyrinthine, no doubt, but also, as readers of this extraordinary parable will remember, one that is shot through with the inexorable crunching of operationalized information such that it's mesh, crush and crunch overdetermines all moments of potential and thus of agency; over-determines, we may dimly hope, not quite to the brink of annihilation. Mindful of the chicken's fate, in which most paths lead to the grocery store, how then to game the machine (no pun intended)? What then of Gramsci's machine operators and their/our, machines?

In the next section we will dwell for a moment on the poignant lines of a desperate writer that close off the Borgesian "garden," even as 1) the thoroughgoing instrumentalization, rationalization and codification of the commodified life-world Earth reaches a new pitch, while 2) humans become functionally reduced to standing reserve in informatic capitalism and informatic capitalist war, and 3) they/we become func-tionaries of its proliferating apparatuses—written, reading, writing, read and forced to play against the odds. "Functionary" is Flusser's word for the photographer dominated by the omnipresent program of the camera, but it is also Gramsci's term for the prole subjugated to the machine and the manager subjugated to the interests of ownership. As we shall see, the functionality of the functionary and the condition of the photographer who plays against the program of the machine has become the general case. The instrumentalization of the mentality by systemic rationality leads to both the extreme rationalism and simultaneously to the extreme irrationality noted by Adorno and Horkheimer and experienced by the subject forced into a continuous calculus of risk and reward, the subject forced to game.

2

A Message from Borges:
The Informatic Labyrinth

The telephone book listed the name of the only person capable of transmitting the message.

—Borges

Codifying race

Recall that at the outset of the path through "The Garden" (but already in the thrall of the middle of the action), the protagonist spy for the Germans, Yu Tsun, steadied himself with his own counsel: "*The author of an atrocious undertaking ought to imagine he has already accomplished it, ought to impose upon himself a future that is as irrevocable as the past.*" Composing himself thus he is able to send, through "the uproar of war" the message that is his to send. He sends that message by means of a man, a genius "great as Goethe" (and one who, by a twist of fate, was also able to reveal to Yu Tsun lost secrets of his own Chinese ancestry) precisely by killing him. This man's name happened to coincide with the name of the English town Albert that German intelligence revealed needed to be bombed for the war effort. Captured and then imprisoned in England after the murder and condemned to the gallows Borges' character writes:

I have communicated to Berlin the secret name of the city they must attack. They bombed it yesterday. I read in the same papers that offered to England the mystery of the learned Sinologist Stephen Albert who was murdered by a stranger, one Yu Tsun. The Chief had deciphered this mystery. He knew my problem was to indicate (through the uproar of war) the city called Albert, and that I had found no other means to do so than to kill a man of that name. He does not know (no one can know) my innumerable contrition and weariness.[1]

"Innumerable." A word that, in qualifying contrition and weariness, stands out in a universe becoming increasingly codified, calculated and calculating. In a world overrun by various forms of calculus and instrumental enumeration, it indicates something that cannot be counted. One may wonder: Is there anymore anywhere a beyond number? Something that evades enumeration and that exceeds what could only be algorithmic governance? Something not subordinated to calculation and encryption in a world at war, a something that persists as an incalculable remainder? Already, in 1941, under emergent regimes not just of instrumental rationality but instrumental mediation, that question became *the* question—at least for the blind librarian named Borges, who was what he read. Very likely his own serious political failings gave him pause.

Readers of "The Garden of Forking Paths" may remember, that Borges, through Albert, offers them a challenge midway through the story: "In a riddle whose answer is chess, what is the one word that is inadmissible?" And Albert, who is, in fact, a regular Einstein, provides us and the baffled Yu Tsun with that answer: "Chess," of course. Some readers of the story, taking the bait, and engaging in a meta-analysis of the divergent paths indicated there have said that the answer to the riddle of "The Garden's" own narratological and indeed cosmo-logical question is "time," but to judge by the rules set out, they are mistaken: that word is actually given in the text—as the solution to Yu Tsun's ancestor's labyrinth. "Time," unnamed by the ancestral author of the labyrinth/novel inside of Borges' text, fragments, forks, runs parallel, reconnects, and though reportedly unwritten there, is indeed written by the author of "The Garden." It is offered as the domain name for a core mutation in the flux of things that explains the narrative form created by Yu Tsun's ancestor and author of the labyrinth, but not that of "The Garden" itself. What might seem like another promising candidate for the answer to the riddle of "The Garden," "history," seemingly absent from the narrative proper and thus quite possibly the medium that was required to be re-imagined in order to make the various elements of the story yielding Yu-Shun's innumerable contrition and weariness cohere is also disqualified. "History" as it turns out is written in the very first line of our text as part of the title of another text that frames all the other mediated layers of text and acts of reportage dramatized within. The story begins, "In Liddell Hart's *History of World War I* ..." and so on.

"History," written within "The Garden" is not the answer to the riddle of the garden of forking paths wherein whose labyrinth all possibilities are inscribed, but more than 75 years from the moment of this inscription, it seems likely that the answer to Borges' riddle is "information." The word does not occur, but every word, thought, image and act in the story, including the programmatic intelligence required to send a message "through the uproar of war," or what we might call "noise," is a negotiation of its multiplex churn. Information is what must be gathered, negotiated and transmitted. It supersedes time and history; its surge transforms intelligence, character, the terms of engagement among people, and narrative form. In informatic war, where life is taken for the purpose of taking more life, and communication means the transmission of information, people are shown to be functionaries of its protocols and indeed media. The treatment of Albert, killed for the accident of his name with the express aim of targeting a military strike, concisely demonstrates that the medium is the message and the message is murder.

What might lie beyond the cruel calculus of the informatic combinatory of contingency and necessity that constitutes the substance, plot and drama of the war of maneuver and of the existential riddle posed by "The Garden of Forking Paths?" Only a residue or remainder, the closing inscription of Yu Shun, appearing at the end of the story and just beyond the threshold of communicable knowledge: precisely the "innumerable contrition and weariness" that "no one can know." All the rest it seems is history, written by those with Liddell Hart.

With or without heart, things come to pass, numbers get crunched. The "innumerable contrition and weariness" that "no one can know" indicates the emergent historical sensibility of an emotional dominant that will at once result from and partially elide massive information processing. One might think of "Bifo's" analysis, in his book *After the Future*, of the rampant depression and burnout characteristic of our times, or his scathing treatment of Lenin as a depressive who combated his bouts of nervous breakdown with responses of ironclad will. We could venture—and Borges' story would support—that another name for this "innumerable contrition and weariness" today is Anne Cheng's "racial melancholia." It is a central, though underappreciated fact, that in the bibliophilic, nearly sightless Argentine's story of informatics, the principle antagonists are racialized: "Madden [the character who pursues and captures Yu Tsun,] was implacable. Or rather, he was obliged to be so. An Irishman in the service of England, a man accused of laxity and perhaps of treason, how could he fail to seize and be thankful for such a miraculous opportunity: the discovery, the capture, maybe even the death of two agents of the German Reich."[2] Against centuries of British colonialism, racial oppression, Edmund Spenser's genocidal "View on the Present State of Ireland," an Irishman "in the service of England" is indeed "obliged" to be implacable. His body and tongue, coded for suspicion by his racial legibility under English hegemony, obliges him. Referring to his own part as a spy for Germany in the info-war, the protagonist Yu Tsun, who is one of the German agents Madden has the good fortune of an opportunity to kill, remarks about his own intelligence activity:

> I didn't do it for Germany, no. I care nothing for a barbarous country which imposed upon me the abjection of being a spy ... I did it because I sensed that the Chief somehow feared people of my race—for the innumerable ancestors that merge within me. I wanted to prove to him that a yellow man could save his armies.[3]

The contradictory implication that Yu Tsun honors his again "innumerable" Chinese ancestors by struggling against proto-Nazi German racism in a way that, by cruel irony, supports the German Reich, (at the time of the writing of this story the then current German Third Reich was organizing a holocaust) in no way mitigates the multiple imperatives of these codes. Rather, in making Yu Tsun's negotiations of race, power and abjection parallel to Madden's, we see coded bodies caught in an informatic meshwork, organized by and operative in a matrix of codification processes that overdetermines their options and drives them in ways that "no one can know." Yu Tsun's struggle against racialization supports the Reich's racist pursuits; he fights racism in support of racism—that is the hand he's been dealt, and that one is still dealt today. Madden's support of the English, serves a nation that would have exterminated him. Sound familiar? Reading, writing, written and read, all characters navigate a fully codified world, and somewhere do the math of risk management in order to respond to and send messages. They are awash in information, overrun by a matrix of code, destined by some incomprehensible emergence to function as computational media.

Borges' garden of forking paths, less the garden of Eden and more a fully immersive discrete state machine, shows clearly how human qualities are becoming coded, instrumentalized, and structurally converted into tools of communication—each semiotic instance offers a fork. The phonebook where Yu Shun finds an Albert along with his address becomes a database, the pistol used to shoot generates a "report." History's new mise en scène, with multiple channels and ambient code all bent by and towards the instrumentality of war nearly eliminates prior natural relationships to organic things such that an encounter with the uncodified becomes remarkable. On the path to Albert's, for example, a fleeing Yu Tsun has a moment to reflect upon what he sees, "I thought that a man can be the enemy of other men, of the moments of other men, but not of a country: not of fireflies, words, gardens, streams of water, sunsets."[4] The uncodified natural world contrasts starkly with the adversarial capture and mobilization of all that can be informationalized. The codified world, shot through with information, demands of those historically enframed by ambient codification both strategy and willfulness, yet it makes of its subject-as-game-theorist's singular intentions, only a pathway, a plot, for warding off contingency, "The author of an atrocious undertaking ought to imagine he has already accomplished it, ought to impose upon himself a future that is as irrevocable as the past." Such a plot offers not an existential explanation of the reason for informatics but only a practical program for its reason. Here again, as with the case of "more eggs," we begin with the desired end state and have the application of human will to the society of things: "the machine operator's to his machine." But the machine, no longer fixed in the factory, is ambient and omnipresent: The natural world appears marginal and strange when set against the relentless and menacing function of an increasingly codified world that demands to be read and written. And re-written. Action itself is captured by code, encrypted, and undertaken only for the sake of transmission. Thus what "information" explains is precisely this shift from temporal openness to programming, from fireflies to assassination. What still needs to be explained is the infiltration of informatics into lifetime itself and the innumerable remainders.[5]

Today, as we pass the hundredth anniversary of the Russian Revolution, when the abject fail to send their messages in the old school ways or on Instagram, other attention algorithms such as shooting up their schoolmates or killing their colored neighbors, or going on a killing spree in a queer club they might have otherwise found freedom in, present themselves as means of (re-)mediating their agency. Got to send our messages—or so they must feel. "White people" for example, white men, self-identified by virtue of being content to be the authors of atrocious acts (the very thing that constitutes "the white race") find that even their once seemingly irrevocable authority has been cut and mixed and thus needs buttressing. Not quite the abjection of being a spy perhaps, but the abjection of non-recognition, of not having one's message received and acknowledged by the presumably sovereign community of white brethren and their murderous bond. On second thought, this extension of invisibility and non-recognition even to the white man is another version of the abjection of being a spy, of traveling incognito and never being able to come home. It drives white-identifying types to deport, incarcerate, murder, to vote for fascists, to declare war. They become spies, reading information off the skins, clothes and accents of others, coding their own actions in a struggle for legibility. They want to send a message through the uproar of what for them is still civil war.

Even as Borges was writing "The Garden of Forking Paths" in recognition that linguistic codes, including racial and national markings, were being functionalized as information, and even as eggs were being encouraged to engage in risk management and advertising to assure themselves of getting more eggs, the full mathematicization of these codes of representation was being consciously undertaken. Norbert Weiner, Claude Shannon, Warren Weaver, Alan Turing, among others were grafting signs to number in unprecedented ways, translating and indeed transducing messages using modalities that were number based and "content indifferent:" just as ALBERT the message was sublimely indifferent to Albert the man. Statistical methods, punchcards, paper tapes, discrete state machines cryptography, cybernetics, and artificial intelligence: Electricity, it seems, could be used to generate on a large scale not just content indifferent light, but content indifferent numbers—and that would change the world. It was this indifference that made the difference that Adorno and Horkheimer called incalculable.

Admittedly much work on information and computation, on cryptography and cybernetics, was not immediately economic, undertaken (and funded) as it was for the war effort(s), or at least in relation to it (them). Computation and information were considered means to new forms of steerage, from cryptography, to cybernetics, to control and to the atom bomb. But were these mid-century info masters populating Princeton, Bletchley Park and the Macy conferences creating *ex nihlo* or even *ex mathematica*?[6] Or, were they formalizing a systemic shift in the operational logistics of a world—already grown abstract and increasingly codified by the exigencies of wars organized by crises in capitalist production that, without a doubt, included vectors of racism, colonialism, gender oppression and homophobia? For the thought experiment at hand it seems advantageous to wager on the latter thesis, that information emerges not just in the foot print of evaluation, but of *valuation*—but more on that anon.

Guy Debord, arguably a brilliant theorist of data processing, understood with perhaps still unsurpassed clarity, some of the social consequences of digitization, even if he did not think in precisely those terms. What he called "the spectacle," "the accumulation of capital to the point where it becomes an image," became symptom, modality, and goal of capitalism. Spectacle had, in other words, a digital logic and was ideologically if perhaps not entirely technically a pre-DC2 digital incarnation. The spectacle, a historically new form of social relation, was an intensification of commodification. Retrospectively the spectacle meant a heightening of the incipient digitization of daily life, and the emergence of what today we might call data visualization. My conflation here of mass cultural forms with the more restricted and seemingly precise notion of data visualization reserved for computational design is purposeful. Data processing does not all take place at the same level, or with the same level of legibility for all concerned. Debord's spectacle, as theorized in *SOS*, had deep links to ideology, that is, to forms of thinking and knowing, themselves organized to legitimate and sustain the material practices of capitalism and yet it also marked a wholesale liquidation of certain analytic capacities. The spectacle was not a narrative or any particular world view; the spectacle was rather "all that appears," all that could appear, in a new stage of capital that for Debord was also the colonization of the senses and of time. For Debord the spectacle was "the guardian of sleep." This modality of appearance, all of the practices that went into the creation of the spectacle as social relation, in turn, depended upon, and indeed were, the worldwide expansion of quantification. That is, it was part of the evolution of the commodity form and the expansion of the logic of exchange-value. The spectacle was in short for Debord the key interface with capital—the further codification of appearance by capital. Its multiplex operation extended from the commodity form to the screen and colonized perception, awareness and the imagination.

The cues around the block that for Christian Metz "invented cinema" were in fact digitized at the box office; before the rise of "digital culture;" digitization was already taking place and the cinema and spectacle were paradigmatic interfaces. Building on Debord, I understood in

The Cinematic Mode of Production that those analogue images, subject to background digitization by the box-office, the studio and the bank, were slated for further digitization and a dramatically increased functionality by means of culturing, that is expanding, the digital feedback mechanism known as the market increasingly mediated by the digital computer. Qualitative theory was necessary to challenge the onslaught of quantification.

> Marx's project is the project of a conscious history whereby the quantitative realm that arises from the blind development of purely economic productive forces would be transformed into a qualitative appropriation of history. The *critique of political economy* is the first act of this *end of prehistory*: "Of all the instruments of production, the greatest productive power is the revolutionary class itself."[7]

So, quantification against "the qualitative appropriation of history," quantification against the revolutionary class and the revolution. The greatest productive power, says Debord, is the revolutionary class itself, a class that for Debord needs to awake from the spell of the somnambulism of the spectacle, and "take up arms" against the society of the spectacle for its dialogue to be heard. This is the class recently re-imagined by Hardt and Negri as "the multitudes" and by Franco Berardi in a totally alienated form as "the general intellect in search of a body." For these latter thinkers the revolutionary class today is composed of atomized bodies and nobodies. The revolutionary class is also not that revolutionary, and not a (self-conscious) class. Negri's social factory, my own attention theory of value, Virno's virtuosity, Berardi's cellurization of labor, Lazzarato's new work on "machinic enslavement," and a litany of other terms developed over the last couple of decades, have testified that the deterritorialized factory and the radical fragmentation of production (and of productive bodies) are among the fundamental features and problems of post-Fordism. Virtuosic social cooperation in the social factory, the "communism of capital," all transpire under the fractal logic of quantum profiteering. Race, as Wendy Chun smiths it, appears "as a technology," and intersectionality becomes a qualitative means by which to overcome hegemonic categoricality. These are among the social practices that will give rise to social media (social-media), the abstraction of and the technical realization of a computational processing of information that was already present in Borges. Everywhere we struggle with the imposition of algorithmic overdetermination, yet who has really figured out how to send a message that does not also entail murder?

Derivative revolution

The abstraction and formalization of social practices as social-media marks the subsumption of social life that announces the arrival of full-blown computational capital. As the late Randy Martin, Bob Meister, Benjamin Lee, Robert Wosnitzer and others involved in the New York based "Cultures of Finance" group suggest, we are, with the financial-ization of culture, for the moment at least irrevocably in the domain of the derivative. Everyone is seeking a hedge on volatility—such is the current condition. But derivative revolution can be captured as capitalist production and is locally navigated upon an ocean of inequality ... Borges could not be a Marxist, but he well understood how subjective residues were deposited from the willful navigation by agents of infor-mation's capacity for sublime content indifference.

In addition to the fragmentation and indeed fractalization of the freedom seeking media edge-worker in processes of production distributed across the entire landscape of the social—even through the unremunerated labor of virtuosic cognitive-linguistic production—we need to understand within this transformed media-scape that the status of the object, and more particularly of the commodity has lost the very solidity that seemed to define it. Only an awareness of informatic transformation at the ontological level will allow us to fully grasp the dissolution of the prior epoch and its metaphysics in the vectoralized informatic swarms of capital. Swarms that when all is said and done, or even before, may have, in their executive opinion, better uses for you and your molecules than you do. All that is solid melts into computation, and attention metrics emerge to account for—as a system of accounts for—the AI-directed extraction and amalgamation of sensual labor. Everything sensible and indeed insensible becomes at once a solicitation to work and an advertisement for itself. Informatics is the key transition to the distributed production and consumption of integrated commodities, the bundling and re-selling of attentional products.

In the last chapter of *Message* there will be more to say about dif-ferentiable objects and integrated commodities, understanding that in post-Fordist economies of distributed production and valorization a new morphology of social form is emergent even if perhaps the basic rule set of capitalism has remained constant. One stumbling block on the path to unraveling the mysteries of computational capital and financialized communication is precisely this prevailing confusion that conflates the object form and the commodity form. This misapprehension of the essence of the commodity has led to the mistaken notion that cognitive capitalism, semio-capitalism, neuro-capitalism and/or attention economy imply the death of the commodity-form. This confusion is analogous to another mistaken notion, namely, that under post-Fordism value has become immeasurable and that work has disappeared. In reality, the growth of social-media and financial derivatives are, from the standpoint of capital, nothing other than the development of new metrics for the evaluation—and indeed valuation—of a new phase of commodification and new forms of productive labor.[8] In understanding that the discrete object (a coat, to use a famous example) represents an instance or stage in history of the commodity-form (and as a particular value in time is essentially a derivative in a calculus of value), it will be useful to recognize that Marx never presented the commodity-form as one with the object. Rather the commodity-form was itself a decoding of the capital-mediated object's unsettling appearance and dynamics as a relation between use-value and exchange-value. The commodity exists in a regime itself organized by the complex—and indeed dynamic—logistics of wage-labor and private property. Thus, while the commodity-form expressed the abstract formation of a phenomenon most readily visible as the industrial object, its ostensibly objectivity was the consequence of a set of historical practices that were themselves but a stage in capitalist accumulation. The object was a result of the physics of a moment in the history of capitalization and resulted in that period's metaphysics—it being understood that the subject was the other side of that equation, and money was the vanishing mediator, the general equivalent. Post-Fordism's emergent dynamics include shifts not just in the objective character of the commodity, but also in the character of labor, the wage, affect, social currency. The mode of production has become computational. This fractalization of the relations of production produces a matrix of dividuals and monetization interfaces. The endeavor here would include the mandate to understand the central role of screens and computation as a dialectical development in capital, as well as the, often violent, (re-)organization and maintenance (policing) of categories of social difference that indicate the experiential dimension of derivative finance.

* * *

The next chapter considers the informatic shattering of humanist thought already conceived (and indeed accomplished) by Alan Turing by mid-century.[9] The emergence of computational machines is at once a formalization and a becoming conscious of operations already implicit in capital—a formalization of its unconscious processes, and yours, that allows for its expansion and intensification, and opens a pathway toward the dissolution of subjects and objects by matrixial proliferation. Contemporary consciousness is the result of the massive formalization through abstraction and relentless codification by means of digitized writing machines of those calculative practices of lived cost-benefit analysis that are now fed back into the social metabolism (through "feeds"). This recursivity between machine and person extends the calculus of profit, ramifying new sites of production and presenting a whole new set of problems—a set that quite frankly, includes "you."

Recognizing the extension of digital operations into the core of what used to be "the self," we might then pause a moment on Roberto Retamar's scathing critique of Borges and his right-wing affinities. For the most famous Marxist literary critic of Latin America, Borges' pages "are the painful testimony of a class with no way out, diminished to saying in the voice of one man, "The world, unfortunately is real; I unfortunately am Borges."[10] Retamar's indictment of Borges' right-leaning betrayals of Latin American revolutionary becoming might suggest that the writer-spy Yu Tsun's "innumerable contrition and weariness" was more than a tad autobiographical. Perhaps in its own way the geopolitical garden of forking paths shattered Borges too. Poetic then indeed that Retamar closes his groundbreaking essay on Caliban with a lucid antithesis to the career of a Borges described as "a colonial and a representative of a dying class."[11] Dreaming of a different historical role for Ariel, Retamar counter poses against Borges' role as Latin America's preeminent writer, Che's word's offered at the University of Las Villas on 28 December 1959 and designed to interrupt the codes of capitalist war by transforming the very source of the codex:

I am convinced of the overwhelming necessity of the revolution and the infinite justice of the people's cause—I would hope for those reasons that you, today proprietors of the university, will extend it to the people. I do not say this as a threat, so as to avoid its being taken over by them tomorrow. I say it simply because it would be one more among so many beautiful examples in Cuba today: that proprietors of the Central University of Las Villas, the students, offer it to the people through their revolutionary government. And to the distinguished professors, my colleagues, I have to say something similar: become black, mulatto, a worker, a peasant; go down among the people, respond to the people, that is, to all the necessities of all of Cuba. When this is accomplished, no one will be the loser; we all will have gained, and Cuba can then continue its march toward the future with a more vigorous step, and you will not need to include in your cloister this doctor, commandante, bank president, and today professor of pedagogy who now takes leave of you.[12]

Retamar concludes: "That is to say, Che proposed that the 'European university' as Marti would have said, yield before the 'American university.' He proposed to Ariel, through his own most luminous and sublime example if ever there was one, that he seek from Caliban the honor of a place in his rebellious and glorious ranks."[13] Che too saw that social difference was historically constituted but he proposed a different matrix of relations than did Borges: "become black, mulatto, a worker, a peasant." Open the university to the people and enable Caliban's code to rewrite the world. In other words, don't be satisfied to be what you have read; write otherwise. Interrogate the terms of codifications, the codifications of class, race, identity; and rewrite them as necessary. Relating the narratives of such codification directly to number, in the brilliant book *Who Counts*, a book on genocide in Guatemala and the socio-semiotic struggles around numerology including between Western and Mayan mathematics, Diane Nelson teaches us something we should never forget: Double-entry bookkeeping is also an ethno-mathematics, but with an army.[14] We will hold fast to this notion of the enthno-mathematics of capitalist computation—their narratologies and practical results—in subsequent sections.

3

Alan Turing's Self-Defense: On Not Castrating the Machines

I forgot my destiny of one pursued. I felt myself to be for an unknown period of time an abstract perceiver of the world.

—Borges

Alan Turing's dismissal of the provocative question "Can machines think?" in "Computing, Machinery and Intelligence," his masterful essay of 1950, decisively reformats the question of consciousness. In his essay, Turing dismisses the question of the thinking machine as not useful—because, as he demonstrates with startling economy, the terms of the question itself are improperly understood. In fact, he manages this dismissal while unequivocally answering the question regarding the possibility of the existence of such a machine in the affirmative.[1] His interrogation of the presumed uniqueness of "man," also has implications for the unconscious as that which gives consciousness depth and presence, though he does not address the unconscious directly as such in the piece. In keeping with Turing but with our own purposes firmly in mind, we will want to note the existence of what I call the computational unconscious, because it names precisely the haunting of contemporary thought by the unthought and largely unthinkable history of computational praxis that materially underpins current thought, knowledge and computation. I will endeavor to clarify this assertion below.

In "Computing, Machinery and Intelligence," Turing goes so far as to posit a version of a vast computational unconscious as a statistically likely ontological condition that can be summed up as follows: we do not know that we are computers. This radical anti-humanist position staked out by Turing is often missed but the implication regarding a generalized misperception of the nature of computation is clear. For Turing, the notion of intelligence, resting upon the notion of human intelligence and thus upon the humanist tradition, is simply *a* notion of intelligence that depends upon the non-perception (ignorance) of the possibility that human behavior is a consequence of the rigorous execution of the operations of a rule-set. Turing held that at the very least, the contrary notion, that there was not a set of rules governing human behavior, and that human behavior was thus not a computational effect, could not be proven. As he writes regarding the hypothetical rule set for the laws of human behavior, "The only way for finding such laws [of behavior] is scientific observation, and we certainly know of no circumstances under which we could say, 'We have searched enough. There are no such laws.'"[2]

To emphasize the point that we have only really just begun an investigation into the laws of intelligent behavior, Turing adds:

> We can demonstrate more forcibly that any such statement would be unjustified. For suppose we could be sure of finding such laws if they existed. Then given a discrete-state machine it should certainly be possible to discover by observation sufficient about it to predict its future behavior, and this within a reasonable time, say a thousand years. But this does not seem to be the case. I have set up on the Manchester computer a small programme using only 1000 units of storage, whereby the machine supplied with one sixteen figure number replies with another within two seconds. I would defy anyone to learn from these replies sufficient about the programme to be able to predict any replies to untried values.[3]

In 1950, in a single act of cryptographic *sprezzatura*, Turing puts his formidable reputation on the line to demonstrate that the best mathematicians of the day cannot reverse engineer a few lines of his code that takes one of 10^{16} possible inputs and returns one of 10^{16} possible outputs—no matter how extensive a chart of inputs and outputs they might be able to assemble. If that relatively controlled environment of "only" 100 million billion input variants along with an equivalent number of possible outputs does not yield to empirical scrutiny such that the program can be reverse engineered, how much less, the data field of human history? Clearly the prior 1000 years has not been enough time to crack the code of human behavior (should it exist) by examining inputs and outputs, and possibly the next 1000 may not be enough. But ignorance is no excuse for the law, as the old anti-Republican joke goes, and ignorance of computational process (non-conscious cognition, as Kathryn Hayles recently ventured), which the evidence suggests is how Turing conceives of Darwin, is no excuse for a law that claims human exceptionalism; it in no way guarantees that a program of sorts (a rule set) is not churning in the background iterating complexity along perfectly rule-bound lines. This insight implies a radical liquidation of the humanist tradition along with all of its exceptionalizing essentialisms by positing a trajectory of procedural emergence. Turing, it seems, would be in agreement with McLuhan regarding the misidentification of historical agents (the autonomy of subjects, the essences of beings), but his insight has even greater ontological depth because of the granularity implied by his notion of media.

It is within the domain of a rationale that understands that entities are not givens but emerge from the operation of rules, that Turing replaces the question "Can machines think?" with "the imitation game." This game involves the question of whether or not an "interrogator" can discern if the entity they are typing a conversation with is a human or a machine. This shifting of the "nature" of the question of machine intelligence is a bold move, involving what Katherine Hayles refers to as a "sleight of hand" that, as she notes, already situates the formerly human being in a networked "posthuman" condition no matter the outcome of any particular instance of what came to be called the Turing Test.[4] As humans are placed within a circuit of symbolic exchange with machines, the full integration of humans with (writing) machines is suddenly a given in a way that looks both forward and back in time. Turing's reframing of the question can machines think, is for him necessary in order to answer the question, because in his own view we understand neither the meaning of the word "machine" nor, perhaps even more dramatically, "think." But for better or worse, we may discern from the above example of Turing's challenge to reverse engineer a rule set, that what is at play here is, from the point of view of metaphysics, a bit more than a magic trick. Turing's argument is at once ontological and teleological, if only weakly with respect to the latter. How little we understand "machine" and "think" indicates that the stakes involved in this understanding may vitiate ontological presuppositions that extend to the essence of humanism and humanistic thought and that include notions of governance, hierarchy, divinity and "man." The challenging of these presuppositions explains why Turing published this essay in the philosophy journal *Mind*. In the guise of a casual inquiry into the nature of computation, the essay orchestrates high metaphysical drama; it troubles not only the nature of machines but of "man."

Among Turing's examples of human elements, which, in the terms of the imitation game are no longer essential verities but rather virtualities or virtualizations, there are subtle but significant inclusions of gender, race and nation. For example, the imitation game in which an interrogator must specify the difference between man and machine is based on a game that already implies a form of cross-dressing and gender performativity: "The interrogator stays in a room apart from the other two. The object of the game for the interrogator is to determine which of the other two is the man and which is the woman."[5] What is important here in the erotics of this tropologic parlor game is first that gender is deduced from input and output, in short, from the interplay of codes, and furthermore that in making the determination of gender it is possible to be "wrong" (while still being subjectively "right"). Human intelligence is AI in drag. But eliciting the "wrong" identification is in fact victory for the impersonator, making the drag performance at once more real than real, and, in the context of the larger argument, the truth of intelligence. From this insight, plus a few decades of thought and passionate struggle, we glimpse a path to the groundbreaking work of Judith Butler. If gender is code all the way down, obviously there is no ontological right and wrong—just and always an exchange of information and thus simulation and its consequent semiosis.[6] And as Butler lucidly demonstrated more than twenty years ago, this semiosis includes not just gender but "sex." It's performance all the way down.

This de-ontologization of gender early in the history of computing did not, however, prevent the engineering of the female voice of computation within the developmental framework of heteropatriarchy—there are many examples from the starship *Enterprise* computer ("... working") to Siri. As Emma Goss brilliantly puts it, "The ultimate marker of artificial intelligence ... was based on the idea that a computer could perform femininity better than a real woman."[7] Looking at the history of the utilization of the female voice in communication and computation from early phone operators, to mid-century female programmers to Siri, Goss argues that with electronic communication and computation there emerged an idea that "women's intelligence could be electronically engineered"[8] and that women were "artificially intelligent."[9] She writes, "People [who get] fed up with the shortcomings of voice-communicative technology, recogniz[e] that their 'smart' phones are not very smart at all. Rather than blame the engineers for the faulty technology, people have come to blame "her," the voice, the artificially intelligent woman."[10]

Thus we begin to see that the conscious development of machine intelligence required a disruption of many of the ontological presuppositions of hegemonic Western society and also that many age-old assumptions reasserted themselves in the making of new technologies. Additionally, we find that just as the de-essentialization of gender was implicit in Turing's understanding of machine-think, but did not guarantee a progressive politics (at least so long as an essentialist metaphysics with regard to one's own humanity remained), so too was the de-essentializing of race and disability. Against the numerous "disabilities" presumably inherent in machines that would exclude them from being counted as thinking, Turing comments:

> The inability to enjoy strawberries and cream may have struck the reader as frivolous. Possibly a machine might be made to enjoy this delicious dish, but any attempt to make one do so would be idiotic. What is important about this disability is that it contributes to some of the other disabilities, e.g., the difficulty of the same kind of friendliness occurring between man and machine as between white man and white man, or between black man and black man.[11]

Turing's logic here is indirect but rigorous. Because of prejudice regarding perceived disabilities, the friendliness between man and machine cannot be like that friendliness between white and white or black and black. The unsaid here is the relation to the unformulated combination, the (non-) "friendliness" between white and black, a relation which by implication is analogous to the prejudicial relation between (so-called man) and (so-called) machine that Turing inveighs against. This argument also marks the assignation of the category "disability" as a form of prejudice, one that is a condition of ignorance.

These anti-essentialist notions tear up the founding of social difference on humanist ontology (more or less the same humanism that presided in the colonies, over segregation and apartheid, and that everywhere rears its ugly head today). Here anyway, Turing's anti-essentialist notions are without doubt a consequence of the critique of metaphysics implied by the slow revelation of the programmability of the discrete state machine. When Turing is pressed, that is, when he presses himself to provide an actual example of a "learning machine," that is, of a program capable of self-modification through interaction with the environment and therefore of intelligent self-transformation, he uses the analogy of a human child. But he also says:

> The idea of a learning machine may appear paradoxical to some readers. How can the rules of operation of the machine change? They should describe completely how the machine will react whatever its history might be, whatever changes it might undergo. The rules are thus quite time-invariant. This is quite true. The explanation of the paradox is that the rules that get changed in the learning process are of a rather less pretentious kind, claiming only an ephemeral validity. The reader may draw a parallel with the Constitution of the United States.[12]

While it is unclear to me whether Turing means to suggest that the main body of the constitution is the unchanging portion, while the amendments are the examples of machine learning (amendments which would include the abolition of slavery and women's suffrage), or that the Constitution in its entirety is the variable in the more abstract machine that is the state and society or even the meta-program of "human behavior," the difference hardly matters here: Not only is the state founded on a machine that can learn; it can also think. Though subject to hardwiring, the program can be modified. Rule sets persist; programs can be modified and machines can learn. Currently inscribed in that circuit is this category called "man."

From these examples touching on gender, race and nation, we see that already with Turing, the substrate of social and historical existence not only tropologically informs Turing's thought but is also radically redefined by computational logic. Where before there were men and women, blacks and whites, gods and states, with Turing there are rule sets. Rule sets are prior to emergent instantiations and they condition them. Turing's brilliant abstraction and reduction in the "Turing Test" of intelligence to communication and of communication to performative simulation in "Computing, Machinery and Intelligence" is of a piece with the harnessing of language as programmatic medium, in a way that retroactively renders the operations of the symbolic as itself a simulation that "is" "human" intelligence. Kittler, whatever his flaws, has a point when he observes that the machinic typewriter with its transformation not only of language but of philosophy and mind is, by separating writing from the organic body, the mechanical preconditions for machine-based computation. "Turing merely got rid of the people and typists that Remington & Son needed for reading and writing."[13]

One cannot disprove the possibility (indeed likelihood) that what passes for human intelligence is the computational effect produced by the execution of a rule set or even that what we categorize as human intelligence was always already machine-mediated. For Turing, the ramification of scientific rationality into the natural world provided increasing evidence that the universe functions according to rules and that human beings were unlikely to be an exception. It is no wonder that he felt he had to debunk various objections to the possibility of machine thinking, since humans were in some sense understood as machines or at least the result of machinic operations. The ripostes and put-downs to common objections arising to stave off the horror of this radical and profound anti-humanism were craftily indexed in Turing's essay by categories that included "The Theological Objection" and, my favorite, "The "Heads in the Sand" Objection." For, at the end of the day (of Humanism), the thinking machines, those "machinic assemblages" were us.

As for "The Theological Objection," which as he renders it reads, "Thinking is a function of the immortal soul. God has given an immortal soul to every man and woman, but not to any other animal or to machines. Hence no animal or machine can think," Turing writes:

> It is admitted that there are certain things He cannot do such as making one equal to two, but should we not believe that He has the freedom to confer a soul on an elephant if He sees fit? We might expect that He would only exercise this power in conjunction with a mutation which provided the elephant with an appropriately improved brain to minister to the needs of this soul. An argument of exactly similar form may be made for the case of machines. It may seem different because it is more difficult to "swallow." But this really only means that we think it would be less likely that He would consider the circumstances suitable for conferring a soul. The circumstances in question are discussed in the rest of this paper.[14]

Turing's razor sharp understanding that the implications that computational intelligence implies an attack on theology, metaphysics and the primacy of the human by way of an impeachment of the conceit of a Divine Subject leads him to write, "In attempting to construct such machines we should not be irreverently usurping His power of creating souls, any more than we are in the procreation of children; rather we are, in either case, instruments of His will providing mansions for the souls that He creates."[15] He then drops the ironic tone and gives the example of Galileo as a victim of an ignorant theological framework that has since (almost?) disappeared. His example of Galileo under the attack of the Church serves as a direct analogy with Turing's own critique of what amounts to a secular theology of anthropocentrism, and very unfortunately, was also a tragic predictor of his own fate. Galileo faced the Church inquisition for challenging the theology that placed Earth at the center of the universe along with the implications for power and governance therein, while Turing himself challenges the secular theology that places an unbearably narrow and willfully ignorant definition of humanity at the center of intelligence and that has built Western "civilization." And persecuted he was. It took England until 2009 to apologize for it's own normative (why not say "humanistic") inquisition against Turing's homosexuality, one that forced him, in 1952, to accept "chemical castration" and likely drove him to suicide. Such was the automated thinking endemic to the program of the humanist state. Yet heads remain in the sand.

Turing's description of the "Heads in the Sand" objection reads simply: "The consequences of machine thinking would be too dreadful. Let us hope and believe they cannot do so."[16] Turing comments:

> This argument is seldom expressed quite so openly ... But it affects most of us who think about it at all. We like to believe that Man is in some subtle way superior to the rest of creation. It is best if he can be shown to be necessarily superior, for then there is no danger of him losing his commanding position.[17]

He adds, "I do not think that this argument is sufficiently substantial to require refutation. Consolation would be more appropriate: perhaps this should be sought in the transmigration of souls"[18]

My sense of this gloss and its shade, at once scathing and hilarious, is that, like the pseudo-theological remark above about intelligent machines "providing mansions for the souls that He creates"[19] it is more than half serious. With Turing we find the sublation of humanist ontologies by a theory of emergence. As the metaphysical artifacts of a particular moment of emergence become outmoded, they will find new basis in computation and will be revealed as heuristic conceits and/or disappear. From the perspective of computation, all machine states are iterations of the crunching of a program—whatever it might be. The soul is not what we thought it was, but those who still need such an interface as a skeuomorph might find it in transubstantiation. That is, in the artificial intelligence of machines grasped through the framework of the soul, particularly as there is increasingly less and less evidence with which to mark a firm boundary between bodies and machines. The soul will require some redefinition beyond the hegemonic framework for there to be progress. And as the black radical tradition might remind us, the notion that soul is not exclusively the province of those with legal claims to humanity, has done significant work.

Turing's brilliance partially entailed the application of mathematical thinking to that symbolic system known as "language." But one must understand that the re-conceptualization and subsequent machinic reduction of representation and particularly of linguistic messages leading to the instrumentalization of representation had long been taking place. The communicative relation as metaphysically constitutional was posited (by for example Nietzsche who disallowed the distinction between the doer and the deed) and increasingly presupposed. From the emergence of print as an economic exploit forward, the denaturing of "natural" language into code was a long time coming. From Sassure's "arbitrary nature of the sign," which severed signifier from signified, to what came to be called the critique of the metaphysics of presence in post-structuralism, this denaturing at first felt like the ancillary dismantling of one more pillar of tradition in the general liquidation of tradition by capitalism (or by science or modernity, as it might have been said) before coming to be seen as the complete subsumption of the history of the human species (and with that the subsumption of history and of the species) by computation, Nietzsche with his typewriter collapsed the philosophical distinction between being and act and became, above all else, a writer—a "general without an army," as has been said, "determined to emphasize maximum influence on the future." Jacques Derrida brought home the idea that in the signifying chain, no one is home. There's no body there in language, just the referent under erasure. Hélène Cixous showed that all Western philosophical binaries rested on gender binaries, and were not indices of truth but rather indices of power—the power of hetero-patriarchy manifest in phallogocentrism and the metaphysics thereof. Thus, in another case of the medium is the message, the very operation of language in the enforcing of sexual difference exceeded it's denotative meaning, imposing the paradigm of the gender binary everywhere. William Pietz's essay, "The Phonograph in Africa" brilliantly recounts the colonial resignification of recordings of native speech for purposes of further colonization by which an imperial overcode resignified and thus denatured a "natural language" by treating it as a pass code. Those (natives) still foolish enough to believe in essences and presence (or at least in the merely discursive realities of suddenly provincial customs and gods) were hoodwinked with phonographic recordings of tribal leaders' voices commanding people to offer hospitality to colonizers. This marked an emerging and increasingly self-conscious tradition, or rather military-political strategy, dedicated to the resignification of existing codes that was capitalized on by Hitler, Mao and Voice of America, and is again being redeployed in a new Amerikkkan synthesis. Ontology was mobilized as politics, and, as Allen Feldman keenly observes, metaphysics in its reconfiguration becomes a medium of war. Barthes' "Myth Today," Adorno and Horkheimer's "Culture Industry," Deleuze and Guattari's "overcode", Kittler's work, Nietzsche's *Geneaology of Morals*, Butler, Cisoux, Sylvia Wynter, and the subsequent would-be wholesale deconstruction of the humanist project, testify to the trend of the repurposing of representation for sets of interests that are not representable within the natural(ized) domain of the represented. Rational-representational systems were mobilized at a higher level than was available to those who were most interpellated by them, one that exceeded the discernment of most of their practitioners. POTUS's irrational universe provides an ample demonstration that the inevitably historical rationales of his psychopathology has a structural and systemic fit organized beyond the horizon of liberal perception—and undoubtedly his own. Then as now, across the board, the medium was the message, which for McLuhan meant precisely that even though a new order was transmitted by changes in mediation, that message, the one regarding the changes imposed by a new media form, was not being consciously received. Today, with the overcoding of every communicative act by financialized computation we may perhaps receive the message of "our" media: it is capital, the political economy of murder by installments. The totalitarian necro-political global regime becomes the hidden content of every message. Communication itself brings it home.

Meanwhile one finds multiple efforts at constructing a physics of metaphysics in answer to the shifted properties of the ontological ground re-iterated and thus transcoded, transformed and re-ordained by computation. Regis Debray examines the technical mediation of images and signs by logical-material systems that render the metaphysics of prior media regimes skeuomorphic, mere theatrical simulations that facilitate the capture of those subjects (themselves both signifiers in all senses of the word and skeuomorphs) who, to make their way, still require an orientation in imaginary universes by ideologies now structurally superseded. The materiality of communication again shows the material-practical basis of the subject in ideology. But as we are also aware the intensification of through-put vis-à-vis screens places the subject in crisis. The various forms of subjective dissolution and implosion are also the message.

Allen Feldman's *Archives of the Insensible* understands the contemporary deployment of metaphysics (the constitution and deconstitution of juridical entities) as a means and modality of war. Guantanamo, for example, is in the business of *producing* terrorists. We have the intentional engineering of subjects: the terrorist *and* the sovereign subject by the carceral machine—the terrorist is retroactively engineered and the sovereign is proactively engineered. Where with Turing and the development of computers, subjectivity was decoded and simulated (that is revealed as a simulation), subjectivity is, with the integration of computers and their calculi into the web of life, encoded and simulated (that is projected as an actionable fact), as a driver of economy and of war. In a general sense we observe that from government sponsored nationalism, to character identification in Hollywood films, to the idea of the computer desktop or file, computational interfaces disbursed throughout the socius utilize retrograde modes of subjectification (orientation, suture, interface) as well as advanced techniques of assemblage and blurring to perform socio-economic functions whose larger consequences structurally exceed the understanding of the subjects posited, interpellated, fragmented, dis-/re-/al-located ... and above all—above all (?)—functionalized in the informatic matrix that instantiates them.

However, it must be immediately added that the functionalizing of what Althusser calls "concrete individuals" and in another, not unrelated context, Hortense Spillers calls "the flesh" via forms of codification whose invisible processes are shrouded in obscurity and (most often) received/ discerned/interpreted and "understood" only through dependence upon various metaphysical presuppositions that no longer (fully) obtain (e.g. readers of *The New York Times* who think they are merely informing themselves when they read on a platform dedicated to neo-liberal class war), in no way means that all bodies, despite being subjectively and objectively instantiated today by computational modes, are instantiated equally. Patriarchy, racism, heteronormativity, neo-imperialism, political economy, borders, forced migration and the generalization of war amply testify to the intensive material and algorithmic production of social difference. Neither should radical overdetermination by social-media imply any naturalization to the hierarchies imposed, acted upon, produced and reproduced by existing codes and consequently essentialized (or, when convenient, de-essentialized) through computational social process. Just, as Marx taught us, there is not an atom of matter in exchange-value, there is not an atom of nature in computation nor an atom of truth in the metaphysics thereof. Here we arrive at the concept of the fold and the paradox of undecidability: There is exactly no "nature," available in the computational construct; one could say that "nature" is always already a simulation—given up to us by the very means that foreclose its being. (There are times when this reflection is not relevant, and even uncalled for, but such an immersion in an ontology completely isolable from computation is no longer fully, if even at all, possible for "us.") What appears at the horizon of this knowledge during this time, signified by the concept of its very operation (as subjectivity, as computation, as mathematical proof) is the question of a beyond at once necessary and under erasure. Computation is not just a difference engine, but an engine of *differánce*. Simulation = ~~Nature~~.

At its metaphysical best, when, for example the nature that is not simulated but is simulation itself appears to glimmer at the horizon of codification (as the computational multiverse), it comes to occupy the same status as History in Fredric Jameson's *The Political Unconscious*, or the Real in Lacan, or the innumerable in Borges. Jameson's reading of Althusser in *The Political Unconscious* argues that History is both non-narrative and non-subjective, saying it is, rather, an absent structure: "History is *not* a text, not a narrative, master or otherwise, but that as an absent cause, it is inaccessible to us except in textual form, and that our approach to it and to the Real itself necessarily passes through its prior textualization, its narrativization in the political unconscious."[20] History, as distinct from narrative history, is thus posited as the event horizon of knowledge, such that any instantiation is always already a symbolic act in a cosmos where the Real remains unsymbolizable. The Real haunts symbolization, even though symbolization cannot transcend itself to render the Real. Like the Real, History may be troped, but not identified—there is no unmediated access. The dream work of the political unconscious and its representational systems gives it form; the forms are always ideological. In our own moment we observe that it is only the movement of the process of symbolization emergent from the trace through its archive that by means of its own churn gives rise to the computational model. Concisely put, the reality of simulation is also a simulation.

With computational simulation, generalizing itself, for example in the work of Max Tegmark, to cosmic proportions in which the universe is itself a super computer (numbers all the way down, with traditional physical entities such as atoms and quarks, phenomenal forms of data visualization), there is ultimately nothing but numeric operations underpinning ALL. In this totalizing projection of the computational universe extending to all possible knowing we have the retroactive dissolution of metaphysics and the foreclosure not only of Being, but of Nature, History and the Real—all of which must be written with scare quotes to signify that they are not just placeholders for something beyond the horizon of discernment, but that they are indeed empty—former iterations of the impossible, now outmoded, themselves only computational simulations. The hollowing out of prior ontologies, first conceptually and then practically by means of machine operations creates a tremendous crisis of values—in the socio-ethical and the economic. What computational procedures and results will be valued and how? Derivatives, synthetic finance and social media provide answers—no doubt woefully inadequate ones. How to value a person, people, peoples? What forms or formulations might provide an adequate account? The unpleasant question of our time seems not to be Ezra Pound's "Jefferson and/or Mussolini?" or even "Neo-liberalism and/or #45?" but rather, "the slaughter bench of history and/or the slaughter bench of information? Better I think to see the rise of computation not as introducing a crisis of value but as a response to a crisis within the domain of value and valuation—a revolutionizing of the productive forces whose measure has not yet been taken. Here the injunction would be to finally come to terms with the computational unconscious, or what Adam Smith called the invisible hand.

4

Shannon/Hitchcock:
~~Another Method for the Letters~~[1]

Where there is no speech there is no truth or falsehood.
—Thomas Hobbes

That order [the sociopolitical order of the New World], with its human sequence written in blood, represents, for its African and its indigenous peoples a scene of actual mutilation, dismemberment and exile.
—Hortense Spillers

The problem for an unexpected

Soon we will have occasion to delve further into the relationship between history and information, between capital and computation—and thus also between the unsymbolizable and the innumerable—by which I mean to spend a few more words on the parallel mirrors of an infinite regress where the real and the virtual become indistinguishable and thus, for the abstract (and perhaps it must at least be admitted, psychotic) mind, one. We must come to better understand the emergent interface between statistics (stochastics) and *poesis* — for it is along these fractal lines that we encounter what used to be called "politics." We will see that it is necessity itself that must fight the odds and that necessity demands a re-evaluation of the rise of computation—one that historicizes and socializes the anti-social and anti-historical entity called information. We do this by dismantling the supposed objectivity and universality of forms of mediation.

First, however, we review the achievements of Claude E. Shannon, whose 1948 paper, "A Mathematical Theory of Communication," is the landmark essay regarding the conversion of natural language to number—a conversion that weighs the odds of any message whatever. Shannon's "translation" of linguistic symbols into mathematical ones is no ordinary translation. Rather, it signifies the wholesale conversion, that is, the numerological transduction, of the very process of textualization. The reconfiguration of textualization advances a prior period of textualization that was, at least until the rise of visual culture, itself the main process through which history has been understood. Indeed, philosophically, linear writing becomes understood as the precondition of "history," an analogue of as well as a program for linear time and temporal development. Not content with the denotative contents there inscribed, Lacanian Marxism, as we briefly saw in the last chapter, found History in the ellipses and gaps, recorded in the only way it can be—ideologically and in absentia. Nearly all surviving history and experience was rendered or refracted in those "ideologemes" of linguistic form passing through what Friedrich Kittler aptly calls "the bottleneck of the signifier."[2] Included here were not just histories but novels, poems, critical theory, indeed all writing—the empire of signs in total. Shannon's mathematical theory of communication would result in the translation, which is to say conversion, of the repository of textuality that inaugurated history and implied History into an ocean, nay, a cosmos, of ones and zeros—with nary a quark left unturned.

The paper regards the written word and seeks "a general theory of communication"[3] that is content indifferent with respect to the message. The theory needs to account for the possibility of sending any message whatever. Noting, among other factors, "the savings possible due to the statistical structure of the original message," Shannon writes, "the . . . semantic aspects of communication are irrelevant to the engineering problem. The significant aspect is that the actual message is one *selected from a set of possible messages*. The system must be designed to operate for each possible selection, not just the one which will actually be chosen since this is unknown at the time of design" (italics added).[4] Furthermore, "We wish to consider certain general problems involving communication systems. To do this it is first necessary to represent the various elements involved as mathematical entities, suitably idealized from their physical counterparts."[5]

Let us attend carefully here: "The actual message is one selected from a set of possible messages. The system must be designed . . . for each possible selection, not just the one which will actually be chosen since this is unknown at the time of design." The advantage of statistics will emerge from the fact that some messages are more likely than others. A particular novel, then, is the one selected from a set of possible novels— not all writers are yet aware of this fact. Even the text before you was selected from a set of possible texts. And *Psycho* was selected from a set of possible images—as we shall demonstrate, a not entirely random thought. On the one hand, we are dealing with a question involving any message whatever, in short, any possible combination of symbols that might be found, say, as in Jorge Luis Borges's "Library of Babel," the library that most closely approximates quantum multiverses in that this infinite library contains all possible books. Pondering this infinite library, the lone narrator poignantly remarks, "If an eternal traveler were to cross it in any direction, after centuries he would see that the same volumes were repeated in the same disorder (which, thus repeated, would be an order: the Order). My solitude is gladdened by this elegant hope."[6] On the other hand (I will limit myself to two here)—and this is the key insight in Shannon's paper—unlike as in the library of Babel, all messages are not equiprobable. If they were, there could be no useful mathematical theory of communication, because the organization of signs would be entirely random. Shannon's insight builds on the fact that such random occurring is not, in fact, the case: some messages are statistically more likely than others, and there are concrete ways to delimit the random factor by studying the frequency and sequence of the occurrence of letters in natural language. To get a sense of how Shannon proceeds from Gutenbergian homogeneous segmentation to create statistical models, I quote at length:

> We can also approximate to a natural language by means of a series of simple artificial languages. The zero-order approximation is obtained by choosing all letters with the same probability and independently. The first-order approximation is obtained by choosing successive letters independently but each letter having the same probability that it has in the natural language. Thus, in the first-order approximation to English, E is chosen with probability .12 (its frequency in normal English) and W with probability .02, but there is no influence between adjacent letters and no tendency to form the preferred diagrams such as TH, ED, etc. In the second-order approximation, diagram structure is introduced. After a letter is chosen, the next one is chosen in accordance with the frequencies with which the various letters follow the first one. This requires a table of diagram frequencies pi(j). In the third-order approximation, trigram structure is introduced. Each letter is chosen with probabilities which depend on the preceding two letters.[7]

3. THE SERIES OF APPROXIMATIONS TO ENGLISH

To give a visual idea of how this series of processes approaches a language, typical sequences in the approximations to English have been constructed and are given below. In all cases we have assumed a 27-symbol "alphabet," the 26 letters and a space.

1. Zero-order approximation (symbols independent and equiprobable).
XFOML RXKHRJFFJUJ ZLPWCFWKCYJ FFJEYVKCQSGHYD QPAAMKBZAACIBZLHJQD.

2. First-order approximation (symbols independent but with frequencies of English text).
OCRO HLI RGWR NMIELWIS EU LL NBNESEBYA TH EEI ALHENHTTPA OOBTTVA NAH BRL.

3. Second-order approximation (diagram structure as in English).
ON IE ANTSOUTINYS ARE T INCTORE ST BE S DEAMY ACHIN D ILONASIVE TUCOOWE AT TEASONARE FUSO TIZIN ANDY TOBE SEACE CTISBE.

4. Third-order approximation (trigram structure as in English).
IN NO IST LAT WHEY CRATICT FROURE BIRS GROCID PONDENOME OF DEMONSTURES OF THE REPTAGIN IS REGOACTIONA OF CRE.

5. First-order word approximation. Rather than continue with tetragram, · · ·, n-gram structure it is easier and better to jump at this point to word units. Here words are chosen independently but with their appropriate frequencies.

REPRESENTING AND SPEEDILY IS AN GOOD APT OR COME CAN DIFFERENT NATURAL HERE HE THE A IN CAME THE TOOF TO EXPERT GRAY COME TO FURNISHES THE LINE MESSAGE HAD BE THESE.

6. Second-order word approximation. The word transition probabilities are correct but no further structure is included.
THE HEAD AND IN FRONTAL ATTACK ON AN ENGLISH WRITER THAT THE CHARACTER OF THIS POINT IS THEREFORE ANOTHER METHOD FOR THE LETTERS THAT THE TIME OF WHO EVER TOLD THE PROBLEM FOR AN UNEXPECTED.[8]

In brief, items 2—6 in capital letters are samples of signs randomly generated by means of probability tables (or an equivalent method; see below), with probabilities weighted as described; item 1 is a string of letters generated completely at random. It is well known today that as a result of habituated literacy, the brain "knows" how to fill in the gaps in a message that might be generated by dropped or out-of-sequence lettering, and when scanning the lines above we can literally feel that capacity being activated even if it does not fully realize what we ordinarily think of as an intelligible message. As we shall see, Shannon understands literacy to imply unconscious statistical knowledge about the operations of language. If we recall from Jacques Lacan that the unconscious is structured like a language,[9] here we begin to understand something new about how a language is structured. It would appear that there are rule sets, otherwise known as laws. And these laws (laws that ultimately conform to the law of the Father) are the laws of probability. Shannon's examples are the pre-Oedipal stammerings of the computational unconscious.

Normal behavior (organized by laws, the law) delimits the kind of things that actually get said (through repression). Desire—though perhaps no more random than life itself in that it emerges out of randomness but then follows its own logic, its drives—is polymorphous and must therefore be managed by its chances at a successful (or is it profitable?) outcome, which is to say managed by what could be grasped as an algorithm first formulated and once known as the "reality principle."[10] Likewise, the realities of normal English (what it is permissible to say) will structure the likelihood of the occurrence of any message whatever through statistical modeling. As we shall see, it is on the basis of such research and experimentation that Shannon's machinic utterances resemble real language. The reality principle is another name for an algorithm of psychic repression, and translating forward from this earlier paradigm implies that so too is the statistical ordination of language. Not just anything can burble forth—we cannot have our computers speaking in tongues.

The mathematical theory of communication is content indifferent, but what does content indifference communicate? Here, with Shannon's phrase in item 6, "THE HEAD AND IN FRONTAL ATTACK ON AN ENGLISH WRITER THAT THE CHARACTER OF THIS POINT IS THEREFORE ANOTHER METHOD FOR THE LETTERS THAT THE TIME OF WHO EVER TOLD THE PROBLEM FOR

AN UNEXPECTED," constructed by means of second-order word approximation, we have the heretofore unavailed of opportunity to usefully confront the following imperative that was a staple of literary criticism for the decades spanning the early 1970s to the late 1990s: psychoanalyze this! It is understood now (or should be) that psycho-analysis was an analogue technology straining to make itself adequate to a set of mathematical vectors grounded in the capitalized logistics of the bourgeois family that included the calculus of sexual difference, of inheritance, property, and pleasure as well as that of class and the disavowal of race and, as important, particularly when history gets to Lacan, that of the image. One could say that psychoanalysis was derived from the prolegomena of the emergent information economy's restructuring of interiority and allowed the analyst to take a derivative of ambient information at any point in the garden of forking paths.[11] This derivative was of course the discourse of the modern subject, the discursive modality of risk management that produced modern subjectivity through the repressive hypothesis and later via the phar-macological industrialization of self-help and ultimately by the neurotic abjection imposed by the full financialization of daily life.[12] Psycho-analysis then was an analogue approach to incipient digitization, a way of narrating ambient unconscious forces. Although things are no longer organized at the highest levels in accord with its paradigm of the subject, which accords with a fantasy of subjective sovereignty—think not "the ego" but rather algorithmic governance—we might want to explore what goes on, that is, to think the logistics of informatics for the/a subject, as if it still mattered, because to some people it does.

PSYCHO: "pure cinema" as meditation on castration
and paradigm of codification

"WHO EVER TOLD THE PROBLEM FOR AN UNEXPECTED?" Well, let's just say, "THE HEAD AND IN FRONTAL ATTACK ON AN ENGLISH WRITER [SUCH] THAT THE CHARACTER OF THIS POINT IS THEREFORE ANOTHER METHOD FOR THE LETTERS."

Shannon's procedural generation of signs in accord with statistical rules applied to Markoff states provides a kind of cipher for what may as well be inscribed as an ur-text of the computational unconscious—these signs are as good as any. Put it this way (stay with me here—remember, this text is *selected*): just as it is possible to read Norman Bates as Alfred Hitchcock's conscious creation, designed precisely to decode and then encode the effect of a newly mobilized gaze on the law of the father in order to create what was referred to as "pure cinema" (we will do this momentarily), we might engage Shannon's symbolic creations in his paper and "do a reading." Hitchcock, also looking for a general theory, for "pure cinema," set out to register the preconditions, symptoms, and consequences of an algorithm called psychosis (a freewheeling variant of the reality principle in which a gender-troubled masculine-identifying subject is at pains to impose reality in his own terms because the larger, collective reality is just too much to deal with and must therefore be radically denied). Psychosis results in the improper translation and thus the short-circuiting (vis-à-vis the cut) of the rules imposed not just by propriety, civilization, and patriarchy, but by signification and the law. Indeed it sacrifices these rules outwardly in order to preserve them inwardly, endeavoring to constitute itself as sovereign in impossible circumstances. In *Psycho*, Norman's psychosis is shown to be the result of Norman's mother cutting the normative dispensation of the signifier scripted by the law of the father—she gets rid of her husband, Norman's father, and after an unusually intense bond with young Norman (ordinarily precluded by oedipalization), takes another lover, therefore depriving Norman of, in short order, the nuclear family, the name of the father and access to the mother. In brief, unrestrained female desire blocks Norman's ascension to full masculinity and a woman will have to pay—that's the story. The story is thus one of failed oedipalization and an inability to attain to the symbolic order, which subsequently, in what was to become *the* formula for classic horror, causes further cutting.

As we all know, the fatal cuts slice Marion (Marrying?) Crane. She becomes in the taxonomy of the film yet another bird to be stuffed, at least as far as Norman, castrated by his mother and held in the "half-light of the imaginary," is concerned. Like what Laura Mulvey said of cinema itself, Norman will cut the woman to the measure of desire. Marion who herself cut the law of the father and stole forty thousand dollars to support her own illicit pleasure with lover Sam (himself laboring under alimony payments, and unable to afford to marry Marion and make things legit) has in her flight from the law aroused Norman, and, after checking in to the Bates Motel, takes a shower. Called upon to be man but cut off from an ability to "properly" constitute his masculinity by an overbearing mother, Norman makes a few cuts of his own. Psychosis thus results at once from the cut in normative behavior organized under patriarchy but is also an intensification. In this tale it results from the provocation by and subsequent liquidation of female agency ("sexuality"). The deviation of the psychotic's desires from the code of patriarchy, and their re-conversation into that same code, otherwise known as "the law," is here expressed in the sequence woman = crane = bird = stuffed. If normativity can't answer and control female sexuality, psychosis will provide other methods. Norman's removal of the copy of the painting *Susanna and the Elders* to reveal the peephole through which he may gaze at and thus objectify Marion, concisely suggests not just an image for the cinema, but that the (white Western) male gaze has long engaged in quasi-psychotic sadistic objectification: Norman literally reveals what lies beneath the Western tradition and looks right through it.

But with new media come new opportunities. The light from the peephole evokes the light cone of the cinema and the affordances offered the voyeur. Like cinema, and in an homage to the quagmire of castration, the desire that is his gaze executes with the cut. Hitchcock's own algorithmic program in *Psycho*, otherwise known as the plot, but I mean more than mere narrative here, iterates a main character: NORMAN BATES—written in capital letters here to denote that it is the output of an algorithm of psychoanlysis as operative in the newly mechanized (cinemated) visual sphere. NORMAN BATES is a name that, as the eloquent Saul Bass-designed credits slicing through the signifiers in the titles of "P̶S̶Y̶C̶H̶O̶" might indicate, bears the mark of the psychopathological cutting of the signifier—a visual editing of a phrase that can be reverse engineered to its proper form of signification. The slashing of the signifier "psycho" in the same set of titles might indicate that, under the force of the cut, "Psycho" removes "path." Following the path of *Psycho* the signifying chain NORMAN BATES can be restored to an "original state" when signification functions normally, that is in accord with the everyday operations of the law of the father, and is thus organized not according to a short-circuiting of law by mobilized (female) desire (a castrating mother and a sexually modern Marion Crane)—but by warding off such a brazen cut, and living peaceably in accord with the law as it purports to operate in the reality of pre-cinema. This reverse engineering of psychopathology—Norman's psychopathology, cannily attributed to the rest of us by his exemplary role as cinematic voyeur who, to preserve his own fragile homeostasis, to ward off castration, has a tendency to overobjectify (desubjectify) women—clearly allows the audience to grasp from the coded message that is NORMAN BATES a sort of corollary to the law of the father and its necessary legacy repression of desire up until modern, cinematic capitalism.

NORMAN BATES is an algorithmic encryption of the law placed under duress by cine-mediated scopophilia and the mobilization of desire beyond the traditional capacities of the symbolic order to contain it; the code is the result of an old law caught in the press of modernity and new media. Norman is the result of a linguistic short circuit (hence his stutter), a cutting of the symbolic order (as ordered by the name of the Father). Even the situation of the backwater Bates Motel produces a persistent ressentiment regarding the irrelevance imposed upon its location by the new modern highway that cut off Norman's access to power. What then would Norman's name be if, in accord with longstanding patriarchal custom, castration were "properly" reserved for women alone? Reverse engineering law-breaking Norman would be an act of decoding (interpretation) that reveals Hitchcock's under-standing of the law itself—its flailing operations in a cinemated world. Let us then interpolate the proper letters back into NORMAN BATES, who, as victim of some unfortunate cuts (for him and for his victims yes, but fortunate in all financial senses for the history of cinema), is probably no more than two standard deviations from the norm by which the patriarchal regulation of desire by the ordinary signification process is imposed. Let us sound our own unconscious and restore the path to psycho. A moment's thought reveals the following elisions or cuts: THE MAL MASTUR, an abridgement that, when properly recombined, solves the puzzle and reveals the fuller text of the everyday law of patriarchy: NORMAN BATES without the castrating (cinematic) cut imposed by female sexuality and its imperative for the reorganization of male desire fills the lacunae in the code and gives us our result: THE NORMAL MAN MASTURBATES. Unappealing as it may be (to some), such is the corollary and consequence of the law of the father, the situation imposed by the otherwise unacceptable terms of female sexuality and the cinematic obscene. When all goes smoothly in patriarchy, the "normal" pathway to taking the woman as object suffices—that's everyday objectification. But when a modern (cinematic) woman, pursues her newly mobilized desire and breaks the bounds of the law by trying to cut out her own version of THE MAL MASTUR (dreamwork for the bad master, the name of the father, of course) in pursuit of her own satisfaction, the result is a new plot: a procedure that also sends a message: NORMAN BATES![13]

In a classic case of psychoanalysis blaming the victim, female desire, in revolt against capitalist heteropatriarchy (the law of the father and the big other), produces the male psychopath (and makes for good-profitable cinema in its day). Its disruptive consequences can themselves be decoded, that is, reversed engineered, to reveal the law of the father. The code is broken and re-inscribed. Norman Bates is the logical consequence of the increasing power of female desire organized around the objectification of women, or here, the axiom that in heteropatriarchy, to ward off castration and still comply with the law, the normal man masturbates. Without going so far as to speculate on what a world might look like rid of normal men, we can say that precisely this is the project of *Psycho*—to use psychoanalysis to decode the consequences of the unmoored mobilized gaze of cinema on the Oedipus complex and thus to encode "pure cinema." This project, with a different inflection, would shortly thereafter be taken up by "second wave" feminist film theory as it attempted to decodify the male gaze, derive the psychologistics of gender oppression from the analogue (and re-enforcing) screen image, cut to the measure of desire—and thus to requisites of "the patriarchal unconscious".

We note in passing that this image, cut to the measure of desire, was itself subject to box-office digitization. Mother rids herself of Norman's father, and Marion rebels against all that is personified in money, but the male gaze must impose its continuity and seek its compensation. In *Psycho* the more acceptable, sober regard belongs to psychoanalysis itself and even more emphatically to money. After her murder, Marion is apprehended from the point of view of money in the shot-counter shot sequence immediately following the annihilation of her gaze. Her agential lifeblood flows from her cut-up body into the dark abyss of the bathtub drain and, in an astonishingly eloquent cut, that itself marks the literal liquidation of female subjectivity, the camera gaze follows the bloody swirl down into the void and emerges out of her now dead eye. The counter shot to this shot of Marion's annihilated gaze and total objectification is the money on the bed. Indeed, Hitchcock's own heuristic, albeit bound by whiteness, would seem to be that the cinema, as a new order of codification (and here we get closer to what I meant by viewing plot as algorithm), restores the law of the father that it itself interrupts through the mobilization of the gaze and the reorganization of desire by means of the cut, precisely by traversing the psychotic—namely, the reality denying domain of the cut that reorganizes both perception and the signifying chain. As a break with and a short circuit of the law of the linguistic sign, the cinema is an invitation to psychopatholgy. With it, the ambient program of psychosis is at once executed and canceled by the successful work of art—make that the commercially successful work of art. The short-circuiting of the law of the father by the liberation of cinema eye and its modernity can be recodified by the cinema, by capitalist cinema. The psychotic denial of female agency is decoded, re-inscribed, and raised to the level of cultural paradigm.

Hitchcock used the Lacanian algorithm of the symbolic order organized in accord with the law (rule set) of the father governing desire to concoct his signifying machine. As mentioned and as is well known, the (white) woman in jeopardy became a general formula for cinema with gender-troubled protagonists but one might also say action films and all the rest. This formula is also reversed, particularly in horror, which, with its increasingly venerable history, provides gender-troubled antagonists and phallic women heroes—what Carol Clover famously called "the final girl." Laurence Rickels' fine intertitles, "The New Norman in *Dressed to Kill, Blow Out* and *Body Double*," followed by "The Feminist Reproach in *Slumber Party Massacre*," understand the mutability of the code.[14] These rules (property, marriage, policing, privilege, sovereignty, the regulation of sexuality, the phallus)—threatened yet also enforced by the cut— were the weighted factors that staved off randomness. The stochastics of heteropatriarchy overdetermined the film program—also known as the plot. Queer becoming happened in the margins and interstices by refusing the codifications and re-codifications of normative positions. But it was precisely the cutting of the law of the father by new imaginaries that led to the cutting of the signifying chain that led to Norman Bates and a reassertion of the law of the father as "pure cinema." The medium then, in its pure form, or at least in this "pure" form is itself psychotic.

As a medium, cinema first cuts the law but is then recut in accord with the law. Interesting then that Lacan, as Lydia Liu recently argued, concocted his theories of the symbolic order and the unconscious from the insights of cybernetics and information theory, which he used to comprehend Freud.[15] It is therefore not entirely imprecise to suggest that the fundamentals of Shannon's mathematical theory of communication provide the means for the decodification and recodification not just of psychoanalysis but also of *Psycho*. And indeed many of Hitchcock's films were thoroughgoing exercises in decoding and recoding of psychologistics in a cinemated world.

~~ANOTHER METHOD FOR THE LETTERS~~

So we have, albeit in a limited way, a sense of how dominant cinema codes its objects and through that treatment creates a world for its subjects. We will return to the cinema as a more general form in a later chapter. As for Shannon's THE PROBLEM FOR AN UNEXPECTED, THE FRONTAL ATTACK ON AN ENGLISH WRITER (or is it THE FRONTAL ATTACK ON AN *ENGLISH* WRITER?), ANOTHER METHOD FOR THE LETTERS …—these iterations too are the result of the operation of an algorithmic machine. But is it the effect of the machine operator on their machine (Antonio Gramsci) or of the machine on the machine operator? Like NORMAN BATES, it too is the result of cutting up of language and the law. Here, however, not with the lens and its images, but with statistics and their mathematical odds. In moving from the machine age to the digital (DC1 to DC2), we should bear in mind the shifting relation between the worker and the machine during the move from manufacture to fully industrialized capital when Marx observed that the machine as fixed capital became "a vast automaton" and the worker became its "conscious organ." Indeed we are looking at the agency of machines, agency that good historical materialists will recognize as the agency of fixed capital and thus as the agency of dead labor—amortized subjectivity. The subject, organized by the machinic cut in the life-world, and then re-vised by the cinematic cut in the visual field, will now be reformatted by the statistical cut in the signifying chain by means of a mathematical theory of communication that is purportedly content indifferent. If NORMAN BATES is the cinematically encoded output of a message that properly expressed reads THE NORMAL MAN MASTURBATES, can we then ask what is the unadulterated, that is decoded or "proper" expression of Shannon's

THE HEAD AND IN FRONTAL ATTACK ON AN ENGLISH WRITER THAT THE CHARACTER OF THIS POINT IS THEREFORE ANOTHER METHOD FOR THE LETTERS THAT THE TIME OF WHO EVER TOLD THE PROBLEM FOR AN UNEXPECTED?

To propose an answer to this, my central question here regarding ANOTHER METHOD FOR THE LETTERS, let us look a bit more closely at the exact method by which Shannon's example passages were procedurally generated in order to attempt a similar reverse engineering. In reference to the passages excerpted above Shannon writes:

> The resemblance to ordinary English text increases quite noticeably at each of the above steps. Note that these samples have reasonably good structure out to about twice the range that is taken into account in their construction. Thus in (3) the statistical process insures reasonable text for two-letter sequences, but four-letter sequences from the sample can usually be fitted into good sentences. In (6) sequences of four or more words can easily be placed in sentences without unusual or strained constructions. The particular sequence of ten words "attack on an English writer that the character of this" is not at all unreasonable. It appears then that a sufficiently complex stochastic process will give a satisfactory representation of a discrete source. The first two samples were constructed by the use of a book of random numbers in conjunction with (for example 2) a table of letter frequencies. This method might have been continued for (3), (4) and (5), since diagram, trigram and word frequency tables are available, but a simpler equivalent method was used.
>
> To construct (3) for example, one opens a book at random and selects a letter at random on the page. This letter is recorded. The book is then opened to another page and one reads until this letter is encountered. The succeeding letter is then recorded. Turning to another page this second letter is searched for and the succeeding letter recorded, etc. A similar process was used for (4), (5) and (6). It would be interesting if further approximations could be constructed, but the labor involved becomes enormous at the next stage.[16]

Shannon's purpose here is to develop statistical rules that will allow for maximum economy in the transmission of a message through a communications channel by reducing the number of bits required for each symbol. In short, the less information required to send a message, the more message content that can be sent over a given channel. The procedurally generated statements above express the effect of reducing the randomness of trying any sign arbitrarily. To properly select it from a set of signs in the making of a message, the selection process is structured by the frequency of the occurrence of particular symbols or sequence of symbols and thus the likelihood or probability of a term occurring following the occurrence of a given sign or sequence of signs— using standard written English. One can grasp the benefits of such a process in the telegraph in which dots and dashes must be decoded to restore a message. Obviously the fewer dots and dashes required to send a particular message, the more efficient the transmission. Thus the mathematics of the likelihood of usage along with the likelihood of one alphabetic symbol's adjacency to another are statistically tabled to construct a code that will require, on average, the fewest number of bits of information (dots and dashes, ones and zeros) to transmit any message whatever.[17]

The conditions thus formulated, we might return to our method of interpolation with regard to Shannon's example to ask what seems to be an absurd question: what is the machine really saying? Can we grasp this algorithmic output as a narrative? With cinema we had to grasp the narrative as algorithm; with informatics we strain to grasp the algorithm as story. Following Lacan's example of the child confronted at an early stage in his development by the as yet unknown language of his parents, we can ask of Shannon's protomachine, why is it telling us this? If we allow our unconscious to peruse the output and thus audition the machine unconscious, we find that the "POINT" is obviously the mode of inscription of a dot or a dash, a one or a zero, a hole punch in a card or a tape, that is, the binary action that in executing a program modifies the machine's storage by writing a one or zero, one binary sign at a time. Undoubtedly, this is the new head (as opposed to the old human one), which is also a FRONTAL ATTACK ON AN ENGLISH WRITER [such] THAT THE CHARACTER OF THIS POINT IS THEREFORE ANOTHER METHOD FOR THE LETTERS THAT [alters] THE TIME OF WHO EVER even those who TOLD THE PROBLEM FOR AN UNEXPECTED message including and perhaps especially Africans, African slaves, and their descendents, first peoples, minorities, colonials and all the Others of the "West."

Well okay, the interpolative method may have its limits, despite the brilliant use of it by scholars like Saidiya Hartman and poets like M. NourbeSe Philip, author of the poem *ZONG! ZONG!* is based on the text of the manifest of the slave ship *Zong*—a ship that, by the way, contains an error of transcription in its own name, originally *Zorg*. The original name was copied incorrectly in a port where it was being restored, a name that, irony of ironies, meant "care" in Dutch. Care, recoded as slave ship, banking on an insurance payout, notoriously sank its human cargo in the ocean and manifested as poem—a poem that through speculation shows the true meaning of Dutch care. A slave manifest manifested in poetry as lamentation, protest, and counter-history, a bubbling up of unimaginable pain through the seals of its encryption. One might listen carefully to item number 5 (above), the procedurally generated language with one degree less order than the line that steadfastly contains "the time of who ever," and faintly hear the poetry that is at once reprimand and lament: REPRESENTING AND SPEEDILY IS AN GOOD APT OR COME CAN DIFFERENT NATURAL HERE HE THE A IN CAME THE TOOF TO EXPERT GRAY COME TO FURNISHES THE LINE MESSAGE HAD BE THESE. "The line message had be these," says the line, but did they? Another irrelevant connection, you might at this point think, really a method of no method, working on the thinnest threads of connection in the cut-'n'-mix vortex of signification that, despite the poetic resonance between the horrific informatic reduction of Africans to cargo in brutally measured hulls, the cruel numbers of murderous accounting ledgers, and the reduction of living language to content-indifferent numbers for instrumental purposes, brings us not one iota closer to decoding a text for which there can be no original. The bottleneck of the signifier was far too narrow for most of what actually happened. And written history, we have been a bit too smugly told, is written by the victors. Counter-history can only be glimpsed in the gaps, the ellipses. We must sound the algorithms and audit the computational unconscious. No doubt procedurally generated language, written by the victors' machines, has eliminated the ellipses and all forms of the unconscious and can mean only one thing. It all but closes off the bottleneck to history. In this it is like the official version of history but better purged of any remainder, stain, or excess, which despite those feints and glimmers, the sounding of an unconscious that is no longer there, it can also mean in the light of day only one thing (particularly, need the world remind you, as God is dead, *telos* is nothing more, and computation reigns), that is, precisely, really, ultimately just what it says—just what it says and no more, which is to say, metaphysically speaking, absolutely nothing. Computation as pure simulation destroys linear history and eliminates the unconscious by operating exclusively on its own symbols. Today, "real-time," financial-ized, networked simulation operates on a churn of content indifferent 1s and 0s increasingly removed from anything "historical." The generalized expropriation of language by the full colonization of the life-world by computational capital renders all meaning solely the meanings of money. The significance of "meaning" is one-dimensional—automated, functional and anti-hermeneutic—without content. The linguistic signs may simulate qualities, but they are iterated by stochastic methods, that is, weighted yet ultimately random events of pure quantification. In brief, those words don't mean a thing.

Or so it may seem in your nihilist cosmology. But let's not forget that in the name of efficiency, of economy, in the name of shipping the greatest number of signs in the smallest possible container, the mathematicians decided what was normal. They decided what was normal about language. They looked about and comprehended normal men. They told themselves some stories and encrypted these stories in their calculations. Uncanny then, to find out that the ur-text for Shannon's experiments with word sequence was Dumas Malone's *Jefferson the Virginian* (1948), the first volume of Malone's six-volume biography of a man who was the author of the *Declaration of Independence*, the third US president, and a slave owner, one Thomas Jefferson.[18] "The content of a medium is another medium," says Marshall McLuhan;[19] the content of Shannon's code is Malone's; his world, encoded and recut. Malone was a highly distinguished historian who served on the faculty at Yale, Columbia, and the University of Virginia, who was also director of Harvard University Press. He was, in brief, an establisher of the establishment who wrote a huge book on an even more established establisher of the establishment. His volumes were widely praised for their lucid and graceful writing style, for their rigorous and thorough scholarship, and for their attention to Jefferson's evolving constitutional and political thought.[20]

Jefferson the Virginian is a narrative of "America," of the new world order. But as Hortense Spillers so eloquently schools her readers in her dismantling of American grammar, in the quotation that serves as an epigraph to this chapter "that order, with its human sequence written in blood, represents, for its African and its indigenous peoples a scene of actual mutilation, dismemberment and exile."[21] What then is represented by the re-inscription of that imposed order by the mathematical theory of communication for African and indigenous peoples? Even early on some reviewers faulted Malone, believing that he had a tendency to adopt Jefferson's own perspective and thus to be insufficiently critical of Jefferson's occasional political errors, faults, and lapses. Some said that he was biased in favor of Jefferson and against his principal adversaries,

Alexander Hamilton, Aaron Burr, and John Marshall.[22] It was said that Malone had not adequately treated Jefferson's life as a slave owner and the paradoxes inherent in his views on liberty and slavery. Malone did not examine the facts related to Jefferson's long-alleged relationship with his slave Sally Hemings. Famously, Annette Gordon-Reed, in her 1996 analysis of the historiography of the controversy, blew Malone's text wide open and showed that he had accepted testimony by Jefferson descendants, who said that two Carr nephews were the father(s) of Hemings's children, but had dismissed accounts by former slaves, including Sally's son Madison Hemings, that named Jefferson as father, although these accounts were better supported by available facts.[23]

One could indeed wonder here what differences might have emerged and what actual mutilation might have been avoided if Shannon's research on the predictability of standard language had been based on a text that included the history/ies of Jefferson's slave ownership. And what if the ur-text for "The Mathematical Theory of Communication" had included slave narratives and slave speech? What if the psychotic discourse of "American Grammar," as Spillers so deftly names the paradigm of unreconstructed American semiotic iteration that in its syntagmatic emergence continues to disavow the presence of the historical violence of slavery and simultaneously performs the recapitulation of white supremacy in every possible meaning, had not been the "normal" language decoded and then recoded according to the same, now fully digital law? If Shannon's order had not been drawn from that new world order, would the autocorrect in your iPhone work differently? Would the entire universe of statistically transmitted language have been more nurturing of black life, more amenable and just plain friendly to global blackness? On this latter point, there can be no doubt. As smoking gun and as incremental excision of black, Latinx and native life/history, Shannon's foundational moves are both paradigmatic and symptomatic. As the textual reference template to generate statistical information regarding textual predictors by doing research on subjects given certain letters of a text whose subsequent letters had to be guessed, *Jefferson the Virginian*, like so many other default encodings fatally skews the results. Racism sediments into the architecture of modern machines.

Regarding the clear success of his method, Shannon stated that "results of this order are typical of prediction by a good subject with ordinary literary English. Newspaper writing, scientific work and poetry generally lead to somewhat poorer scores."[24] We clearly see here how even for

Shannon, rhetorical difference and indeed social difference, both in terms of the form of the original text and in terms of the "good subject," affect the mathematical outcomes. When these same equations are used to produce texts, to (re)generate texts from reduced or encoded texts, the texts themselves become inputs into the socius that affect the outputs, which is to say that, in the name of efficiency, of economy, and the most efficient shipping of signifiers, they tend to reproduce their own semiotic architecture at the level of statistics, and these statistics endlessly feed back into semiotics, consciousness, and lived experience. Thus #Blacklivesmatter becomes a statistically improbable event. Until now.

Shannon remarked, "anyone speaking a language possesses, implicitly, an enormous knowledge of the statistics of the language. Familiarity with the words, idioms, clichés and grammar enables him to fill in missing or incorrect letters in proofreading, or to complete an unfinished phrase in conversation."[25] What goes unremarked about this generalized unconscious knowledge is that social differences among speakers imply both differences in the types of implicit "knowledge of the statistics of the language" and different statistics. These differences, we wager, are not content indifferent. Understanding the culture-programming-culture loop, Beyoncé's comparison of herself to Bill Gates in *Formation* ("I just might be a black Bill Gates in the making") may not be too far off. She too has a brilliant program—one that has grasped the potentials of the programmable image in a new way. Despite the fact that it is precisely sociohistorical and political differences that are disappeared from the communications model by the assumption of a norm on which to base the content-indifferent model, these differences nonetheless function as programs. In place of psychoanalysis or cinematic apparatus, Shannon creates a statistical model of implicit linguistic law. But his modeling of this unconscious knowledge as universal and content indifferent is possible only because of the unconsciousness of his method with respect to the new world order—so clearly and differently perceptible to decolonization and anti-racist struggle—and thus inscribes the computational unconscious through machinic repression. The measure of the results, better or poorer scores, are not matters of objectivity but value judgments encoded in the conception of the task at hand, in the very idea of what is to be shipped. This adoption of one standard over another in the handling of cargo obviously has a direct relationship to history, authority, hegemony, race, gender, and class. It is a relationship of no less consequence than that of the normativity of white heteropatriarchy, the psychosis of which was interrogated in the linguistic domain by feminist critiques of phallogocentrism,[26] and by theorists of decolonization, anti-imperialism, deconstruction, and postcoloniality. These were thinkers, in short, who were neither fully overtaken by the informatics of linguistic efficiency (only one way of putting a price on time) nor seeking a Hollywood ending (reconciliation by means of sublimation) to their struggles.

While it might be argued that these questions regarding the social and historical character of another method for the letters are matters for sociology, history, or aesthetic theory, that is, for the humanities rather than for the objective or virtual worlds of mathematics and computation, it is worth noticing that it is precisely such a conceit that eliminates the social from the now fully e-numerated linguistic in the first place. Communication is treated at the outset as if it were content indifferent, and then, once a whole system has been built upon that axiom, the fact that the system works is taken as proof of concept. But for whom is this efficiency when deep in its DNA is its founding ideology of value neutrality and the assumption of the right to set standards? "*The author of an atrocious undertaking ought to imagine he has already accomplished it, ought to impose upon himself a future that is as irrevocable as the past,*" wrote Borges. The structural exclusion of social difference, the weighted bias against the non-normative, which is to say the non-hegemonic, modes of signification, at once constitutes a baseline, imposes a past and a future, and shapes the current mathematical and computational consciousness. In the imposition of normativity we saw that *Psycho* treats the exception that proves the rule, Shannon's rules admit no exceptions. Such normative encodings render a world where what can be recognized as plot, as thought, as information by its "conscious organs," all but excludes as idle speculation, irrationality, baseless outrage, bad scholarship, or just plain noise, the possibility of interrogating, much less smashing, the structural and epistemic limits of the code's very mode.

5

The Internet of Value, by Karl Marx: Information as Cosmically Distributed Alienation

I thought of a labyrinth of labyrinths, of one sinuous spreading labyrinth that would encompass the past and the future and in some way involve the stars.

—Borges

There is a deceptively simple but nonetheless correct equation between what has become the media-environment and the unconscious, discernable from the evidence that is the global warming of the material substrate of our thought and now entering a new stage variously christened, the anthropocene, "the capitalocene," "the white supremacist capitalocene," (Mark Driscoll), plantationocene, chthulucene (Haraway). There is also a growing recognition that these hot materialities are indeed the return of the repressed of centuries of idealism, alienated science and all its attendant if unfathomable colonial violence. However the argument of *Message*, that both "the environment" and "the unconscious" are computational and together currently comprise elements of a single system, goes further than just to suggest that these two ostensibly separable conceptual entities (the first demonstrably everywhere as indicated by "the anthropocene," and the second, only just proposed in this text as "the computational unconscious") are of a piece. Let us recall through the lens of Stanislaw Lem and Andre Tarkovsky (*Solaris*) that according to Marx (arguably the first great figure in software studies) "nature is man's inorganic body"—and the history of the species is also the history of the transformation of this inorganic body—its reprogramming. No wonder that in the fictional, if allegorical, science of "Solaristics" that investigates the uncanny star Solaris, the very appearance of the cosmos becomes an expression of the species' repressed. In an interactive and recursive relation, Solaris mysteriously sends emanations of the scientists' unconscious back to their observatory to haunt them.

Marx's de-encryption of private property anticipates this insight into the historical materiality of the as yet untheorized unconscious that would later emanate from the outside when in the 1844 manuscripts he cracks the code (codification) of private property to show that private property, rather than being a natural form (along with its affective dimension, "greed" existing as a natural attribute), is "not the cause but the effect of alienated labor." The long history of alienated labor is the antecedent of the universalist generalization of private property that comes into being only by separating the workers' product from the worker and giving them less in return and recursively iterating through cycles of expansion for centuries without end. The analogy Marx uses to discredit the naturalizing mythos of private property as the cause of avarice and wage labor is one with theology. "[T]he gods in the beginning are not the cause but the effect of man's intellectual confusion. Later this relationship becomes reciprocal."[1] Private property as effect is naturalized and soon taken up as an explanatory cause by political economists and nearly everyone else and this is the source of intellectual confusion, to say the least. As "man" is inscribed in "nature," "nature" is inscribed in "man," says Marx, in a reciprocity based for him upon a confusion of first principals.

Such recursive mistaking of mediation effects for causal agents—private property, avarice, the subject, the nation—has been a leitmotif thus far in *Message*. We observe that this type of mistake, characteristic of idealism, has all too often naturalized murder. With colonialism and the forced shattering of indigenous traditions, various "mytho-ontologies" have undergone a narrowing and "refinement" through disenchantment by dominant science working to exclude nearly all other mythic domains of ordination and narration save its own. This science however has fully incorporated a transformation of "man"/"nature" by history that has for at least seven hundred years been dominated by what we may now recognize as the informatics of capitalism—an incorporation that in its dynamics and consequences is both unconscious and the unconscious that has consequences beyond all calculation. Science separates race from colonialism and slavery, gender from heteropatriarchy, homo sapiens from the environment and humans from their media. No wonder we are zombies in the face of climate change—the somnambulism imposed by the spectacle and the separation from embodiment imposed by information leaves us with an impoverished idea of the bio-dynamics of capitalism and encloses us in a mytho-ontology that presupposes greed and private property but has translated those presuppositions into computational operations.

We could recast history here and say that this appearance of being outside the world and the reality of being incapacitated by it, results from the automation of planetary life by alienated computation. As Marx puts it "It is only to be expected that a living, natural being equipped and endowed with objective (i.e., material) essential powers should have *real natural objects* of his essence; as is the fact that his self-alienation should lead to the establishing of a *real* objective world—but a world in the form of *externality*—a world therefore, not belonging to his own essential being, and an overpowering world. There is nothing incomprehensible or mysterious in this. It would be mysterious, rather, if it were otherwise."[2] "Man" emerges mediated through his objects, his externalities—a logic that places "man" outside of "nature" and makes clear why dialectics is forced into the uncomfortable claim that capital was simultaneously the best and the worst thing that ever happened: the liberation of the productive forces and all that, capital as the condition of "man." Self-alienation from nature produces both the human and nature—an "originary" binary that in truth can only be imposed retroactively as the result of alienation. This alienation is, for the early Marx "objective man," and as Sean Cubitt has brilliantly shown, it constitutes the environment as an externality of capitalism and colonialism that, in a second moment, even when re-deployed by environmentalists for protection and saving, continues to presuppose capitalism and colonialism in the very notion of "the environment" precisely because the environment is conceived as an externality.[3] The conditions under which the environment is an externality are consequent from colonization—in the *longue durée*, the practical continuation of the severance of man ("man") from nature ("nature"). Thus any invocation of "the environment," presupposes it as a colonial externality. The notion itself, despite the best intentions of some, results and persists from the unchecked proliferation of narratives by abstractions embedded in the material operations of political economy broadly conceived—abstractions that are themselves part of systemic colonization of the planet and the mind by capital. These abstractions contain within themselves the naturalizing notion of originary severance that is private property, the still eminently practical means by which people continue to be separated from resources that they might otherwise access (and arguably the means by which the categoricality of distinct speciation comes into being). The list of what has been severed from access is long but it includes air, water, land, earth, life and nature. Dominant self-conceptions and the concept of the environment—to say nothing of the actually existing planetary relations—urgently require decolonization.

Commenting on the power of concepts to inform consciousness and differentiating her Chthulucene from the name of monster in the racist imaginary of a story by H.P. Lovecraft, the cyborg known as Donna Haraway writes:

> "My" Chthulucene, even burdened with its problematic Greek-ish tendrils, entangles myriad temporalities and spatialities and myriad intra-active entities-in-assemblages—including the more-than-human, other-than-human, inhuman, and human-as-humus. Even rendered in an American English-language text like this one, Naga, Gaia, Tangaroa, Medusa, Spider Woman, and all their kin are some of the many thousand names proper to a vein of SF that Lovecraft could not have imagined or embraced—namely, the webs of speculative fabulation, speculative feminism, science fiction, and scientific fact. It matters which systems systematize systems, which stories tell stories, which concepts think concepts. Mathematically, visually, and narratively, it matters which figures figure figures, which systems systematize systems.[4]

It matters which systems systematize systems. If I understand her correctly, Haraway's injunction to make kin at the end of her essay is a recasting of her notion of the cyborg that understands "we" are trans-species, trans-material assemblages and that "our" current essentialisms regarding who "we" relate to and who "we" are, are not only profoundly refugee unfriendly (she has in mind refugees: human, animal and all types) but are killing the planet. I couldn't agree more.

*   *   *

The alienation of "man" from "nature" brought about by the alienation of man from his product by wage labor (at once capitalizing and digitizing) leads Marx, twenty-odd years after the 1844 manuscripts to the following observation regarding the misunderstanding of nature, man and capital: "[T]here is not one single atom of its value [capital's] that does not owe its existence to unpaid labor" (Vol. 1, Ch., 24, 405). This means two things 1) that all the value of capital is theft and 2) that nothing of the environment, no matter, is in and of itself of value to capital. Not only is exchange value content indifferent, it is without material content. Value conferred by unpaid labor accretes to capital via the repurposing (re-ordering, in-forming) of materials, that is to say, the repurposing of raw materials, that is, of matter, for social purposes. Value is not in things but in what has been done to things in their working up within the socio-historical context. We understand from this deduction that capitalist valuation is exclusively, inexorably a socio-historical relation. It is a *form*, an *informing* of matter. More precisely still, it is socio-historical relation indexed by number and organized as early computation.[5]

Marx says explicitly, "As use values, commodities are, above all, of different qualities, but as exchange values they are merely different quantities, and consequently do not contain an atom of use value."[6] Therefore: 1) The only externalities that can be accounted for in capital are in fact internalities—that which can be valued: the numerable. Use-values can only be represented to capital as exchange-values. Human life itself is only visible to capital as labor power, that is, as exchange value (and living is visible, only as risk). These exchange-values, though external to matter and use, nonetheless index attributes of matter and use by number (notionally as value, practically as price); they are actually moments in capital's calculus of value that can be compared to one another via management. This management has come to be known in sophisticated forms as derivatives, and include the options and contracts of synthetic finance, but also prices, methods of bookkeeping, the laws governing ownership, and really any structure intent upon the profitable management of rights to property. These contracts of ownership linked to exchange values are thus internal to capital's system of valuation, and its system of valuation is its system(s) of account, which is to say, of representation. This content indifferent system of executable representation (calculation, accounting, calculus) permeates discourse and creates ideology. Clearly the extension of these representational capacities into the visual domain through spectacle, cinema and computation opens up another huge field of analysis. Additionally, 2) there is another set of externalities that Sean Cubitt (above) has discussed with great acumen and precision regarding the environment, as have others, writing in the register of transnational feminism such as, Rosalinda Fregoso and Melissa Wright, regarding femicide and disposable life, which is of value only in as much as it is of no account. These realms of no account are the realms of the innumerable— the environment itself, the place where waste can be dumped, people can be starved, raped, harvested and murdered, oceans and atmospheres polluted, all with impunity, all without being held to account. These externalities in the form of lands, animals, peoples, ecologies, experiences, histories, cultures, genocides, fireflies are included as excluded in capital's conscription of systems of representation. When our very language has been conscripted as a means of capitalist production and reproduction, when it is expropriated and recoded by content indifferent management, the difficulty and perhaps impossibility of making the second externality count is effected to the point of exclusion and these outsides become accessible only by what might be figured as an anti-racial-capitalist, decolonial feminist-queer poetics and politics, where intellection, engaged in active self-decolonization endeavors to neither presuppose nor conform to programs of capitalist conscription.

Our foray into the immateriality of exchange value—an immateriality precisely resultant from the material organization of production and reproduction—along with our sense of exchange-value's structural exclusion of the surround opens the way forward to another key point for *Message*. With respect to the viral onslaught of value as an immaterial abstraction that nonetheless works its way through the presumed externality that is the environment and nearly all other externalities as well, it is today possible to specify value's relation to information. For it is the incipient digitization of the life-world by capital, its development of machines of account—machines that had to be made increasingly interoperable—that paves the way for the "discovery" of information. In reality capital first developed machinic modes of perception and cognition that were sensitive to what would be "information" and then necessitated its invention through the development of general theories of information. Information is a real abstraction.

Information is a real abstraction, the consequence of the historical working up of the material world, not the cause but the effect of alienated labor. As noted at the outset, the specific history of information as an emergent mode of financialization is not properly speaking the subject of *Message*. That history remains to be written! I am only trying to indicate the path. Some writers who sense the close proximity between information and capitalism are already on it. In his brilliant book, *Control*, Sebastian Franklin writes:

> The specific valorizing logic of control can thus be understood according to the following proposition: if labor under capital is always already digital, then the digitization of practices not formerly understood as labor—communication, sociality, identity, formation,

attention—forms a necessary precondition for their conceptualization as such. In other words, *digitization* is a precondition for *subsumption*.[7]

Digital Culture 1 is the precondition for Digital Culture 2, the commodification of the life-world is the precondition of post-Fordism, of "immaterial labor," and of racial computational capital. The exchange value of a commodity, the quantity of "the universal form of value" that it embodies, is immaterial, but is nonetheless a number. What this means is that the value measured in a quantum of money is a number assigned to a process. "The value of commodities is the very opposite of the coarse materiality of their substance, not an atom of matter enters into its composition."[8] We see clearly then that there is no substance to exchange value—despite its material mediation it is nothing but the quantitative index of a social relation. This social relation, however, is itself material and historical—"objective" in Marx's sense.

This quantity of Value, V, indifferent to any and all materials but nonetheless requiring the operations of a biological and material substrate that crystallizes a constellation of social relations (originally the commodity in *Capital*, originally wage-labor in the 1844 manuscripts), is, in essence, an abstraction—a number assigned to a matrix of social relations through the very operation of these relations: exchange value, abstract universal labor time, the basic building block of a humanity measured by clocks. It depends upon the historical emergence of a set of increasingly coordinated practices and interconvertible measurements that have become generalized, and universal in the sense that they are inexorably transmitted across the planetary situation. This requires what in a long ago essay on Dziga Vertov I referred to as the meshing of what Ernst Bloch called non-synchronous temporalities, as well as the incipient digitization presided over by the world market. The organization of the world by means of digitization has been going on for some time. Franklin's *Control* clearly articulates Charles Babbage's view of God as a grand programmer, his "view of the universe as fundamentally digital," and in a lucid argument about the incipient digitization brought about by capitalism he "posits Babbage's world view as a proxy for capital's optimizing gaze."[9] Given the encroachment of digitality and Marx's clear notion that value is an immaterial number assigned to a matrix of social relations, we prick up our ears then when we hear Norbert Weiner conclude in his essay "Computing Machines and the Nervous System," that there exists an immaterial domain called "information" present in relation to any given phenomenon: "Information is information, not matter or energy. No materialism that does not admit this can survive at the present day."[10]

The wager then is that not only does "not an atom of matter enter into" the composition of information, but that information emerges in the foot print of capitalist valuation—it is not "nature" in any naive or unmediated sense but rather value achieving a new order of self-consciousness, self regulation and interoperability. The connection to cybernetics is now clearer. Weiner writes:

> We have already spoken of the computing machine and consequently the brain as a logical machine. It is by no means trivial to consider the light cast on logic by such machines, both natural and artificial. Here the chief work is that of Turing. We have said before that the *machina ratiocinatrix* is nothing but the *calculus rationcinator* of Leibnitz with an engine in it; and just as modern mathematical logic begins with the calculus, so it is inevitable that its present engineering development should cast a new light on logic. The science of today is operational; that is, it considers every statement as essentially concerned with possible experiments or observable processes. According to this, the study of logic must reduce to the study of the logical machine, whether nervous or mechanical, with all its non-removable limitations and imperfections.[11]

The reference in Weiner is Turing's 1936 paper, "On Computable Numbers, with an Application to the Entscheidungsproblem," in which the machinification of computation was proposed as a universal possibility—one that gave rise to what became known as the "universal Turing machine."[12] This paper generalized the thinking already present in Charles Babbage's and Lady Lovelace's steam driven analytic engine, effectively showing not only that all mathematical process could be machine driven but that it was fundamentally machinic. *The abstraction that was the calculus of Leibnitz and Newton was thus always already the thinking of machines.* Marx argued that the organization of machinery created a "vast automaton" out of fixed capital in which workers were only its "conscious organs" and capitalists did the thinking of capital. So too then, the mathematicians—those who so rigorously enumerated the calculus of space and time. They did the thinking of machines. Given the mesh between industrial history, the machinification of thought and capitalist accumulation, the conjecture that computation is the auto-poeisis of capital implies that information is its representational medium.

Built on machines, but an immaterial isolate of machines, computational process proposes to be content indifferent and medium indifferent—the universal Turing machine implies (in the abstract) that one computer is as good as another. Our abiding insistence that this indifference to history and specificity is not the case in computation is the equivalent to an insistence that there is or must be a persistent form (persistent forms) of non-capitalist valuation. If there is not a single atom of matter in exchange-value, then neither is there a single atom of matter in information or computation. Weiner says as much. What then of the rest, of the body and the flesh—of what matter is matter? Regarding the immense edifice of computation from the standpoint of life not (not yet? not completely?) taken up as labor by capital, that is, from the standpoint of what Neferti Tadiar calls "remaindered life," the machine as The World Computer, is at once basis and externality.[13] It is violently alienated intelligence as condition of possibility.

In addition to splicing machines and brains into the same circuit, informatics can therefore be understood as the "subjectivity" of the objective situation of "man,"—non-conscious thinking (at least so far as humans have been concerned), emerging in a world grown increasingly complex and abstract: in a word, "operational." The *machina ratiocinatrix* speeds up (motorizes) the calculus in a capitalized world, "essentially concerned with possible experiments or observable processes," because, dependent upon innovation capital must stave off the falling rate of profit. But just because machine-mediated logical operations are non-conscious in a human sense in no way implies that they are not self-conscious in a machinic sense. They are self-reflexive in the same manner that, as Turing pointed out in his essay published in *Mind*, computation works on its own operations and store of information. They are also not without vectors of intention, for what else is logical problem solving but an algorithmic approach to representations of life—a program. As Turing emphasized, humans are often surprised by the outcome of programs they themselves set in motion. The human mind does not and cannot immediately grasp the logical implications (outputs) of a program and its inputs. Today, actually existing computers outpace the narrowly biological mind's capacity in this respect by orders of magnitude—in algo trading, but everywhere else as well. This machine-thinking, that outpaces life, is precisely the thinking of sedimented, dead labor.

Of course, machine-thinking is today nothing if not cybernetic. The machine operator who once worked on "their" machine now works in the machine. Machine thinking has re-sculpted perception and mind for seamless interface and near total capture. The amortized conscious-ness of sedimented historical sensual labor, expropriated by capital, welds itself to current thinking and by enveloping, enclosing, ramifying and programming it, organizes it in ways that are at once extremely subtle, broad-spectrum sensual, and nearly impossible to disarticulate from any possible form of awareness. That's why the kids are all sick: "augmented" reality. But we must wager that "we" retain the capacity to note the spectral character of life as well as the encroachment of what Achille Mbembe understands as necropolitics in which death and power over death is the vernacular of power. When death is the medium of expression, how might the living signal our aspiration?

For Marx, the information that is the exchange value of a commodity has a legible dimension/approximation (its price), and a dimension that relies on social relations that are fundamentally unconscious. "The commodity is exchange-value but has its price."[14] Price is not one with value, but is, rather "notional." This means to say that when the commodity realizes its price in a sale, the relations and ratios informing the sale are gleaned from background information processing and abstraction, some of which is pre-conscious or unconscious. Seizing upon these same relations with machinic computation posits that they might be given symbolic form in a register that departs from the market—one that is representationally adequate to the market but not, in the first instance, the market. We may position the history of information theory as the effort to formalize these relations in executable form while eschewing the dialectical call for understanding an abstraction, a machine or an abstract machine in relation to its social embedding. Dialectics surfaces the repressed of information, namely noise. "Information" was and remains a way of treating the social as an externality—as noise. This tension between the formalizations of political-economy via the principles and practices of exchange value (and now financialized computation) with dialectical critique precisely describes Marx's struggle with representa-tion (*darstellung*): how to represent capital in a way that at once follows the movements of production and the capitalist market and comprehends it such that the hegemony of that market might be transcended.

Dialectics endeavors to outpace the market and outthink computation. But we need to be aware that the insights of dialectics are hardly immune from market digitization. Take for example the insight, "Money does not effect the actual circulation of commodities in space and time. It merely realizes their price in a way that transfers the title of ownership to the commodities to the purchaser, to the person who has offered the means of exchange. What is circulated by money is not commodities, but the titles of ownership to them."[15] Almost 150 years later, we can clearly grasp from Marx's statement about the social dimension of exchange, what is becoming an axiom of crypto-currencies: monetary circulation is a matter of informatics and contracts. The traffic in rights to ownership mediated by money are antecedents to forms such as the bitcoin blockchain and Ethereum's programmable blockchain and "smart contracts" developing in the twenty-first century. The current thinking on crypto refers to this immanent restructuring of finance by computational money-forms as "the internet of value." The visionaries here are not imagining crypto as a mere replacement of "fiat money." Building on the practices of post-Fordist economy and cognitive capitalism, it is clear that money executes a transfer of rights by means of quantification and more or less understood that social process will be ever more intimately wedded to financialization and encrypted as money in real time. A new computational layer of communication and datavisualization that formally binds financialization to representation (of intention, identity, visibility, aesthetics, etc.) is in the works: "the internet of value." A century and a half ago Marx's dialectical method resolved aspects of property relations that are now being self-consciously utilized in the build out of crypto-currencies. However, none of these currencies are post-capitalist—at least not yet.

The degree to which the inner dynamism of the commodity form can be elaborated is testified to in the writings of Marx and beyond—it is elaborated even in communist revolutions. However, one thing is clear: this "thing" called value is constituted by both a social relation and a civil contract; it is thus, also, a tacit collective agreement that there are pre-individual and trans-individual forces at work in the market. Theses organizational forces, manifest in and through wage labor, alienation and private property (a causal chain, if one recalls the exposition in the 1844 manuscripts, that becomes recursive) and the logistics thereof, are the precondition of the exchange of equivalents in the market. The market as information machine, as itself a computer, an understanding already achieved by Hayek in 1945, was less a discovery of informatics, than a pre-condition for the emergence of informatics. Dissolving here (a la *2001*) from the primeval bone toss of Marx's dialectical analysis of industrial capital to the orbiting space stations of Google, Facebook and bitcoin, one could say that the becoming economically conscious of the fine lattice-work of informatic relations and the understanding of them as simultaneous means of production and communication is in fact the significance if not the meaning of the internet—at least from the standpoint of capital. As I said of cinema in the *CMP*, the dominant mode of representation has become the dominant mode of production. Taken as a whole, the internet is the nonconscious cognition of "man,"—the cognitive process of the market in the largest sense, that then processes its conscious organs.[16]

As a kind of aside, my own view of the nonconscious status of AI, is one of extreme skepticism. Let's pull our heads out of the sand, shall we? Just as machines operate at orders of magnitude faster than human brains (beneath or beyond the level of human discernment) so too does the daibolical intelligence of the market. Marx clearly understands these market relations (their intelligence) as forcibly imposed.

"[T]he totality of the process appears as an objective relationship arising spontaneously; a relationship which results from the interaction of conscious individuals, but which is neither part of their consciousness nor, as a whole subsumed under them. Their own collisions give rise to an alien social power standing above them. Because circulation is a totality of the social process, it is also the first form in which not only the social relation appears as something independent of individuals, as, say, in a coin or an exchange value, but the whole of the social movement itself."[17]

In brief, this analysis of circulation, its elision of conscious relations, and its imposition of market conditions on human existence accounts for and historicizes both Adam Smith's invisible hand in which the pursuit of individual interests serve the general interest and Hobbes' naturalization of the war of each against all and brings us into the present. By drawing an arc that spans from Hobbes' Leviathan and Smith's invisible hand to Google's invisible mind, we may grasp that Marx's analysis of the social totality is indeed a proto-theory of both AI and of the unconscious: the commodity form is a symptom (a fetish) requiring the depth hermeneutic of the dialectic. For us it also provides the basis for a theory of the computational unconscious and a means of historicizing information as the product of alienated labor. The unconscious is structured like a language, a computer language. This computer language is in us more than "us."

Thus one sees through Marx's analysis of monetary circulation, the instantiation of the individual:

> "Money ... as the individuality of general wealth, itself emerging from circulation and merely representing the general, as mere social result, implies no individual relation at all to its owner, its possession is not the development of any one of the essential aspects of his individuality, but rather possession of something devoid of individuality ..."[18]

The subjective dimension is given as follows:

> "Money is therefore not only *an* object of the quest for enrichment, it is *the* object of it ... Avarice is possible without money, but the quest of enrichment is itself the product of a definite social development, not a *natural* in contrast to an *historical* development. This explains the lamentations of the ancients about money as a source of all evil. The quest for pleasure in its general from and avarice are two particular forms of greed for money. The abstract quest for pleasure implies an object that can embody the possibility of all pleasures."[19]

Marx continues, "The greed for money or quest for enrichment is necessarily the downfall of the ancient communities ... " It is itself the community and cannot tolerate any other standing above it.[20] "Where money is not itself the community it must dissolve the community."[21] Given this notion, or at least intimation of a communal totality—here viral, cannibalistic and alienating, "the false community of the spectacle" as Debord would say or "the communism of capital" as Virno has it—there is the strong suspicion on the part of economists and entrepreneurs (but also among some revolutionaries) that some (non-humanist) episteme (Althusserian science?) ought to be adequate to these relations; this episteme is generally known as social, or political, or economic science, but has become computer science. Leaving aside for now the question of the singularity, in which the sedimented and alienated consciousness of capitalism as computational power becomes irrevocably self-conscious (I just suggested that for all practical purposes, it has) and which by definition would outpace our thought, we should be able to grasp clearly that any version of Marxist social science (at least) needs to become

Marxist computer science; Marxist critique of political economy needs to become Marxist critique of the digital/attention economy of racial computational capital. Thus we require a Marxist theory of information. I hasten to underscore here—and this is the point of making this argument for a Marxist theory of information only one chapter in the larger work that is *Message*—that the Marxism I have in mind registers capitalism as racial capitalism, and understands it as axiomatic that the difference made by information is always social difference.

The imperial masters of social, now computer science (not the mere academics relegated to our pay silos and Twitter "feeds," but the practitioner-entrepreneurs), feed their avarice, their abstract quest for pleasure in general and the object that in Marx's phrase "can embody the possibility of all pleasures," by decoding the social/computational logic of the community—of any phenomenon whatever—formalizing it, and developing a proprietary relation to that formalization. They call "their" insights nifty things like "Google" and "Facebook" and "Apple" and help to devour prior social orders by moistening them with information and re-organizing communication. Progress is bound less to their genius and more to their proprietary rights. Can we reengineer these relations?

The control of communication, as Weiner noted, is the very strategy of the "Lords of Things As They Are." This current control of communication has meant the instantiation and control of information, a control that in turn means a control of the market, and of social production and reproduction. The decoding and recoding of social practices in a proprietary vein is the precise logic of the start-up, as well as that of speculative markets, particularly that of the markets for celebrity, "tech" and art. Why? "The abstract quest for pleasure implies an object that can embody the possibility of all pleasures." Content indifferent information is the contemporary analogue for content indifferent pleasure. The greater the accumulation of information, the greater the quantity of abstract pleasure. Without diminishing the brilliance of the achievements manifest in these corporate platforms, which do indeed harness collective aspirations and abstract an eon of collective praxis, we can also see what drives them. They embody the same logic of abstraction that drives many of the rest of us to abjection, sleeplessness, psychosis, insanity, precarity, outrage, breakdown, migration, starvation and/or death, in the unequal distribution of dispossession. Within the dialectics of avarice they offer the lure of increased sociality, and in return they strip-mine our libidos, our neuronal powers, our cognitive capacities, our language, our imagination and our time. In the twenty-first century it is paradigmatically social-media, the grim reaper, which extracts content indifferent value from the myriad qualities of social life to provide an elite coterie of vested owners with what can embody the possibility of all pleasure, namely, money and the informatic control of rights.

Within the space of the social, information, in contrast to what we better understand as the community of exchange values, does not, at least until now, appear as social; it has been expressed as a property of things—"neither matter nor energy" and there with or without an observer (according to its observers, anyway). It is what communicates even between non-sentient things that otherwise do not communicate. It is, as Benjamin critically observed, the antithesis of narrative and the annihilator of experience. We search information in pursuit of life and in flight from death, doing what we can to avoid the crashing of the wave. And while we would be solipsistic and even foolish to imagine that after our own deaths, nothing means anything, it is perhaps slightly less egocentric to wonder, "What of the cosmos beyond the life-span of our visible generations, or even of 'our species'?" In as much as we believe in the immortality of information, is there really any question we can pose that is not also in some way about our own place in the universe, that does not posit our own critical consciousness even after it has logically disintegrated? While there is within this reader-writer an impulse to say yes, it's not all about "us" and better if it isn't, I must confess that I/it is not sure—I/it is perhaps unable to escape the originary ethnocentrism of the sign and its extension into informatics. However, I also recognize that not caring about those in the future is analogous to not caring about those in the present or the past; we may be removed from them in a narrow way, but there are many many tendrils that link our fates together in the web of time. It only matters if it matters. If information binds us together in a negative way, what about the historical emergence that is the con- solidation of the net communal will of what has been? What about the echo and persistence of all the endurance, survival, communication and aspiration that built the apprehension of the indifferent infinity called information? However bound by autopoetic limitations the answers to such a question about cosmic meaning may be, when regarding the relation of information to community our responses do not need to fall back into an identitarian framework, nor, in recognizing the alienation of so much intelligence, do they need to fantasize a return to origins. However, we may and indeed must ask, if death has developed such an articulate, infinite and immaterial infrastructure, wherefore life? If there is so much death in our information, in our images, in our streets, in our borderlands, and in our persons, what of the living that are marooned at the edge of space and time?

Can we say (in agreement with Brian Rotman's groundbreaking work on mathematics as sign system in *Signifying Nothing*) that information, likewise, elides the subject (I, God, totality) even as it smuggles in its ghost. This degree zero of information we should call the myth of non-presence (the presence of anti-presence that ushers in presence under erasure), a deep conviction, or rather a theology of the irrelevance and non-existence of what used to be called the human species, a world-view ceaselessly dedicated to the absence of concrete human agents, but no less ethnocentric for all that.[22] Information, "the difference that makes a difference" as Bateson said, derives from the Latin nominative and the Latin verb *informare (to inform)* which means to give form or to form an idea of. "To give form, therefore I am." As an expression of maroonage we can re-write this grammatological formulation as "Information, therefore I am." The post-structuralist rewriting of Descartes, in which "think, therefore I am," expresses that the subject is an artifact of grammatical function, a phantom ~~presence~~ generated only after the fact of, that is, in the very movement of sign function, of the symbolic, of the signifying chain, expresses that the subject of information as presence is therefore also a myth, an artifact that merely suggests metaphysical presence, rather than a pre-existing agent. I is a predicate rather than a subject who is always already absent— this famously, was "the myth of presence." The spectral I of information, the informatic dividual, megalomaniacal and abject, is indeed the spirit of contemporary capitalism. Secular religion, an ascetic ideal. Knowing all devouring information encompasses the cosmos, therefore I am. And yet, in accord with an idea I develop elsewhere as the politics of the utterance, the strategic voicing of this spirit, this immaterial cybernetic consciousness so firmly grounded in and dependent upon the totality of the material array, matters profoundly. Does it hew toward all that appears, that is, to the spectacle and data-visualization? Or, might this spirit, Turing's trans-substantiation, also be a specter, the product of so much disavowed violence that may yet devise strategies to hew toward all that is disavowed, disappeared, invisibilized, haunting and forgotten, as these unremembered violences are nonetheless part of this history of its moment of emergence and therefore part of what it is?

The perception of information *qua* information, the analytical instantiation of the category itself, clearly has its origins in history and in sociality. Today there is almost no escape from the legacy of that perception: we are all part of the history of technology and all haunted by presence. Such is consciousness. Our emergence as an affordance of fixed capital is bound up with planetary materiality and information. Dominant history has it that the category of information arises and is formalized as an intervention in the merely social by punchcards, quantum physics, cybernetics and communication theory. Indeed, as ostensibly autonomous realms, the cumulative result of these emergent disciplines was a mythic generalization of the logistics of inscription of information as the fundamental cosmic modality. Thus information is now at the foundation of any event whatever—indeed any and every event without exception at least in the multiverse of computational physics. Here we have wagered, a bit more precisely, that information arises in the footprint of the value form and that value as an immaterial number assigned to a social relation was indeed the precursor to the conceptual matrix that became information. Information: a way for value to get more value. No doubt this work of analysis can and will be done better and more thoroughly, but we have established that the cybernetic social totality of the computational multiverse has capitalism in its DNA. (Literally of course, since the discovery of the role of DNA was itself premised on an informatic model).

Information as "the difference that makes a difference" was in fact informatics' very own concept of *differánce*. A deferral of meaning that found dramatic expression in many domains, for example, Shrodinger's cat, who was alive and dead until one had a look. The fact of information has been generalized as a universal principle, visible everywhere one looks and, what's more, everywhere one does not look, but could. We thus concur with critical race theory's critique of dominant discourses of post-humanism in our analysis of information: it places the sovereign subject of colonial humanism (white, male) under erasure while leaving it operative. Technology as "white mythology" says Joel Dinerstein, Posthumanism as having afro-futurist, anti-racist, decolonizing roots in the rejection of the racist category of the human says Alexander Weheliye. Information as the further deracination of exchange value (itself dehistoricized and naturalized in everyday experience), and as the temporary suspension of price from propriety, serves as in an interum calculus that has value inputs and outputs at each end. It casts its net(work), its informatic reticulum, into speculative domains that have financialized protocols operationalized before and after. The endless flux of the cosmic informatic churn, presents an endless array of virtual subjectivities, any of which might become vested. NSF grants and medical research are the most obvious examples of this process, and all research, as Flusser says, aspires to be photographed, which for us, is another way of saying that it unfolds in a capitalist milieu bent upon the bio-mediated extraction of information.

As we shall see in greater detail in the final chapter, the general formula for capital, M-C-M' becomes M-I-M', where I is information. As simple circulation, it returns a value equivalent, but as capital, the very informationalization of money and life also assumes a machinery of value extraction: Facebook, bitcoin, the NSA, Tech. This shift in the general formula of capital, in which surplus value is extracted by means of the human-mediated production of information, is the key to any understanding of post-Fordism and begins to forecast what's beyond. In a nutshell, information as a universal property of things means that the entire universe is posited as an interoperable site of financialization. The machines that measure information and the informatic results they procure/produce are inscribed with ever increasing granularity between M and M'.

Thus information as a presumably value-neutral category represents the cosmic naturalization of digital market relations. Under such conditions, we may be sure that any super-intelligent machine we make, (along the lines say, of any of those discussed in Nick Bostrom's *Super-Intelligence*) will be the algorithmic embodiment of our history—of objectified humanity savaged under racial capitalism—and not the objective (as in ahistorical and value-neutural) embodiment of some deracinated universal Absolute Intelligence—which is to say that it is likely to be totalitarian with respect to any and all inferior races, the so-called human race included. Shanon's words now sound almost as chilling as they were prescient: "I can visualize a time in the future when we will be to robots as dogs are to humans … I'm rooting for the machines!"

Situating the emergence of information theory and practice in the history of capitalism (and keeping in mind the fate of Pavlov's dogs), it is thus legitimate and indeed historically and politically necessary for us to ask: Is it Information that transcends Value, making Value just one instance of Information (ambient in markets); such that a category or superset that contains value as a subset led to the discovery of many other subsets of seemingly immaterial variables that index more general relations; or, does Value transcend Information, the latter of which as a category appears to be even more autonomous and therefore abstract than Value but, in actual practice, only operates/appears within the domain of Value (and markets), and thus not only in the domain of sociality per se but of Capital? Is informatic process the very means by which racial capitalism continues to expand its Imperium? No amount of "OOO" is going to answer that one, I'm afraid. What we need is a critique of Digital Ideology that re-subjectifies and historicizes the ostensibly non-subjective and ahistorical, a critique that, once having out-informed information, is not content to rest there, but is committed to develop new methods, idioms, and practices capable of recognizing the instrumentality of processes of digital occlusion and exclusion, and to actively refuse non-existence by demanding new methods of account. This critique must understand its own embodiment, its own emergence from *within* the framework of racial capitalism even as it writes in the name of an outside.[23]

Otherwise, the world will go on as it does, intensifying its violence, its environmental destruction, its genocide and radical dispossessions. To be clear, this murderous future is the path we are currently on since the planetary communication system—its integrated system of accounts— kills people(s) in its everyday operations. Racial Capitalism is another name for intergalactic information processing as we know it. Computational Capital as communication system, a militarizing apparatus and a distributed factory, crunches numbers and many of these numbers are people. We, the substrates of computational capital ... The devaluation of the 2 billion dispossessed and living on two dollars a day, as accomplished by advertising, nationalism, imperialism, militarization, "aid," borders, internet, educational systems and art, is part of the general, world-wide devaluation of the working day with regard to the fixed capital embodied in machines and their information. The historical devaluation of those in the Global South is thus far only intensified and exacerbated as the processor extends its range and resolution.

Information is alienation distributed. It paints the cosmos with sedimented dead labor. To speak in the vernacular, it is the inhuman perceived by the inhuman in a matrix that encompasses what used to be human. It is an "object" that exists everywhere for a "subject" that exists nowhere. As the communication of the stolen sedimented dead labor that is capital accumulation, it is an abstraction meaningful to an abstract machine—all of which transpires with absolute indifference relative to the use-values afforded, including the use-value known as "you." Your own particular value, based upon your production price and the value that your virtuosic activity gives to the computer that is capital, is calculated as a multiple of removes from absolute dispossession. Even if your multiple happens to go up (even if you are worth 50 or 500 times the lowest common denominator of "human" life), the general value of humans (or is it ~~humans~~?) approaches zero while the extraction of productive activity still remains essential. Because capital depends upon labor, and laborers are increasingly devalued in relation to the cosmic expansion of fixed capital as information, we see increasingly intensive exploitation on increasingly massive and increasingly granular scales. The falling rate of profit brought about the decrease in the relation of the value of labor power as compared to fixed capital is compensated for by the extension of the working day to every and evermore waking hours, and the proliferation of metrics of extraction to linguistic, psychic, neuronal and metabolic levels. Likes, movements, heartbeats, pheromones and prison time are all value-productive for someone as every attack surface of the body and cerebellum is exploited. The devaluation of life on Earth is the mirror image of the cosmic distribution of information.

Computation is the reticulated extension of financialization. We are back to Tarkovsky's *Solaris*, in which the history of suffering is the very medium through which one apprehends the cosmos. Thus we have an image of the world media system and thus we may grasp the emergence and most general function of informatics in computational capital. Despite what the ideologues will tell you, neither your soul nor ambient information have escaped capitalist valuation. The very fact of information and its metrics, both the data and the infrastructure that records, measures and posits it, is the result of alienated labor: sedimented dead labor, theft. Yet some think it is just information that wants to be free.

Does the "notional" assignation of price really begin to extend itself into the subatomic and the universal? Already, the cost-benefit analysis called the atom bomb seemed to say yes. So too does the large space telescope, the Higgs-Bozon particle colliders, and all the seemingly autonomous science undertaken without a serious regard for global inequality. John von Neuman, who Philip Mirowski credits with having invented both the A-bomb and modern computing in 1943, may have been remarking on the relation between the specific and the general case when he said, "I am thinking about something more important than bombs. I am thinking about computers."[24]

And then of course, there is the oh-so-familiar computer-mediated financialization of everyday life. Interface, get paid. Move up the value chain on Instagram or at your institute, get paid. Garner those attention metrics, get paid. In the context of my overall argument regarding computational capital, our re-placing of the "universality" of information by and indeed within the domain of exchange value cosmically posited brings the entire armature of information back to McLuhan's chicken: Information, an egg's idea to get more eggs.

In conclusion, information is but game theory for eggs. Well, at least we have posed the question: "Was information value's idea to get more value?" There may not be a definitive answer, but new pathways for thought and praxis open when the logic gate selected is "Yes."[25]

PART II

Photo-graphology, Psychotic Calculus, Informatic Labor

6

Camera Obscura After All:
The Racist Writing with Light

Taking a chapter from Jacqueline Goldsby's brilliant and disturbing book, *A Spectacular Secret: Lynching in American Life and Literature*, entitled "Through a Different Lens: Lynching Photography at the Turn of the Nineteenth Century" as a starting point, I would like to pursue a point made by Goldsby about the role of these atrocious photographs of racist murder in what, with Paul Virilio, one might call "the logistics of perception"—so I'll start there.[1]

Goldsby cites Jonathan Crary's *Techniques of the Observer* to remind us that "the optical devices used in the nineteenth century were not invented in cultural vacuums," but were, rather, "[p]remised on 'conceptual structures' that reflect 'points of intersections where philosophical, scientific, and aesthetic discourses overlap with mechanical techniques, institutional requirements, and socio-economic forces.' [P]hotographic equipment also presupposes an ideal viewer—an observing subject—whose cultural privileges can be inferred from (and, consequently conferred by) the ways in which a camera makes the world visible to human perception."[2]

At this point in *The Message is Murder* we are quite familiar with the notion of both the machine and machinic operations as culturo-historical forms. We are also increasingly aware of the dire consequences of the uncritical operation of seemingly neutral technologies such as computation and cinema (informatics and optics) because they themselves are racial formations. Ideas operating "in the silence of technologies" are without a doubt ideological in the sense that they are divorced from their material conditions of production and dissemination as Regis Debray taught us, but technologies operating in the silence of social difference are solely techno-logical only in the sense that their emergence as a social formation that sediments those social relations into an apparatus is suppressed. Here we explore the extent to which photography might be grasped as a racial formation.

Building on Crary's insight, Goldsby says, "Thus, when considering lynching photographs and their social effects, we must approach them as artifacts that are more than transparent, self-evident documents of these events of racial murder. Indeed lynching photographs encode more than the deadly operations of white racism. The images also inscribe how practices of racial violence were used to cultivate the experience and meaning of sight itself."[3]

The point I want to emphasize here, that what is encoded in the basic structure of the photographic apparatus feeds back into the social to re-organize and reproduce it, resonates with a possible research project that I will only be able to sketch the outlines of here: With respect to practices of looking, there is a deep-seated dialectic, if you will, between racism and photography. Here we will only explore the most extreme form of this dialectic, leaving the many interventions by the black radical tradition and others who contested the racialization of and by photography for another occasion. Goldsby is, for very good reasons, more interested in analyzing the social dimensions, violences, and occlusions transmitted and enabled by the specific photographs and platforms she presents—and in seeing the whole heinous genre of lynching photography as a significant part of the making of American modernity—than she is interested in making general points about "photography itself." However, in the context of the study that is *Message* we may understand from her juxtaposition of her own claims with some of Crary's that any general points one might make about American modernity and hence about photography are inadmissible without a consideration of racial formations. I take this implication as a key starting point for the evaluation and understanding of the social and historical emergence of a media platform. If the making of whiteness and blackness is mediated by the dynamics of photography, then the reverse is also true: the making of photography is mediated by the dynamics of whiteness and blackness. Photography does not evolve in a vacuum; it is, to borrow from Stephen Heath, a *dispositif,* the social and technical *as* photography.[4] Thus we may expect to find that "race relations"—that is to say, forms of racism—may be not only at the heart of "the meaning of sight" but inscribed in the technological platforms that enable sight and, therefore, in "photography itself."

Some questions: To what extent is "photography itself" a racial formation? What social dynamics have been subsumed in the reification that occurs under the sign of—and, indeed, in the form of the apparatus that is—the camera? How might one rethink Martin Jay's scopic regimes of modernity in terms of racial formation?[5] Or similarly, if Deleuze and Parnet are correct in asserting that a machine is historical and social, i.e., abstract, before it is technical, what kinds of statements can be made about photography that draw from and contribute to the work of a critical race media theory?[6] If Stephen Heath could consider the cinematic apparatus as a *dispositif*—that is, "the social and the technical as cinema"—then can we return to the question of photography and the archive using the incredible momentum of the intellectual ferment of decolonization, black, minoritarian, queer, of-color, subaltern, Marxist, feminist, Global South scholarship to rethink the ontology of photography and other media platforms? Did photography abstract racial and capitalist encodings in a manner consonant with what we have seen thus far with informatics and with the cinema? And if so, what does this prejudice of technology teach us about the organization of appearance, semiosis, and the terrain of communication? What is the message of these media?

Although there is no mention of cameras or photography in Harriet Jacobs' harrowing *Incidents in the Life of a Slave Girl: Written by Herself,* within the narrative a mechanism appears that I would hypothesize shares some aspects of the abstract machine that necessarily precedes the instantiation of the concrete machines of photography. I am speaking, of course, of Jacobs's prison, the crippling attic crawl space above her grandmother's house where mid-way through her account Jacobs hid from her slave-masters—immobilized and unable to stand—during the seven-year period from 1835 to 1842. Confined, as it were, in camera, by the conjunction of vectors of colonialism, political economy, racism, slavery and the law that granted to whites the legal right to hold black people as chattel, Jacobs, while under inconceivable physical duress, watched her own children grow up through a peephole she drilled in a shingle. In this social and technical construction, she observes her children through a camera obscura, unable to touch them, speak to them, or even let them know that she is alive as they face all the travails of growing up black under white supremacy. She lives the life of the negative.

Through social means, Jacobs is converted into a recording device, hidden from view and forced to observe the world through a pinhole in a shingle. And yet she chooses this form of social and near physical death—imprisonment—over her option on the other side of the pinhole: visibility, being seen and, thus, slavery. Reducing Jacobs as closely as possible to a pure observer on one side of the aperture, and to a pure object on the other; this horrifying assemblage—this being in camera—requires the deprivation of one's rights to one's body, a deprivation that itself relies on the development of a particular scopic regime that offers two disparate pathways to social death. On one side, invisible observer; on the other side, abject object. This scopic regime is not incidental but is a matter of life and death; it has the power to produce metaphysical ideas about the human and nature, order and entitlement; it becomes, in short, a foundation of U.S. "civilization." In this racist spectrometry, persons are measured by the biochemical, light-absorbing properties of their skin—let us call it with Lacan (but with a different set of inflections a kind of "photo-graphing."[7] A regime of subjectification and objectification and a metrics of domination.

This everyday photo-graphing endemic to slavery in the United States and to racial formation itself—this constant inscription and re-inscription of black and white and color dramatized by Jacobs in camera—points toward an essence of photography somewhat different than that put forth by Roland Barthes in *Camera Lucida*, a text that often still passes (notwithstanding the writings of Chela Sandoval and Fred Moten) as a definitive statement on the ontology of the photograph today.[8]

To cut to the chase (itself a suspect narrative formula), in *Camera Lucida* Barthes sets out to determine "the essence of photography … *at any cost*" [italics mine] and determines finally that a photograph's *noeme*, its unique quality, is precisely its chemically mediated indexical transmission of a moment of Reality—what he calls the photograph's "that has been" aspect. This, for Barthes, is the distinctive feature of photography itself.

But we must ask: what about the costs of this determination? For Barthes, the personal cost is twofold. First, there is the cost in pain. With *Camera Lucida* Barthes writes a book of mourning for the loss of his beloved mother, the person with whom he was most closely, indeed intensely bonded. The photograph, and here a very specific photograph, is a way back to her. Indeed for Barthes the Winter Garden photograph of his mother (which is not reproduced in the text) provides a way to activate (but also register the loss of) a pre-verbal, para-psychoanalytic, extra-semiotic bond of unspeakable import. And then, beyond the pain of loss there is, in the rejection of semiotic and psychoanalytic explanations for the nature of his desire for and love of his mother, the cost to Barthes's extraordinary intellectual career; for the book is a kind of recantation, an admission that the domain of semiotics, which he spent the better part of his life elaborating, is not adequate for the deepest questions of love, of life, and of mediation. As he concludes, the indexical character of the photograph—its relation to reality, both in the instance of the photograph and as opened by the particular feature he identifies as the *punctum*—"the prick of the Real"—delimits and indeed exceeds the terrain of semiotics. Photography contains within it a relation that exceeds meaning of any kind. However there is, in the determination of the essence of photography yet another cost, and for the rest of us perhaps, it turns out to be the most important one.

∗   ∗   ∗

In *Camera Lucida*, Barthes provides a detailed description of his own experience of being photographed, during which he feels himself physically transform. "Now once I feel myself observed by the lens, everything changes: I constitute myself in the process of posing, I instantaneously make another body for myself, I transform myself in advance into an image."[9] And then, "I don't know how to work upon my skin from within."[10] His account of becoming an object before the lens, of being separated from the world by the play of sociotechnical dynamics on his skin, precisely echoes—albeit in apparent ignorance—Frantz Fanon's description in "The Fact of Blackness" of coming under the white gaze while in France: a description that read in its entirety, suggests the colonial roots of existentialism and existentialist visuality. Here is just a brief excerpt:

> And then the occasion arose when I had to meet the white man's eyes. An unfamiliar weight burdened me. The real world challenged my claims. In the white world the man of color encounters difficulties in the development of his bodily schema [...] On that day, completely dislocated, unable to be abroad with the other, the white man, who unmercifully imprisoned me, I took myself far off from my own presence, far indeed, and made myself an object. What else could it be for me but an amputation, an excision, a hemorrhage that spattered my whole body with black blood.[11]

What, then, is the relationship between photography and modern racism? What Nicole Fleetwood has subsequently called "the Fanonian moment," in *Troubling Vision*, what she reminds us, Henry Louis Gates calls "a Rorschach blot with legs," is an experience of the visible field that no matter how it is inflected, testifies to its ambient striation by the violence of racialization. Thus it seems to me that something deeply hidden, repressed, or unthought inheres in the *dispositif* that is photographic technology. A thoroughgoing analysis of this *dispositif* would necessarily show connections between photography, racism, and political economy—three vectors of objectification—and ultimately should intersect with legal, psychoanalytic, imperialist, and sex-gender systems. After all, Barthes describes being photographed as if it were a process of proprietary alienation: "[T]he disturbance is ultimately one of ownership," he says, and, "I invariably suffer from a sensation of inauthenticity. I am neither subject nor object but a subject who feels he is becoming an object: I then experience a microversion of death […]: I am truly becoming a specter."[12] Barthes also likens the captured light of the photograph to "a carnal medium, a skin I share with anyone who has been photographed."[13]

Well, yes and no. Is aphanisis, the fading of the subject under the gaze of the other a question of psychology or of racialization? Of death or social death? Is the abjection of objectification that comes from sharing the skin of the other a matter of the gaze, or racism, or both? Here we hypothesize that the processes of racist and colonial visuality have been translated into the photographic apparatus, and what transpires under a racializing gaze designed to draw profit from othering, for turning subject into object, can in principle be turned on anyone, even Barthes. But in spite of Barthes' uneasiness one still feels that the blood that spatters his body is mostly black.

The large-scale archival project that these hunches regarding racialization and photography imply would be to establish that the parallel thus far limned between the mortification of the flesh before the lens and the mortification of the flesh under a white gaze—supported by, and indeed developing as a technology of the historical-economic violence of slavery and colonialism—are not merely analogous but are mutually constituting. White psychology and white visuality rests atop black dispossession. The camera itself would be studied as a machine for the generation of what Saidiya Hartman calls scenes of subjection—forms of domination that go undetected.[14] A study proving that photography is itself a racial formation—following say, Goldsby, and in a different way, Ariella Azoulay and Vilem Flusser, for example—would want to show that usage, form, and technical development went along a kind of simultaneous and mutually imbricated trajectory that was fully embedded in racial and racializing social practices. The machine as a racial formation is also a machine of racialization. These procedures would include the institutionalization of photography in various disciplines, the elaboration of a racial imaginary by photographic and other means as well as a critique of assumptions about the ontology of photography. Vicente Rafeal's work on census photography in the colonial Philippines as a technology of racialization comes to mind here, as does the work of Malek Alloula, Jane Gaines, and bell hooks.[15] Each of the three latter writers explores the imbrication of photography in regimes of racist violence. Rafael's astute analysis of the encoding of an American racist imaginary on the Philippine populous by means of photography and the census shows how photography was used to impose a teleological narrative regarding "progressive" waves of racializing colonization that took Filipinos up the racial hierarchy (from Malays to Spainiards, to White Americans). Given the racializing role of the census, we see that Sebastian Franklin's research on Herman Hollerith, the inventor of the punchcard and enabler of first the broad based, searchable data collection of the national census (and later IBM's infrastructural support of the Holocaust), turns up something arresting. "Hollerith utilizes an extended analogy between data collection, on the one hand, and inter-pretation, the objective conditions of society, and photography on the other, noting that 'the enumeration of a census corresponds with the exposure of the plate in photography while the compilation of a census corresponds with the development of the photographic plate.'"[16] The census and the photograph were media of racialization. The image was data visualization.

Goldsby's suggestions that the images produced by cameras also structure the meaning of sight allows us to see that the development and iterations of photographic knowledge—as well as the incorporation of that knowledge into the further development and use of the apparatus— are marked by practices of racial violence that feedback and feed forward through lived experience and technics. As a modest foray into what is a potentially vast undertaking, we can show here that these parallel and seemingly autonomous regimes of racial formation, on the one hand, and photographic visibility on the other, are mutually constitutive in Barthes' work. If such a counter reading of *Camera Lucida* turns out to be correct, then the "essence of photography," precisely defined by Barthes as "that has been,"—and acted upon in similar ways by entire populations—has for many decades meant the practical disavowal of racism by its beneficiaries. While such an account does not exhaust photographic practices, we will show that the essence of photography lies elsewhere, which is another way of saying that the referent of "that" in "that has been" is not what it seems. Photography does not simply index a past; it is profoundly embroiled in the past—all of it.

In *Camera Lucida*, Barthes makes a case for the meta-semiotic "madness" of the photograph and rhetorically generates a meaningful— that is, semiotic—context for the dramatic eruption of the Real itself. Within a carefully weighted semantic field he stages the emergence of "the essence of photography" as the indexical "that has been." He also develops the extremely influential theories of "the *studium*," or the various photographic genres along with their necessarily all-too-familiar (and for Barthes, ultimately uninteresting) avenues of meaning, and of the aforementioned notion "the punctum," which is rendered as "the prick of the Real," "the wound," "the puncture" all of which endeavor to figure a rupture of and a limit to the merely semiotic by the Real. The punctum is activated, in Barthes' view, only by certain photographs, most are subsumed in the studium and the semiotic.

What is crucial here is that for Barthes to produce this reality effect—that is, for him to produce these programs of photographic apprehension— the majority of the images he uses to do this work in *Camera Lucida* are photographs of slaves, racialized bodies and differently abled bodies. This striking fact is somehow most often overlooked, and students at art schools everywhere proceed as if they were learning simply about a technology and not about a mode of sociality. Indeed, careful textual analysis of *Camera Lucida* shows that slavery, race and, ethnicity became the privileged tropes—the discursive apparatus—with which to figure "the essence of photography," for Barthes, "at any cost." Slavery and race become the rhetorical figures, the discursive, and arguably material media for the derivation of the supposedly ontological character of a visual *technology*. Indeed one might say that by making racialized others the stepping stones leading to the essence of a technology, Barthes subsumes and finally disappears the historical realities of race, ethnicity, and slavery (Jews, blacks, Latin Americans, Eastern Europeans) in order to make the ahistorical, that is, *technical* and indeed *chemical* reality of photography appear. At the very least, we can show that in the presumed illumination of *Camera Lucida*, racialization is something like the unconscious of the essence of photography. Indeed the troping and subsequent disappearing of racial difference for "purely" epistemological purposes may well be the most "universal" gesture here—the essence, if you will, of a whole tradition's way of knowing by signifying on the other: Humanism.

For Barthes, the unique quality of the photograph, its that-has-been-ness, along with the ability of the punctum to puncture the merely meaningful and disrupt the normative function of the sign, imbues the photograph with a radical potential for semiotic instability. However Barthes does less with the instability unleashed (instantiated) by the photograph than we might hope. For example, he writes that, "since every photograph is contingent (and thereby outside of meaning) photography cannot signify (aim at generality) except by assuming a mask."[17] He then regards the (is it haunting?) Richard Avedon portrait entitled *William Casby, Born a Slave*, and all-too-summarily concludes his observations with the thought that "the essence of slavery is here laid bare: the mask is the meaning, insofar as it is absolutely pure."[18]

Barthes' inclusion and cursory treatment of the Avedon photo do more than give slavery short shrift, they make slavery appear only to make it disappear again. Slavery rises up only to fall back and make way for an understanding of photography: "Society, it seems, mistrusts pure meaning [...] Hence the photograph whose meaning is too impressive is quickly deflected; we consume it aesthetically, not politically."[19] Ironically, to lay bare the essence of slavery, the photograph and therefore Barthes must be in "mask" mode—that is, on the side of meaning and of society, of semiotics. This "essence of slavery" is neither named nor described. Rather, its meaning conveniently dispensed with, the photograph opens the way for further (aesthetic) remarks on the inherent characteristics of the photographic medium. One suddenly suspects that the trajectory of the text—a striving to represent the essence of photography by replacing obscure projections with a lucid Real accomplished by signifying through racialized representations—is precisely a way of not talking about slavery and is, in fact, a displacement, a *method* of disappearing the history and with it, the logistics of perception that *really* produced the image of William Casby and perhaps in certain respects, all photographic images. It being understood, of course, that a political meaning of this sort, that suggests that photography itself is made with black blood, and that abominably slavery itself is the medium of photographic representation, would subsequently vitiate ostensibly non-partisan knowledge, to say nothing of value-neutral aesthetic inquiry, forever. But Barthes treats the Casby photograph as a *studium*, which allows him to proceed with the analysis of the essence of photography in his famous degree-zero prose.

50 pages later, at exactly the climactic moment in *Camera Lucida* when Barthes discovers photography's essence, slavery comes up again:

> I remember keeping for a long time a photograph I had cut out of a magazine—lost subsequently like everything too carefully put away—which showed a slave market: the slavemaster, in a hat, standing, the slaves, in loincloths, sitting. I repeat: a photograph, not a drawing or engraving; for my horror and my fascination as a child came from this: that there was a *certainty* that such a thing had existed: not a question of exactitude, but of reality: the historian was no longer the mediator, slavery was given without mediation, the fact was established *without method*.[20]

One is reminded here of Regis Debray's statement echoed above: "A fortiori, ideology could be defined as the play of ideas in the silence of technologies."[21] Here, the silent technologies that establish Barthes' certitude "without method" (an ostensibly non-ideological knowing that for Louis Althusser would mark the pinnacle of ideology—and hence of semiotic function) would include all of the recording machines and disciplinary technologies involved in the mediation of people by graphing their skin as image or sign, converting subjects into objects and persons into commodities that together constitute and constellate as photography. In *Camera Lucida*, slavery itself—in fact the slave market—composes photography's primal scene, its degree zero, and is arguably identified as paradigmatic of the essence of photography, but uncharacteristically, in perhaps too quick abandonment of his own brilliant work in semiotics, Barthes reads an (the?) image of slavery—actually, ironically, and uncannily, an *absent* image of slavery—in purely phenomenological terms.

Whether in the semiotic or evidentiary mode, slavery appears in *Camera Lucida* as supplementary to the photograph—a coincident incident that explains photography by being disappeared. In the first instance, the Casby photo, slavery appears as an essence that is visibly communicated, but aestheticized and thus of no more interest (since Barthes meaningfully pursues the photograph as an event beyond meaning). In the second evidentiary example, an absent image of a slave market appears as the cynosure of photography itself—within the framework of the essay, slavery and its absence exist, as it were, principally to establish the that-has-been-ness of the photograph. Thus the disappearance of method in Barthes' establishing for himself the facts of slavery has, in fact, the opposite function in *Camera Lucida*: the discursive disappearance of slavery establishes the facts of photography; *that* is the method. It is only via the epistemic disappearance of slavery— and of all the historical-economic vectors that made *both* slavery and photography possible—that by means of *Inception*-like layers of self-deception, Barthes' phenomenological account of photography as merely a technical medium with a unique property ("that has been") is possible. Had he been able to refuse techno-fetishism, Barthes might have kept his punctum but more accurately have gleaned the essence of photography: "slavery has been." And the slave market has been. Photo-graphing as a medium of racializing objectification and subjecti- fication has been—and it still is. One must steadfastly keep the histories of racial formation and political economy outside of the photographic frame to have evidence without method because otherwise, one might see that *the evidence is the method*: the historical and technical separation of subjects from their skin explicitly places racialization and photography on a continuum.

The imprisonment, social death and annihilation of subjects by the logistics of the gaze are fundamental to that relation we name photography. This photo-graphing of the skin, we must insist, is an ineluctable part of what Flusser identifies as the camera's program. To produce photography as a stand-alone platform, slavery must be at once present and disavowed. Which is to say that slavery is one of the methods by and through which photography came to be what it is, or at least what it appears to be—an autonomous platform. From this it is crystal clear that colonialism, and slavery, and the institutionalization and normaliza- tion of the practices on which these depended and depend, are part of the conditions by which bodies are first liquidated of subjectivity and reduced to images and signs for others to read. Whether in the slave ship *Brookes* where people were so cruelly reduced to numbers or in the maquiladoras where, as Lourdes Portillo shows, young women are photographed as targets for rape and femicide, the inscription of body as sign and its treatment as profitably captured cargo merge. Indeed this lifting off, or abstraction, of what will become racial and gendered characteristics from bodies is part of their de-coding and encoding as information—

it becomes, as we saw in the first chapter, a condition of possibility for Borges "Garden of Forking Paths." These modes of abstraction and alienation are part of the economic and racializing prehistory that gives rise to the society of the spectacle and its de-realization of the world. Social photo-graphing provides the abstract machine for technical photo-graphing; chattel slavery haunts the photographic image. The social relation opens the space for the chemical one and for what Flusser calls, in his description of photography, the thinking in numbers that is accomplished by the apparatus. Before the encoding of abstraction, society becomes abstract in practice. To fail to address this primordial disappearing—both the alienation of the skin and the alienation of the right to one's look, consequent upon the social abstractions endemic to racism and persistently emerging in Barthes' text as an eternal return of the repressed—would be to embrace the essence of the dominant discourse about photography, which as it stands unconsciously recapit-ulates, extends, and naturalizes violent forms of corporeal inscription, racial objectification, and social death as the very media of speculation.

Time constraints force me to note only in passing that such photo-graphy disappears bodies to make subjects appear (the viewer), and disappears subjects to make bodies appear (the viewed). We have seen a similar logic at work in informatics, computation and cinema. The disappearance of the subjectivity of the slave-object becomes the means by which the subjectivity of the slave-master manifests. Likewise the slave's body appears as the means of world making and of slave-master subjectivity through the radical and violent disappearing of the slave's subjectivity. Leaving Hegel aside, we can content ourselves here by clearly stating that materially and psychologically, the objectification and incorporation of the slave is a condition of possibility for the subjectivity of the slave-master. And the disappearance of slavery is the condition of possibility for Barthes' philosophy of photography—that is, for "the essence of photography" as many still understand it. The photograph, as Barthes says, is a *momento mori*, but of whose death?

Goldsby writes, "The secretion of lynching photographs was an explicit exercise of racial domination. If 'reckless eyeballing'—looking at white women in a sexual way—could get black men killed by white lynch mobs, knowledge that photographs of these murders were circulating thoughout the pulbic domain no doubt terrorized black communities ... Indeed the secretion of lynching photographs codified what was emerging as the civil right to look at and interpret the world in ways that perfected racism's hierarchies of privilege."[22] The death of blacks underpins white subjectivity and dominant visuality. As Harriet Jacobs' example shows a century earlier, to an extreme that was all too common, the slave as a subject had to disappear from view in a white-supremacist scopic regime in order to retain subjectivity and even life. What is remarkable in Jacob's case is that she was able to occupy this regime in a fugitive and clandestine way that allowed her to preserve and ultimately constitute her subjectivity in public discourse—albeit at a tremendous price. It would not be incorrect to assert that under this scopic regime, Jacobs' superhuman perseverance—which allowed her to live long enough to achieve literacy, write her life story, and re-appropriate both her body and her gaze—is one of the punctums in the history of photography. Her presence constitutes a wound, a prick of the Real, an eruption of unspeakable black suffering that the dominant discourses on the origins, meaning, and significance of photography have preferred not to detect, to simply pass over in silence. It is as if her life and the innumerable lives that had to bear the pain of white supremacist inscription had nothing to do with the history of images and of image making, of semiotics and code. With Jacob's a subject otherwise erased by slavery's photo-graphic regime talks back.

Without doubt, the camera obscura from which Harriet Jacobs miraculously emerges is an iteration of a visual-political system that extends in one way or another through the history of modern racism and colonialism, a visual-political system marked by gender as well as by race. Much ink has been devoted to the formal differences evident in the ways in which persons of various races and genders are photographed; and it has recently been brought to our attention that film stocks themselves were chemically biased towards rendering whiteness legible in acceptable and valorizing ways. There can be no doubt too that gender dynamics underpinned the formation and, indeed, the form of photography (whether black and white, or "colored") in a manner that was similar to, overlapping with, but distinguishable (at least at a certain level of analysis) from race. Furthermore, these social vectors— vectors that are fundamentally linked to agency and oppression vis-à-vis objectification—are inseparable from the cultural meanings and, indeed, the mysteries of the photograph. During her life, Jacobs is objectified as a black and as a woman: in addition to her enslavement, the slave-master's lust and the slave-mistress's jealousy were what produced the particular circumstances of her incarceration in camera. And as Jacobs lucidly expresses (and Hortense Spillers brilliantly elaborates), the roles of masculinity and femininity associated with whiteness, down to its very psychology were dependent upon the subjugation of slaves, and the brutal theft of material and sexual pleasures. What subsequently is allowed to appear and what is disappeared in photographs—what constitutes photography's "program," as Flusser again might say—has everything to do with the dynamics of agency and desire in this regime. Indeed, though it would take us too far afield, one could imagine that Barthes extraordinary love for his mother also presupposed a set of racial, financial and colonial relations. The fact that such regimes are contested (by their victims if no one else) also places the use, meaning, interpretation, significance, and epistemology of photography on an inexorably political terrain. What would it mean, really, to think of slavery as *a* form of photography or conversely, of photography as *a* form of slavery? The question itself calls for a far-reaching decolonization of visuality and visual technologies, and of the information that informs the photographic apparatus. And again, what would it mean to think of photography as a vector of feminization and commodification, both of which are inseparable from racism in the modern era—from racial capitalism that is also sex/gender capitalism? And what are the long-term epistemological and political implications of a certain knowledge of this triple objectification that recognizes that these photographic racializing and engendering structures of encoding and expropriation are the conditions of possibility for the now ineluctably historical illusion of transcendent, unmarked, objective (photographic) perspectives which, despite their anachronistic ontologies, persist in rendering truths ostensibly "without method?" The recent (and in my view utterly contemptible) emergence of "object oriented ontology" is merely the tip of the iceberg here; everywhere we confront deracinated mediation, data visualization and computation that are at once the means of social connection and the disavowed operation of a globally distributed system of apartheid. Biometrics, signature strikes, profiling of all sorts have become the affordances of an informatic world that takes much of its organizational template from photography and the history of visuality— even Hollereith confirms this. For those of us who concern ourselves with media and politics as if life depended on these (which it does), understanding the historicity of technological formations, cameras, film stocks, information systems, and the myriad other apparatuses of visualization in terms of race, gender, and commodification calls out contemporary media theory's fetishistic technological determinism. To refer to "photography"—or for that matter, "computers" or "the internet"—as if they were standalone media could be dismissed outright as a kind of platform fetishism bent on the disavowal of the immanent and absolute relevance of race, gender, and political economy to any and all technological questioning.

Although we might use Gwendolyn Audrey Foster's idea of a "plantocary of images" or Hortense Spiller's still unrivaled instantiation of "the flesh" as wedges of further inquiry, marking a starting point for reckoning the ontological being and un-representable experience of captured bodies always already overcoded by violent categories (and hence ideologies and moreover practices) of racialization and gendering; my purpose in this brief intervention on photography has only been to "stain the waters clear"—that is, to make the invisible visible in the seemingly transparent window that is the photograph, endeavoring as I have to indelibly mark photography itself as a racial formation.[23] In this view Flusser's account of the photograph as a "triple abstraction," (from the pre-writing pictograph, to the hieroglyph and linear writing, to the materialization of linearly written (numeric) thought in the apparatus) persuasive as it may be, remains woefully incomplete, as it is derived purely from mediatic shifts and devoid of geopolitical concreteness attendant to colonization and social differentiation.[24] Indeed, the history of visuality, including photography, cinema and computation, needs to be entirely rewritten in terms that understand the intersecting roles of racialization, feminization, and commodification. More than that, their convergent operating systems need to be decolonized—disrupted in their function in the broadest possible sense and reprogrammed.

To be sure, no amount of looking—even knowledgably—at Avedon's photo of *William Casby, Born a Slave* could redeem any aspect of the violent injustice, unspeakable brutality and astonishing suffering of the past, or its extension into the present. Recognizing that contemporary visuality, semiotics and computation is bound up with racism and slavery—genetically, so to speak—and that so much of what is seen is actually a *seeing through slavery and coloniality* and that so much of knowing is a *knowing through slavery and coloniality* (that is, by means of slavery and coloniality; *slavery and coloniality as method*) does not amount to reparations. Still, the abiding thought that modern scopic, discursive and computational regimes are inexorably entangled in lived racism, past and present, and that there is no photographic image, and possibly no post-photographic thought, that is untouched by racism powerfully shifts the terrain for the understanding and use of images, archives and machines. May it also enable visions and practices that will help to one day make racism a "that has been" that is no more.

7
Pathologistics of Attention

In the end mass media culture has, bottom line, no other content than violence.

—Laurence Rickels

What white people have to do, is try and find out in their own hearts why it was necessary to have a nigger in the first place, because I'm not a nigger, I'm a man, but if you think I'm a nigger, it means you need it.

—James Baldwin

Their history [drones'] is that of an eye turned into a weapon.

—Grégoire Chamayou

As it turns out in the mise en scène of computational capital, our nonexistent democracies increasingly rely on automation, and more particularly the automation of psychopathology and psychosis, in order to sustain the ir-reality necessary to their function. This, to be sure, suggests that psycho-logistics, falls under the domain of an overarching functionalization of the living by algorithmic governance and pattern recognition in the society organized at the level of meta-data. The shattering of traditional life forms and the imposition of new forms of life (and of statistically distributed death) by placing the bios in information brings broad-spectrum crisis, at least from the standpoint of prior constitutions. In this chapter, we will attend to the immanent organization of the (white, white-identifying) psyche in and by cinematic technologies that are to be understood as emergent interfaces with the data-sphere of computational capital.

Psychopathology, in the modern sense, while an overly general term, most often results from some dissociation of sensibility, or in other words (a necessity, it seems), some slippage of the signifier from the signified. Psychopatholgy was, as Lukacs scandalously wrote in his valorization of Thomas Mann over Joyce and Kafka, symptomatic of the bourgeois flight from reality and from an awareness of the objective conditions that over-determine subjective existence.[1] While this thoroughly modern slippage of language from the Real is intuited by linguistics and latched upon as an inexorable feature of language by post-structuralism, a historicization of these emerging insights into the becoming ontological failure of language to image Being would understand post-structuralism as itself an inflection point in which this generalized slippage intensifies. While the paradigms of reality and truth are irrevocably lost to philosophy in the mid-twentieth-century West (and seemingly to the world at large with the U.S. Presidential election of 2016), one sees, retroactively, that the gradual intensification and awareness of this slippage from the referent was the condition not only of post-structuralism and postmodernism, but of psychoanalysis and modern linguistics *en toto*. Naturally, this view of arbitrary signifiers slipping off of no longer fully presentable signifieds in accord with new organizational principles (drives, fetishes, desires, in psychoanalysis, syntagmatic, paradigmatic functions on the arbitrary nature of the sign in linguistics) could be stretched back into historical time to explain the need for hermeneutical analysis (Marxism, psycho-analysis) as well as the opening of the space (gap) that will give rise to and be ramified by poetry, modern literature, abstract painting, and visual culture. Lukacs was right about one thing at least: High Modernism was symptomatic. It could also be extended forward in a recognition that the scrambling of signification was indeed an effect of an instrumentalization of signs (and then images by higher order programs in a media-ecology of capital) that is only now being understood as such. In this chapter, however, I will be interested less in the formal characteristics of linguistic and identificatory dysfunction with regard to a paradigm of representable truth, and more in pursuit of what I take to be the increasing *automation* of this dissociation of sensibility, that is, of what in the older language of the ideological paradigm was in extreme cases diagnosed psychopathol-ogy—while noting that such automation when considered socially tends to completely exceed its psychic dimensions and extensively develop the patho-logical dimensions at a new scale. Even if the normalization of aspects of psychopathology make it no longer recognizeable as such, we may still sense the pathological at another scale: that of the planetary condition which few would deny is both sick and obscene.

The automation of what I will refer to here as the pathologistics of attention can also be pursued from the standpoint of the experience of today's large-scale psychological afflictions including burn-out, depression, autism, OCD, ADD, sociopathology and the like—all of which, like schizophrenia, must be understood as at once forms of genuine suffering and historically specific incarnations. However, I will not dwell on the psychoanalytic aspects of the generalization of "mental illness" in the twenty-first century as a fundamental condition of possibility for the perpetuation of "our times," (though that is, as Eva Ilouz brilliantly demonstrates, indeed the case) and more on the infrastructure of the logistics of attention that organize and functionalize psychopathologies. As a mediological analysis would take into account, these logistics are not only internal to subjects but are also distributed throughout the mediatic and material forms of the *socius* itself. Thus, we shall turn to the "support, apparatus [and] procedure" of modes of transmission of meaning and the organization of attention—in short, to screens and, more particularly, cinema.[2]

An exploration of the pathologistics of attention through a consideration of cinematic programming seems justified in as much as cinema's identificatory structures were, and in legacy forms remain, fundamental processes for the encoding, dissemination, and activation of visual and mental processes. In short we take the subject as always already cyborg while recognizing histories of its emergence and implosion by means of a series of distributed software upgrades discernible in the form of paradigmatic cinematic tropes and conventions.

The investigation proposes the following hypotheses:

1. Films are programs of visualization and hence for discourse.
2. Iconic films abstract and mobilize paradigmatic programs. These programs provide infrastructure for the organization of attention.
3. Psychological aspects of these programs are functional and legible in the interface of the screen, but the logistics are distributed in the organization of bodies, apparatuses and social relations—in materiality and more precisely in historical materiality.
4. Apparatuses automate aspects of formerly human decision and intelligence. They are programs that have been formalized and sedimented into machinery.
5. Sovereignty is increasingly moving into the material, the machine-mediated, which is to say, the computational environment: platform sovereignty.[3]
6. Convergence, ordinarily thought to mean the convergence of various media platforms into the digital medium known as the computer, is

to be understood as the convergence of linguistic function, scopic and auditory function and financialization with and as computation. These platforms consolidate a matrix of operations. This convergence is a powerful tendency, perhaps not a fait accompli.

These proposals extend from the argument made in *The Cinematic Mode of Production* that cinema "brings the Industrial Revolution to the eye." Aspects of Industrialization, "the factory code," the assembly line, routinization, were built into the cinema, and then later developed in feedback loops with the cinema and computation. McLuhan's "homogenous segmentation" attributed to Gutenberg, what Steigler generalizes and calls grammatization, works for frames and bits—and on bodies. Life processes are broken down and reassembled in discrete units with ever more granularity. By studying a non-random selection of films made at various moments along the evolutionary path taken by cinema, films that not incidentally all have a thematic relation to money at their narrative and libidinal cores, we may sketch with some precision the implication of Karl Marx's idea that "industry is the open book of man's essential powers, the exposure to the senses of human psychology" for contemporary psychology.[4] Film, abstracted and submitted to analysis, shows us the machinic and indeed automated organization of spectatorship and it's psychological interpellations. However, in this case, different in important respects from that of Marx and his fragment on machines, our "open book" is not the assembly line (*chaine de montage*) but cinema and cinematic montage conceived as a key transitional phase between industrialization and the social factory of digital culture (post-Fordism). We will be sketching, dialectically as it were, the (re-)organization of the psyche itself as well as the modes of attention that correspond to said organization in the advance of computational capital.

It is increasingly non-controversial that machine-mediated modes of attention are regimes of capture; the attention-machine as fixed capital absorbs sensual labor. Thus we may observe that montage, deep focus, and the cut, as theorized during the history of cinema and the heyday of film theory, all correspond to neurological and psychological processes as well as to specific forms of attention prototyped then instituted. We may also observe paradigmatic cinematic forms were "destined," more or less, to be utilized in capital's emerging regimes of production and monetization collectively termed attention economy or cognitive capitalism. This is particularly obvious from the standpoint of the present conjuncture in the U.S., where as in Nazi Germany, "adolescene [is] streamlined ... and advanced to the position of superego" and a white supremacist government is (still) in power.[5] Thus, we begin a kind of archaeology of forms of attention—neuro-, psycho-, photo-, cinematico-, informatico-, and capital-logical—that have both paved the way to and achieved a culmination of sorts in the capture of the cognitive-linguistic commons by life-destroying modalities for the organization of attention in racial capitalism.

There are connections to be investigated between the organization of perception by machinery, the strip-mining of attention by images and James Baldwin's observation that American heroes of the John Wayne type never had to grow up. Because of the widespread influence of say the first person shooter, a perspective and relation that has effects resounding through the entire fabric of the socius, the modalities of cinematic implantation and cybernetic visualization include not just the ordinarily acknowledged media platforms but in our own times, student debt, blood computing, drone warfare, and the every second of every day function of representation floating on the surface of an ocean of unrepresented—and in the current conjuncture unrepresentable—suffering of more than two billion people living on less than two dollars per day and the history of the world that got "us" here. Platforms though programmatic are not autonomous but embedded; formal shifts index changes in the sites and modes of the production process and of sovereignty. If this correspondence does not occur in exactly the same way for all viewers, then it occurs within statistically predictable parameters in which real deviation requires the reclaimed and purposefully redirected sensibilities of a critical movement such as feminism, anti-racism or decolonization in feminist film theory, third cinema, postcolonial film theory and the like—bell hooks' oppositional gaze. One thinks of figures like James Baldwin, bell hooks, Solanas and Gettino, and in cinema a long and powerful tradition of modification and refusal of programmatic norms (Maya Deren, Trin T. Minh-ha, Sadie Benning, Djibril Mambety, etc.). It is our urgent challenge to connect the function of apparatuses whose logistics both organized dominant (dominated and dominating) psychic formation and have also been abstracted and encoded in the operation of digital machines, with the expansion of mass immiseration, and the relative unrepresentability of planetary crisis in such a way that would demand revolution (and new foms of revolution) instead of various types of conformity and machinic enslavement.

This study of the pathologistics of attention is therefore necessarily also about the scrambling of the symbolic order; the increasing bankruptcy of sign-function; the de-structuring and restructuring of the grammar of semiotics and the grammatization of social relations such that they can be broken apart and reassembled according to new protocols of value extraction; it is about the proletarianization of the senses that occurs from the dissociation of the senses from prior social instantiations of mind and body; the expropriation of the cognitive-linguistic; the installation of the regime of cognitive capitalism over and on top of, or adjacent to, the persistence of spectacular, industrial, and feudal regimes; the mining of attention as an amalgamating means of command-control-production; the current and ostensibly indomitable reign of short-term thinking; the life-sucking character of financialization; the acid corrosiveness of the Wall Street nanosecond; the ever-advancing seizure of the commons; the rise and rise of white nationalism and the effect of all these projects in relation to mentality, warfare, global dispossession, and planetary collapse. The very organization of appearance as data-visualization under the contemporary forms of inequality presses perception and knowledge into functioning as technologies of for-profit murder through the active cancellation and "dismediation"[6] of the other. This intensive production of the other by the pathologistics of datavisualization is a fundamental productive strategy of a computational capitalism that remains racial capitalism. The other is slated to labor as surface of inscription.

So, in addition to the breakdown and reformatting of language function and the redistribution and/or liquidation of meaning, this essay unavoidably focuses on the psychopathology and the logistics of perception of contemporary, that is, postmodern, fascism, otherwise to be thought of as the totalitarianism of computational finance capitalism—a formation that is, like the psyche itself, at once without us and within us. In what follows we will have occasion to remark upon the solicitation of identification and the fractalization of fascist structures of personality such that they may compensate in "the imaginary" for collective dis-empowerment while preserving property relations in "the real." We have the dialectic between the historical expropriation first of labor and then of attention, on the one side, and the short-circuiting of the body and then of thought on the other side. The historico-technical, and indeed affective, ramification of this gap between the liberative potentials of globalized life and the sovereign planetary interdiction against justice is the definitive means and necessary condition for the production of this, our present time—the time of computational capital—in as much as it is verifiably present at all.[7]

A first cut: gesture, or the fragments of machines

Charlie Chaplin's film *Modern Times* (1936), near silent but made nine years after the official end of the silent era and recently re-historicized in Owen Hatherly's illuminating *Chaplin Machine*, juxtaposes the two major filmic modes of the first half of the twentieth century: montage and deep focus. The unforgettable assembly-line sequence: with the Tramp struggling to keep pace with the work speed up, desperately using wrenches to tighten first bolts and then, neurologically reprogrammed by assembly-line repetition, to tighten blouse buttons; the auto-feeder: allowing the workers to continue tightening bolts while a machine pushes food into their mouths; and the culminating fall: into the machine itself all show the radical imposition of the standardization and routinization process on the body by the machinery of industrial capital. The body and the neurological system are being remade by industrial capitalism to compose what Hatherley reminds us, Benjamin in his notes for a review of *The Circus* (1928) called "the Chaplin-machine." "He greets people by taking off his bowler, and it looks like the lid rising from the kettle when the lid boils over ... 'the mask of non-involvement turns him into a fairground marionette.' Benjamin implies something deeper here, that this is a 'mask' of sanguine inhumanitiy, under which something more poignant is at work."[8] Hatherley quotes again from Benjamin on Chaplin:

> He dissects the expressive movements of human beings into a series of minute innervations. Each single movement he makes is composed of a series of staccato bits of movement. Whether it is his walk, the way he handles his cane, or the way he raises his hat—always the same jerky sequence of tiny movements applies the law of the cinematic image sequence to human motorial functions. Now, what is it about such behavior that is distinctly comic?[9]

The disciplinary aspect of the assembly line, in both its corporeal and temporal dimensions, is translated to the cinema and underscored by physical comedy: Chaplin shows it in the Tramp's at times involuntary rebellion against the machine's strict routinization of his gestures as well as through his total incorporation of machinic function. The Tramp's inadequacy to the disciplinary regime of industrial production—he is at once overtaken by it and inadequate to it—leads him at the beginning of *Modern Times* to a series of nervous ticks, short circuits, and conflicts with his fellow workers. Chaplin's ability to be both his character and himself, by means of the "mask" of machinification, allows for the narrative register to be in continual tension with Chaplin's directorial analysis. Whatever befalls the Tramp, as well as his brilliant subversions, are there to be experienced viscerally, but also to be accounted for and analyzed since the machinic structuring of his everyday is abstracted in the representation that is the film such that the film becomes industry's meta-cognitive account of itself—a reading of "the open book of man's essential powers, the exposure to the senses of human psychology." As the film progresses, the Tramp finally falls into the mechanism itself, passing through its system of gears. Only upon his real subsumption, if you will, does the Tramp thoroughly become one of the machine's products. At this point in the narrative he has a complete nervous breakdown: before being carried away in an ambulance he defiantly oils people with big black squirts in the face as if serving machines.

Importantly, this nervous breakdown does not lead the Tramp to the psychoanalyst's couch but instead to a hospital and then, through a series of employment mishaps, to jail—a place, incidentally, that with its warm dry bed and three meals a day he finds infinitely more congenial than the outside world of the industrial city. I stress this not only because the price of neurological failure for the working machine-man is prison or the street but also because the film's coming break from montage for the utilization of deep focus at certain key points does not employ this important latter technique to psychoanalytic ends, as in, *Citizen Kane* (1941), a film we will explore momentarily. This non-psychologizing response is a matter of class of history and of politics. Rather than psychology in *Modern Times*, it is the physical comedy and the power of the body that are given as the heroic response to the fragmentation of space and time by the machine. It is relevant that Hatherley deftly documents not only Chaplin's stake in Marxism, but the Soviet avant-garde's investment in acrobatics, circus and Chaplin. Chaplin's brilliance is in large part due to his corporeal abilities to reclaim a body that would otherwise be robbed of its gestural capacities and effectively shattered by the machine organizing life in the fragmentary mode of montage. Importantly, this bodily mastery manifest in Chaplin also reunifies space and time. As writer, director, and star, Chaplin's superlative control of the four dimensions (for that, in brief, is, or at least was, cinema) is both an analysis of industrial production and a form of vengeance against industrial capitalism. With Chaplin, the cinema abstracts and recasts a paradigmatic experience of machinic industrialization, using its own industrial methods to create pleasure and critique.

Of the two or three scenes that utilize deep focus, I want to talk about the skating scene. The extraordinary tension that a viewer may experience while a blindfolded Chaplin skates backwards with infinite and graceful abandon as if oblivious to a three-story drop opened by the broken balustrade just behind him creates a kind of poetry of the body in which the human animal, slated, as indicated by the film's opening scene to become a programmable sheep by the industrial-ized temporality of the machine age, is shown to be capable of a near supernatural freedom of expressive movement—a form of joy. Not once but many times, Chaplin skates in speedy backwards arcs, with one leg in the air, seemingly unaware that he is less than an inch from the edge of what could only be a bone-breaking fall. This movement in the round, in a temporally continuous three-dimensional space (rather than a space constructed through shot-countershot or montage fragments), is narra-tologically inspired by love: the Tramp and the Waif are an impoverished couple battling the dehumanization of the industrial city. It is also inspired by their momentary if illicit enjoyment of the luxurious spoils of a bourgeois department store. We see a relation to love and to luxury that despite its bourgeois aspirations is not diminished—because within the confines of history and class narrated here such a life of luxury is at once the best that can be imagined and an unrealizeable dream.[10]

Taking advantage of cinema Chaplin uses industrial modes of production to organize body, space, time, and attention counter to that self-same industry's Taylorist reconditioning of modern man's neurological function. This is a political redeployment of technologies of automation that posits the cinema and visual process as a mode of critical abstraction capable of exercising leverage over the abstraction of the body by capitalized machines. In becoming the content of cinema, the medium of the assembly line is interrogated through the revelation of its message. The decoding of "the message" of assembly-line capitalism— that it is nothing short of the wholesale theft of gesture and life by the routinization of neuronal process—makes this a counter-cinema. "Collective laughter," as Benjamin observed, is [a] pre-emptive and healing outbreak of mass psychosis. The countless grotesque events consumed in films are a graphic indication of the dangers threatening mankind from the repressions implicit in civilization."[11] Unfortunately, it appears that Adorno and Horkheimer's sense of cinema as a conditioning mechanism designed to generalize psychosis ("fun is a medicinal bath") prevailed as the cultural dominant of film laughter and film therapy.

A second cut: castration, or the fetish is a penis but not just any penis

This space-time of realism—which Andre Bazin in *What Is Cinema?* described as a decal or a transfer of reality to celluloid and saw as best represented by deep focus—is perhaps today better thought of as the realism befitting a certain Euro-American transnational era in a particular media-ecology. Real space-time continuity was thought to index real relations. With Chaplin the realism provided by deep focus is far more physiological than psychological.[12] How different it is in a film such as *Citizen Kane*, where the journey through a discontinuous set of continuous space-times, what Deleuze calls "sheets of past," is entered into as if one were to enter directly into different moments of Charles Foster Kane's snow globe—one of his many fetish objects whose formation had to be investigated. The narrative sheets, each of a particular time, together constitute a set of behaviors and events that are to be read symptomatically and that, like the fetish objects in the film provide access to Kane's unconscious.[13] The multiple entries into spaces via shots passing through windows and skylights emphasize and thematize this effect even as they build out a notion of the rich and complex fabric of biography and history composed by events and unconscious motiviations. Narrative space becomes itself an extension of the psyche—an expression of unconscious forces.

This spatialization of the unconscious, developed even further, albeit in different directions by Hitchcock and Antonioni, at once discovers what Benjamin referred to as an "unconscious optics" and posits first space and then later the optical field itself as a means to accomplish two distinct but not unrelated aspirations. At the first level, the space is there to be read as a matrix of unconscious forces working on the subject of the film: this is a poetics of space and space as text—as a hermeneutic for the analysis of the unconscious. At the next level, *Inception*-like, the space not only tells us about the figure in it, but programs the figure for certain actions. We see this programming, for example, in *Zabriske Point* when a character drives past a billboard advertising hourly flights by showing an image of a watch and then unconsciously checks his watch as he passes by. All of these spatial dynamics, already present in panoptic designs and then greatly elaborated not only in fascist architecture but in the candy fascism of shopping malls and much urban planning, have here a second register in as much as these are transcoded and mobilized by the image. They become part of the dynamic semiosis of the optical field, and as already stated, thus become both the legible text of the unconscious and means by which to program the unconscious. We are in the realm of the unconscious optics posited by Walter Benjamin. If for Benjamin and Welles these serve as sites of analysis for the default practices of hegemony—whether or not elaborated as concepts or later as algorithms, they also serve as means of programming.

With *Citizen Kane*, there, in these sheets of space-time, sealed off by the closure imposed by Kane's death and the mystery of the gaps among the fragmentary accounts of who he was, everything is pregnant with meaning, and, as has been observed, the audience plays the role of detective or psychoanalyst while watching the film—and not just this film. In *Kane*, we embark on a search for an explanation of the inner workings of a public and indeed cultic personality, one first introduced to us, it must be underscored, through a *montage sequence*. This sequence of the newsreel at the opening of the film is in contrast with all the rest emphatically not a deep focus sequence of movement and duration. The film within the film, which Deleuze says is about money, is indeed, but in a way that may expand our notion of money since it is here embodied by Kane. The newsreel serves multiple purposes here, to inform us about Kane in using the efficient manner of prevalent and popular genre of the time, but also as a metaphor for how we moderns know. It is not just a representation of Kane, or a representation of Kane as a media mogul and financial titan. It is also a representation of the newsreel as medium and furthermore of montage itself. The newsreel is at once psychologically affective (it piques our curiosity) but is also psychologically opaque (it does not answer our questions) and calls for another mode of cinematic function as a mode of analysis. Montage and the cut become the commercial way of understanding a commercialized world; *Citizen Kane* will want to find another way to know this world. Notably then the montage representation Kane the citizen, the media mogul, the recluse, the man whom later, in a deep focus sequence we will see accused by disillusioned paramour Susan—for whom he built an opera house—of "never giving [her] nothing, but only trying to buy

[her] love," has a public identity built through mechanical reproduction's financially calculated montage effects. Even in the newsreel sequence Kane appears through the montage effects of yet another financialized media: the newspaper ballistics that daily sensationalize the famous Kane's endeavors and shock the modern public into continuously recalibrated modes of recognition. It is also noteworthy, in light of the implicit assertion here that newsprint and publicity running on the program of a sensationalist newspaper function as a form of expanded cinema, that Bazin, a great proponent of deep-focus cinema, found montage overly programmatic, saying that montage foreclosed thought. Bazin, for the record, also accused montage of representing things that do not exist—a point on which he was no doubt correct with respect to the pro-filmic world. Despite the fact that for Eisenstein the instantiation of a concept or the creation of a conditioned reflex, that is, of a new order of reality via the montage of attractions, was a good thing, or at least a very useful one inasmuch as it both expressed the modal power of cinema and could engineer new perceptions (adequate to the times) and thereby be utilized by the revolutionary avant-garde both to foment revolution and create revolutionary sensibilities, the programmatic and behaviorist aspects of montage were correctly intuited by Bazin to be on a continuum with the shredding and reprogramming of space-time that was characteristic not only of the cinema-machine but also of industrialization more generally. Newspapers, newsreels, the fragmentation and re-assemblage of life was a sort of ballistic assault in the spectator, "a tractor plowing over the audiences psyche" as Eisenstein said. Deep focus, on the other hand, allows for ambiguity, according to Bazin, and in *Citizen Kane* the deep-focus suspension of the determinate meaning of the image is in fact used to interrogate a montage sequence. Deep focus interrogates the world sutured by montage and subjugated to the exigencies of the message. The film investigates the newsreel.

For whatever reason, there is one part of the newsreel montage that opens *Citizen Kane* that I have always likened to that of the stone lion sequence on the Odessa steps in *Battleship Potemkin* (1925), those paradigmatic splices offered just after Potemkin fires on the czarist troops. In *Potemkin* we get sleeping lion statue, waking lion statue, and fully roused on all fours lion statue, an extraordinarily dynamic presentation of the objectified masses rising up—the stones come alive. In the newsreel in *Citizen Kane* we have the three telegraphic vocal accounts of Kane given a press interviews: "He's a communist," "he's a fascist," and, in his own words, "I'm an American." Here also we have the masses represented iconically, each time by the figure of Kane in relation to a social system. Is this sequence, these representations of the masses, objectified in the figure of Kane come to life as thesis, antithesis and synthesis. Yet this synthesis of the mass movements (communism) and mass culture (fascism) in the figure of Citizen Kane as iconic American is precisely the mystery that the film seeks to investigate.

So, let's say that the film sets out to contemplate a world in fragments, that is, it seeks a depth hermeneutic adequate to a world of appearances that suddenly are felt to be mere symptoms of a deeper mediological and financial problematic. In short, Wells seeks a psychoanalytic explanation for a mass media produced cultic figure—one who as himself a product of industrial society appeared to be sympathetic to the masses and to workers' struggle but who was a Cesarist in Gramsci's sense, that is, a charismatic leader who opportunistically conscripted the libidinal investments of mass-based struggles for liberation to build his own image in accordance with the laws of private property and profit.[14]

On his deathbed Kane loses his grip on his snow globe. It shatters on the floor as if releasing his dying word: "rosebud." The film proceeds as if rudimentary communist sympathies and blatant fascism when channeled through a capitalist media empire somehow culminate in "an American," and in Kane's case in "an American citizen," and as if this "progression," for lack of a better term, could be understood upon a proper exploration of the question whose answer is "rosebud." This investigation will require the spatio-temporality of deep focus and the long take. As we know— because Wells told his lawyers to tell the press so—Citizen Kane is not about William Randolph Hearst (or Rupert Murdoch, Bill Gates, Mark Zuckerberg, Silvio Berlusconi, or POTUS) but is based on "dollar book Freud." Of course like psychoanalysis, a dollar was worth a lot more in 1941, and we certainly should not miss the proximity of psychoanalysis and money in Wells's riposte.

"Rosebud," the fast darkening name on little Charlie's childhood sled, is revealed to us in the final scene in the Xanadu warehouse of Kane's massive material accumulation, as the lost plaything burns with his other unsalable junk in a vast incinerator. Rosebud is fetish number one among a series of fetishes that are reconfigured in the frozen world of the snow globe and analogously in Kane's fetishistic acquisition of "the great

treasures of Europe," bought, crated, and stored in his palatial Xanadu—
never to be seen again.

Freud, unsurprisingly perhaps, tells us that the fetish is the penis,
but reminds us that it is not just any penis; it is, quite specifically, the
mother's penis, often associated with the last object seen before the
fateful revelation of the mother's lack. Freud tells us that the fetishes
for feet, velvet, and fur originate from the moment just before the male
child looks up the mother's skirt.[15] The fetish is a way to simultaneously know and not know; it preserves a last instance of the plenitude of
childhood (a last glance at feet or pubic hair) while becoming a stand-in
for the now-castrated mother's penis. Thus, the fetish disavows the
threat of castration that traumatizes the male child when he sees that
the penis he believed to be there can disappear. This little excursion
into "dollar-book Freud" is clarifying since Rosebud was indeed the last
thing the young Charlie Kane enjoyed before witnessing his mother's
(symbolic) castration. The mother, domineering in relation to Kane's
shady and very likely abusive father, is both protective of Charlie and in
charge of family decisions. But as the story has it, Kane's relation to his
mother is supervened by an inheritance that in a single stroke makes
him one of the richest people in the world and severs his connection
to his mother. Called over from the plenitude of childhood sledding by
his mother and the man who will turn out to be his new guardian, little
Charlie is informed that he will no longer live at home. Charlie's new
guardian is a bank-appointed custodian of his new fortune. The agency
of this fortune—in short, the alienated power of money expressed
as the will of the banks—separates Kane from his mother, in spite of
his childhood protests to the contrary. The rest of his life, we are to
understand, which tellingly includes his hatred for his guardians at the
bank, will be an effort to recapture the plenitude of the maternal bond—
the time of the maternal phallus. However, cut off from the mother
who transferred her loving protection to the bank, the medium for the
solicitation of love is forevermore capital, and for Kane, who seeks to
make his capital expressive of his own desires, this expression takes the
form of the newspaper: mass media itself will be the financial medium
for the solicitation of universal love. But in order to not be castrated
as his mother was (her agency was vanquished by the phallic power of
the banks), he must prove himself to be more than money, to operate
in excess of the explicit logic of money. This time, thinks Kane, money
must create love, not destroy it. Ultimately, this quest turns out to be

impossible and Kane's epic struggle ends in failure. All the fetishes in the world could neither ward off the death of love among his monetarily controlled intimates, nor the final castration that is mortality itself—a fact that were Kane not such a hideous figure might have been tragic. Kane's sympathy for the workers' movements, expressed via the very means that would require overthrow for such sympathy to be authentic (bank capital and capitalist media), becomes only his self-aggrandizing populism—a way of buying love on a mass scale. Money, newspapers and readers become the media for the working out of Kane's psychic trauma, a life-long struggle to ward of the castration imposed by the banks in the first place. Lacan's "vel of alienation" which poses the question "your money or your life," but takes your life in either case reigns supreme. Charismatically, Kane promotes himself as a great man of the people, but in playing the charismatic leader he leads the public to what Walter Benjamin would call "a processing of data in the fascist sense."[16] Kane's love for the masses, expressed via financializing media, is actually a desire for love from the masses that makes him into an authoritarian personality—the "communist" becomes a Fascist, and that's America for you. From now on, for Kane but clearly not just for Kane, love, masculinity, mass media, and capitalist exploitation will be welded together. This convergence makes each of Kane's libidinal investments within the film nothing more than an exploit. Indeed, the love object, from whose perspective Kane might see himself as loveable, whether in the form of the masses, the friend, or the lover, requires an evisceration of the love object because, in brief, capitalized montage as a protocol for the organization of objects cuts them up and abstracts them. Its sovereign imposition of meaning is the opposite of dialogue. Accordingly, Kane, with his horde of hollow treasures and collection of exploits organized by the cutting power of capitalized media, all meant to signify a humanity that he does not possess, will die a great man: loveless, friendless, empty, and alone.

Freud tells us that all men are great in their dreams. Kane tried to live his dreams as a media capitalist and thus became an exemplary American: neurotic, megalomaniacal, unloving, and unloved. In this he was successful: he replaced his mother's love, severed it is true by the money relation, with what on the surface of a world of montaged fragments seemed like the generalized attention of a kind of affection, but in deep focus appears as a relation of exploitation and indeed of liquidation.

A third cut: the normal man, or mobilized gazes
and the short-circuiting of the law of the father

With the development of the assembly line and mass media, we have examined all too briefly in this chapter, the loss first of the capacity to move and then of the capacity to love. Let us survey the damage that is the price of cybernetics and informationalization by returning to Alfred Hitchcock's *Psycho* (1960), a film about a man trying to overcome both of these incapacities. As we have seen, the famed opening of Saul Bass's cut-up credits of *Psycho* already forecasts the shredding of the symbolic order (both syntagmatically and paradigmatically) and thus of the law of the father—by cinema. Nonetheless, despite the cuts, the symbols remain legible, while also achieving a new order of legibility because of the cuts.

We first glimpse Marion and Sam in a hotel bed during time stolen from the lunch hour. We glimpse them voyeuristically, it must be admitted, as we peer under the curtain and through the window into the bed from ten stories in the air. In fact, it is noteworthy that in the first fifteen seconds of the film we go from a bird's-eye view of the aptly named city of Phoenix to a momentary perch outside a curtained window and then into a sex scene—as the characters, the cinema, and the audience seek their quasi-elicit pleasures and their ends. The audience too is positioned in a kind of no-place that welds desire to the technologically mobilized gaze and, presciently here, turns city space into cyber-space. So, with interests thus aligned (we want sex, not psychoanalysis, in risqué 1960), we pursue Marion Crane, who, untamed by the law, takes flight. After having stolen forty thousand dollars, suddenly out of control and haunted, she drives out of town, driven by the gaze and the voice of the law—only, as luck would have it, to fall into the trap of the stuttering Norman Bates, a man with, as we have already seen, his own scopic and linguistic program who also happens to be a taxidermist. One could say that film in general was, above all things about the cut, but such a statement would never be more true than in the case of *Psycho*.

Let us agree: Marion, whose gaze, mobilized like that of cinematic spectators, finds herself momentarily free to follow her desire but is then pursued by the law while on her flight to pleasure. Paradoxically, this journey to pleasure is cut short by a new law, that of the cinematic cut. This cut is the other side, the dialectical antithesis, if you will, of the mobilized gaze—technically speaking, its condition and limit in the cinema, socially speaking, a new modality of perception and experience in relation to which the cinema is at once an abstraction and an inten-sification. Indeed, as observed in our prior discussion of *Psycho*, it is the film as a narrative structure and indeed as algorithm that forces Marion to stop at the Bates Motel to be properly cut to the new measure of desire by the revenge of the law of the Father. Mobility and the edit: the new grammar of desire and deferral for which the old grammar of the symbolic order and the law of the father must find adequation. This power to fragment and reassemble is at once a condition of possibility of, and subjugating grammar for, an emergent order of desire attendant to modernity. That modality, as the slasher auteurs who followed in the footsteps of Hitchcock during the next half century realized in one way or another, is the deeper message, for we find in *Psycho* an algorithm of financial capture—of capitalized vision. The mode of its implantation in the spectator extends and yet reconstitutes the pathologistical imple-mentation of the gendered organization of pleasure.

Kristeva writes, "As correlative to the notion of repression, Freud put forward that of *denial* as a means of figuring out neurosis, that of *rejection* (*repudiation*) as a means of situating psychosis. The asymmetry of the two repressions becomes more marked owing to denial's bearing on the object whereas repudiation affects desire itself (Lacan, in perfect keeping with Freud's thought, interprets that as "repudiation of the Name of the Father)."[17] Not just a violation of the common heritage that is the human body and its thought, not simply the re-composition of space-time, the grammar of the cinema is a mode of and for the mobilization and reorganization of desire. Marion, the desiring Crane, empowered by her new role in the workplace, cuts the law, but she is not the only one. There are many new mobilizations afforded by new social and financial relations in the mid-century United States. In stealing the money and fleeing Phoenix (the bird reborn from the ashes), she cuts out, but she is also cut out: out of society and, even more shockingly perhaps, out of the film. Indeed, Hitchcock shocked audiences not with the one act of cutting against Janet Leigh but with two acts in one: by brutally cutting her up as he did in the middle of the film, he thus, against the audience's expectations, cut the film star out of the film halfway through the narrative. The second half of the film is the afterlife of both Norman's and the audience's fetishistic appropriation and indeed consumption of the female film star—a sewing up of loose ends with psychoanalysis.

Let us also remember that for Laura Mulvey, at least, visual pleasure is generated by a narrative cinema "cut to the measure of [male] desire," and this is accomplished by the organization of three looks, that of the characters, the camera, and the audience. Mulvey describes the exigencies bearing on both woman and the image of woman with a kind of devastating efficiency. "[T]he function of woman in forming the patriarchal unconscious is twofold: she firstly symbolizes the castration threat by her real lack of a penis and secondly thereby raises her child into the symbolic. Once this has been achieved, her meaning in the process is at an end."[18] As if writing about Marion, Mulvey adds that "Women's desire is subjugated to her image as bearer of the bleeding wound; she can exist only in relation to it and not transcend it." The two sentences immediately following this description of the structural foreclosure of feminine expression almost uncannily describe Norman's fate at the hands of his mother: "She turns her child into the signifier of her own desire to possess a penis (the condition, she imagines, of entry into the symbolic). Either she must gracefully give way to the world, the name of the father and the law, or else struggle to keep her child down with her in the half-light of the imaginary."[19] For Norman, as we are to find out, has a mother who did not "gracefully give way to the world, the name of the Father and the law" and thus he is held down "in the half-light of the imaginary." Accordingly, NORMAN BATES as we saw in a previous chapter, is both the discursive symptom and the visible encryption of the repudiation of the logic of castration—at once pure film, and what film must contain: the film's message.

Norman's endeavors to become a man under the unquiet gaze of his mother lead him to engage in acts whose reality must increasingly be rejected if he is to remain a good boy. One might say that paramount for Hitchcock is the diagnosis of modern psychosis as a structural feature of modernity that is one with the affordances of cinema and a new order of scopic relations; modernity unbinds female agency and threatens castration precisely by placing limits on masculinity and the assertion of masculine power.

So, *Psycho* delivers its brand of poetic justice in accord with midcentury white American patriarchy. A woman breaks the law for pleasure—cut to her punishment. If that punishment is mildly disproportionate, it is because somewhere else, another woman, in this case Norman's mother, was seeking her own pleasure in an effort to mean something more than castration and nothing else—at least to herself. But the law of the father, even if it doesn't function seamlessly, organizes things such that (its own) poetic justice is served and things get sewn up. This is the algorithm that scripts NORMAN BATES. The repudiation of the Name of the Father creates NORMAN BATES and its reassertion organizes the fragments and the cuts, as it organizes the cinema. It is, in short, an algorithm for taxidermy. In the media of patriarchy, one woman's exercise of agency is shot down by another woman's exercise of agency and Hitchcock stuffs it into a film. The angel of this justice, the particular medium that provides its deliverance, is first Norman, who as we know is a psycho and, not coincidentally, a voyeur. He also happens to be an embodiment of cinema: a practicing taxidermist. Cinema (*Psycho* is, after all, a "classic") is thus the second medium of poetic justice and here, since, Norman's visual practice is exactly analogous to cinema itself. Cinema transcodes the psychoanalytic (itself an investigation of the visual field) to make it a program of an apparatus that organizes the visual field and Hitchcock is its vehicle.

At the risk of repetition, let's review how this works. On the other side of the wall, is Marion in her hotel room, literally in camera. A moment earlier in the bunker full of stuffed animals for grown-ups, where Norman's efforts to rescue his failed manhood through taxidermic exercise are housed, Marion had questioned the sandwich-bearing Norman's masculinity by implying that he was subservient to his mother, adding, "a son is a poor substitute for a lover."

But now, with Marion's presence expelled from the den of struggling masculinity, she may be beheld in the cinematic gaze (at this moment in history the culminating technology of dominant Western visual practice); she may, in short, be taken as an object in a way that is at once consistent with the rape of Suzanna yet responsive to feminine agency. Notably, the viewer's gaze, directly aligned with Norman's, puts both in the position that Hitchcock stated he wanted for his audience: "aroused by pure film."[20]

According to Jean-Paul Sartre, if one sees the eye, the gaze disappears; however, if one falls under the gaze, the eye disappears. Thus, seeing the eye, objectifying the body of the other, is a way of warding off castration through the repression and negation of the subjectivity of the Other. That is why Jacques Lacan tells us in *The Four Fundamnetal Concepts of Psychoanalysis* that the gaze is also an annihilating gaze. As Mulvey tells us, "Desire, born with language, allows the possibility of transcending the instinctual and the imaginary, but its point of reference continually returns to the traumatic moment of its birth: the castration complex. Hence the look, pleasurable in form can be threatening in content, and it is woman as representation/image that crystallizes this paradox."[21] Cinema, she explains, has developed various strategies of objectification and identification to manage the image of woman, to tack back and forth between voyeuristic pleasure and reinforcement of the male ego: in brief, the sadistic narrative that unmasks the woman and deprives her of power and the fetishistic manipulation of her image via the close-up that removes her from three-dimensional space cuts up her body and renders it two-dimensional and iconic.

In the shower scene, the literal liquidation of Marion's agency gives us a concrete image for the gendered praxis of this gaze as fomented and codified by cinema. As the knife cuts, at once analogously to and here simultaneously with the way in which the cinema cuts up the image of woman, the camera continues by following the blood swirling in the water of the bathtub down into the void of the drain, only to leave the blackness of the void by exiting the pupil of Marion's now dead eye. As the camera zooms out from Marion's pupil, we see her final twitches before she becomes a corpse. The counter-shot to her annihilated gaze/ her dead eye, as noted previously is suddenly that of the newspaper with the money in it, as if all of that psychodrama is now to be grasped from the standpoint of money—was a dialogue with money. Through the sequence of cuts, her subjective (and threatening) gaze has literally been converted into the eye-object. Thus, in abridged form, we have the whole film. The shower sequence is the film within the film that gives us the fundamental relation of the eye and the gaze in an economy of gendered looking circumscribed by capitalist patriarchy. The rest of the material is (a brilliant) elaboration.

Traditionally speaking, then, Norman's attention to Marion is not properly economic—his attention to her exceeds somewhat his contractual duties as hotel clerk. In this, he is Kane-like, using the economic resources at his disposal to work out his psychic need. But, as if to emphasize the extra-economic dimension of Norman's use of Marion, the forty thousand dollars that Marion stole is buried under the mire in the trunk of the car, still wrapped in newspaper—wrapped in the symbolic order of the business world—and despite the fact that it structured the action remains well beyond Norman's grasp. Indeed, although aware that it was the new highway that changed the fortunes of the Bates Motel and left it in the backwaters of commerce, Norman is unaware that it was the money-relation that drove Marion to his lair. Norman's gaze, then, from the point of view of our own times, in which we have come to understand that looking is posited as labor, seems atavistic if not exceptional, part of yesterday's problems and an older regime of looking, as it is not directly productive of value. His attention is not contributing to the shareholder valuation of Facebook it is simply working out his psychological issues. He is not being exploited in his look. Indeed, in a certain respect he is looking freely, an illusion that the conventions of cinema also supports. He knows neither that capitalist patriarchy made him a psycho nor that his gaze is productive of value.

However, if we take seriously, as we must, Sylvia Federici's critique of Marxism and the labor theory of value, for example, then we know that women's work, although unwaged and unrecognized by capitalist modes of valuation (monetization), is nonetheless the bedrock of social reproduction.[22] Woman as unwaged, unvalued, and unrepresented labor not only bears the gendered burden of social reproduction, but also here, archetypically, is the bearer of the burden of the look. Marion bears the burden of the look unto death (though she would have preferred to bear it back to the bank) and thereby serves Norman's desire to reproduce himself as a desiring subject, in this case a man. As the exemplary spectator, his looking and Marion's bearing, now algorithmically coded in the logistics of a film that will become a new paradigm for cinema in general, serves as an architectonics of the male gaze, female objecti-fication (repudiation) and the narrative that will be organized around it. Thus, though atavistic in some respects in as much as this gaze is extra-financial in the first instance, recursively, Norman's gaze is the very formula for the financialization of libidinal logistics. Norman objectifies Marion for what seem to be his own reasons, but the money was watching all along. And cinema harvests his gaze.

In a famous passage about Hollywood narrative cinema that today we must make redound to a critique of Marxist poetics as well, Mulvey reminds us that with the image of woman, "her visual presence tends to work against the development of the story line. This is because the narcissistic needs of the male ego are sutured into an identification with the male character: his gaze, his control of the narrative and his organization of three-dimensional space."[23] This describes Hollywood's male lead but also, we should note, Marx's figure of capital which revo-lutionizes the productive forces presumably without women's domestic work. In Psycho, Marion's act of theft cuts the law of the father and inaugurates a narrative that is used to reveal the logistics of the law, which is to say, the forces of normalization under patriarchy.

The law of the father, via a stochastic-cybernetic system of capitalist patriarchy—what a moment ago I ironically referred to as poetic justice—reestablishes itself. Systemically speaking, the homeostasis of capitalist patriarchy is reestablished among the cinematically mobilized eyes in a no longer traditional world through a kind of Norbert Wienerian self-regulating damping effect via the program known as "the plot." And in a restoration of the law (if you remember the end of the film), psychoanalysis makes sense of it all. As if to say "The symbolic order is dead; long live the symbolic order!" Marion short-circuits the law and is herself cut up by a character who would represent patriarchy but has himself been short-circuited by it via another figure of modernity, the castrating phallic mother. Indeed, we have observed that in restoring what was cut out in the repudiation of the Name of the Father ("the mal mastur" which recombined gives "the normal man masturbates") the main character is himself reinscribed in the cinematic cutting-up of the symbolic order by the very cinematic optics of modernity that both threaten and enable his fantasy.

So from 1929–1960 we see three pathways in the cinema, at once diagnostic and therapeutic: the corporeal short-circuit with Chaplin, a megalomaniacal narscissistic cathexis to mediation with Wells, and a psychotic-schizoid taxidermy of the gaze with Hitchcock. As we shall see in the next chapter, serious as these maladies of capitalism are, they must be understood as specific rather than universal, local and particular, rather than global. For, contrary to all fact, they erupt as if in an all-white world. It must be said now and said very clearly that despite all of its subtlety and nuance, this world is dedicated above all else to the preservation of its whiteness. Thus it is a world also dedicated to the repression and negation, not just of the white woman, who though profoundly diminished in Hollywood remains partially visible, but of everything not white constitutionally excluded from the frame. Arguably then, whatever is in the frame is also a representation of racial violence. Unfortunately, this tendency can be extended to representation more generally: images, whatever they may contain, are *of* racial violence—they emerge from and signify in a context of ongoing racial violence. As we have seen, a similar hypothesis may be applied to language, photography and computation. At bottom global semiosis rests heavily on the exclusion unto death of hegemony's others.

8

Prosthetics of Whiteness: Drone Psychosis

The violence of whiteness

Well, if in 1960 while psychos roamed, the normal man masturbated, what does he do today? What does anyone do? "But by the grace of the good object, there go I," says Laurence Rickels in a clear indication that these two trajectories are of a piece. Particularly after half a century of cinema, digitization, visual saturation, and visual financialization, what are the dominant scripts for power? *Citizen Kane* or *Psycho*, Kane or Bates? Neurotic megalomania or psychosis? Two still functional programs for white subjectivization, and for fractal fascism, for infinite dividualization, and for death by representation.

In today's world in which the entire visual field is posited as a site of value extraction, it is no secret that pornography represents 30 percent of Internet traffic at minimum.[1] If we consider that computer energy usage has expanded to account by some measures for almost 10% of total energy consumption planet wide, that's a significant amount of fossil fuel devoted to masturbation. Still, if reaching orgasm in order to ward off psychosis were the main use of fossil fuels, the world might be a better place. However, the effects are somewhat more serious than "mankind" on the verge of psychosis caught in an orgiastic and masturbatory thrall: unless one begins to understand that this thrall is one with necropolitics. Structural violence, systematically deployed and titrated with highly fungible vectors of racism and sexism, is embedded in the techno-visualization of everything that appears with the express goal of capturing sensual labor and the consequence of liquidating both subjects and the subjectivity of their objects. Bernard Steigler's notion of the stripping of the libido and the proletarianization of the senses by what he calls "retentional systems" would be useful here, as would Herbert Marcuse's idea of one-dimensional man, but more to the point perhaps is Arthur Jafa's sublimely poignant *Love is the Message, The Message is Death* (2016).[2]

From Kane to Bates, we witness the mediatic functionalization of white subjectivity and the virtualization of the object world. Even Chaplin's resistance to machinic desubjectivization takes place in an all-white world. The three films, part therapy for and part intensification of specific historical pathologistics, provide programmatic compensatory means to ward off the radical disempowerment wrought by ambient social programs. The result is nothing short of the codification and automation of neuronal-psychic function by the cinematic apparatus. The programs of subjectification, archetypes analyzed, inscribed and mobilized by cinema depend upon the denial of even the existence of people of color.

Indeed, the forms of neurological and psychic dysfunction and reformation described thus far—people fragmented, castrated, and cut up by money and machines and driven to seek subjectivity by pathological means—are relatively easy to understand, delimited as they are. Not to minimize them, since they violently imposed various regimes of the body, psychology, personhood, and desire upon subjects as well as upon those who became and suffered as objects or invisible ground for said subjects, but we must remark here that they are local manifestations specific to a white supremacist imaginary, in which human drama can be adequately represented in the absence of the non-white world reduced, as it almost always was and is, to an invisible supporting role. Nonetheless, their mainstream expression and dissemination make them valid precursors to the contemporary psychosis of today's mainstream. Yesterday's white supremacist capitalist patriarchy still configures today's white supremacist capitalist patriarchy in the United States, Europe, and beyond, a formation that is symptomatically specific to one class fraction but nonetheless potentially deadly to every planetary denizen (if also to itself) for all that.

Outing the whiteness (for those who may not have noticed) of the examples from the previous chapter should delimit their relevance even as it emphasizes their complicity with the hegemony of a racist imaginary—a racist reign of images. Along with Frantz Fanon, we must recognize the limits of psychopathologizing discourse, which is to say the limits of psychoanalysis. For Fanon, no talking cure was going to cure the sicknesses of either torture victims or sociopaths; only insurrection and revolution could overthrow the forms of egoism, objectification, hatred and desire endemic to colonialism and fascism and only violence could overthrow colonial violence to bring about the needed paradigm shift.[3] So in tracking the white psychopathologies that lead toward the dissolution of their hosts, we are witnessing along with the fomenting of a subject that is capitalist, patriarchal and white, the implosion, the practical deconstruction, of whiteness. It's sickness, emptiness and breakdown. The technical apparatus is there to sustain this crisis and render it profitable through the therapeutic structures of the plot.

Two points: one about whiteness and what Anne Anlin Cheng astutely calls the "melancholy of race."[4] This will be an additional and indeed constitutive pathologistical vector that, in addition to the production of the Tramp, the Citizen and the Psycho characterizes the operating system of the representational dominant. Then there is a second point concerning a generalized liquidation not just of particular human beings, but of human being and of being itself.

In *The Melancholy of Race*, Cheng reminds us that the melancholic is both sad and aggressive:

> Dominant white identity in America operates melancholically—as an elaborate identificatory system based on psychical and social consumption-and-denial. This diligent system of melancholic retention appears in different guises. Both racist and white liberal discourses participate in the dynamic, albeit out of different motivations. The racists need to develop elaborate ideologies in order to accommodate their actions with official American ideals, while white liberals need to keep burying the racial others in order to memorialize them. Those who do not see the racial problem or those who call themselves non-ideological are the most melancholic of all because in today's political climate, as Toni Morrison exclaims in Playing in the Dark, "it requires hard work not to see."[5]

Although Cheng is interested in "the question that Freud does not ask: What is the subjectivity of the melancholic object?", for the moment I want to remark that the canonical cinema of the United States can be thought of as a melancholy canon, organized as it is to profitably portray white narratives as universal narratives in a society profoundly structured by racial inequality—organized, in other words, to not see.[6] bell hooks and many others hence have commented on "the oppositional gaze" responding to Hollywood cinema, particularly the oppositional gaze of black spectators watching white films. "We" must learn to better recognize how whole systems of visualization and thus the organization of attention are structured around a disavowal of racism or of the existence of racialized bodies and oftentimes the active annihilation of racialized bodies.[7] Frank B. Wilderson III, in his *tour d'force* analysis of *Monster's Ball*, in which "prison is seen as black, but *scened* as white suffering,"[8] and the requirement of black death is "rendered as a romance"[9] notes that:

> From the two fisted modernism of white film theory's interventionist agenda to its recent invigoration—or ennui depending on ones perspective—… their differences … maintain between them an uncanny solidarity in relation to the "estate of slavery." That solidarity is evidenced by the fact that the Slave remains unthought, foreclosed by the inspiration of *we*.[10]

Though it is impossible (for me at least) to recapitulate Wilderson's full argument here, he persuasively (indeed overwhelmingly) argues this and more: "Like the reconstructive (socially transformative) gesture of Lacan's 'full speech,' the politics of heteropathic cinema is none other than a narrative instance of Whiteness. And the frame, in its internal assemblage—what is know as mise en scène—and in its external movement—the shot—is none other than a formal instance of Whiteness … In point of fact, the 'composition effects' of [Stephen] Heath's cinematic frame are not available to the Black unless the Black has been structurally adjusted with the frame, made to appear as 'man,' 'woman,' 'proletarian,' child,' 'gay' or 'straight' and so on. Such a structural adjustment makes the Black 'palatable' and allows for his or her cinematic 'conversion [from] seen into scene.'"[11]

As with film and film theory, so too with media studies and philosophy—these also float on a sea of blood and endlessly re-enact the decimation and disappearance of the slave, the colonized, the native. In *I Am Not Your Negro*, Raoul Peck's powerful film based on writings and lectures of James Baldwin, Baldwin appears on *The Dick Cavett Show* to speak about racism. After he finishes, Yale philosopher Peter Weiss is called in as the next guest, to chastise Baldwin who, in his view, dwells too much on race. The philosopher then delivers a few thoughts on the general existential situation of loneliness and the problem of becoming a man. Baldwin deftly eviscerates this position clearly demonstrating the primacy of race: "What I was discussing was not that problem really.

I was discussing the difficulties, the obstacles, the very real danger of death thrown up by the society when a Negro, when a black man attempts to become a man."[12] One is given to understand that like Sidney Poitier's jumping off the escape train to remain with his white friend (Tony Curtis) who couldn't catch on in *The Defiant Ones* (1958), (a scene criticized by Baldwin and replayed in *Not Your Negro*), the gestures of most contemporary philosophy are likewise there just to make white people feel better.

Cheng, citing Thomas Mann, who says that "What we call mourning for our dead is perhaps not so much grief at not being able to call them back as it is grief at not being able to want to do so," shows that "it is exclusion, rather than loss, [that] is the real stake of melancholic retention."[13] Indeed, melancholia approaches psychosis when the lost/ excluded object rises up to challenge the melancholic, who in truth no longer desires (or can abide) its return. Wilderson goes even further saying, "But if David Marriot, Frantz Fanon, Hortense Spillers, Orlando Patterson, Saidiya Hartman, Ronald Judy and Achille Mbembe are correct, then 'human figures in their actions" [(Heath)] cannot have their Humanness guaranteed if those actions are not a priori imbricated in the mutilation, the genealogical isolation of the Black."[14]

Take, for example, Clint Eastwood's all too convincing portrayal in *Dirty Harry* (1971) of a sad cop, Harry, whose disillusionment and melancholic self-loathing have almost cost him his job on the San Francisco Police Department. When one of the rare black characters in Hollywood cinema asserts himself, albeit scripted in the most stereotypically racist of ways—a black bank robber running from the interpellation of a white man who just happens to be a cop—the line of sight through the peephole of *Psycho*, a masculinity machine if there ever was one, becomes the sight line down the barrel of Eastwood's .44 Magnum. The title of the sequels, *Magnum Force* (1973) and *The Enforcer* (1976), are telling, because the psycho—with whom the audience is supposed to identify—does not simply deny reality (the possibility of other ways and practices beyond his ken); he imposes his vision on others, if necessary, by making them dead. Eastwood's persona from Dirty Harry forward is that of being too much a man for these muddled, liberal, and overly tolerant times—his career turns out to be a "heroic" elegy of his racial melancholia, which is to say the melancholia of his racism. As one blogger appreciatively writes, "Dirty Harry put a bullet in the heart of the flower-power generation,"[15] and it's true: white psychosis overcame the global sixties, and too many Americans identified with a killer, a kind of psycho, as therapy for their own racism.

Here we can grasp the virility at the end of Peeping Tom's camera (*Peeping Tom*, 1960), that Tom uses to film women as he murders them. The camera's bayonet blade extension is a concise image for the virility in the extension of Eastwood's racist gun. The combinatory of psychosis, as repressive instrument of subjective agency by regimes of domination understood as race and gender is a toxic, violent and in reality, murderous algorithm.

Eastwood's racial melancholia is of a profoundly different order than that of African American filmmaker Charles Burnett's characters in his extraordinary *Killer of Sheep* (1979). This film, which approaches Cheng's interest in the question of the subjectivity of the melancholic object, which expresses a desire to return agency to they who are deemed inadmissible in the melancholia of a white supremacist community— and we might add, with Wilderson in mind, a white supremacist platform. The film could be read as a kind of black *Modern Times* in which the desultory Watts community in the mid-1970s is also metaphorically figured as consisting of sheep (and on occasion killers), but here the physical machines hardly work and it is the social machine that overdetermines the action. The grammatization of the body and of everything else is of a different order than Chaplin's rendering of the machinic interface with the body. Here the interface is ambient and existential—to some degree it is unrepresentable except through the trace of its consequences. The film is a kind of bearing witness to the lived temporality, disempowerment, and affective experiences of racialized exclusion and the implacable histories of anti-blackness in the United States. It's neuro- and psycho-pathologies, along with beauty and joy hazarded against danger (the kids jumping across the roof gaps, the slow dance of the protagonist and his wife) emerge in the context of stultifying lack of wealth or opportunity and the relentless weight of apartheid. One might find in this film a distinctive composition that creates an apperceptive space of black knowing, which in certain real ways is outside the economy of visual forms and structures, the "composition" proffered at the Hollywood box office (even as it is arguably partially a result of this very economy). The incommunicability and persistence of the legacies of slavery, racism, and Jim Crow are among subject matters and indeed the very contents of this film. The difficulty of generating a subject-constituting line of sight, image, a fully resolved perspective or an iconic representation testifies to a nonhegemonic visuality, an unrealized subjectification, and the presence of counterhistories that mobilize a perceptual mode palpably apart from that which will align itself with—and hence be at once repurposed and devoured by—the mainstream of white supremacist visuality. Here, in the sense that Nicole Fleetwood uses the term in *Troubling Vision* we have a "non-iconic" presentation of blackness, one that through the troubling of hegemonic vision through what in both cinematic and existential terms is a kind of decomposion and dissolution makes palpable lived experiences heretofore unrepresented.[16]

The annihilating gazes abstracted and informed in *Psycho*, *Dirty Harry*, *Peeping Tom*, etc., are a condensation of a specific mode of white life's universal application of a violently imposed sexism and racism to the organization of its perception. These "pure gazes" mobilize racism and sexism on various platforms to fully render their objects—even as they blur the distinction. These dynamics of visualization functioning for the presumption of post-Fordist tramps and the profit of today's entrepreneurial Citizen Kanes, and the pleasure of psychos everywhere, are at a second level ways of achieving visibility, notoriety, subjectivity and likes. Both the objectification and the violating gaze that targets its objects and annihilates ground are among the dividends of violence that continue to be paid by pathologistics evolved from the legacies of colonialism, of slavery, of imperialism and humanism. These pathologistics take forms that recapitulate while disavowing their foundations in racial violence and capitalist exploitation.

Today, these vectors of for-profit programmatic annihilation consolidate to form, among other manifestations, the predatory gaze of the drone in a global war to be human. The history of the drone, as Chamayou says, "is the history of the eye turned into a weapon."[17] This full automation of the gaze represents a kind of third stage of what Bernard Stiegler refers to as proletarianization. We have observed the proletarianization of gesture, of the senses and perception, and now we are asked to confront the proletarianization of critique itself, of reason. The drone and its function by means of signature strike, that is, by means of an algorithmic decision-making process, effectively cuts "human" decision making out of the equation through its own autonomous operation. This is by no means a special case, rather it is a clear expression of the general case in which visuality and the senses have been supervened by computation and data-visualization to the extent that thinking and critique are short-circuited as subroutines subjugated to the programmed exigencies of machines.

These pathological programs of visualization, which flourished under Barack Obama and show no signs of abatement, continue to function in ways that are equally as important as the digital computer. The drone, effecting what Allen Feldman calls a liquid archive, couples all the capacities of computation for aerodynamic navigation, videography, cartography, facial recognition, and weapons deployment to create technologically enabled psychosis, or what we might call cyberpsychosis.[18] The drone and its melancholic functionaries—its cybernetically incorporated pilots (who will go home to kiss their kids (or have psychotic episodes) in Arizona after pulling the trigger on someone else's family half a universe away, along with their entire staff of statisticians, researchers, and commanders who serve both machine and country—draw on a panoply of mutable, and thus programmable, raced and gendered assumptions, as does the press that covers or ignores these exploits and the nation that sanctions them. With a signature strike, initiated by pattern recognition (as when a wedding party strays from what a surveillance algorithm has established as normal movement), the space of critique, of consciousness in its everyday form is further foreclosed. In short, data processing can morphologically produce whatever variant of racist/sexist phobic rage is required for any operation, it being understood, of course, that an operation here means the liquidation of the visualized target (except as in the utopian case of Alex Rivera's *Sleep Dealer*, where a Chicano drone pilot is struck by conscience and ultimately sides with his victims). The violent and fully incorporating logistics of the automated gaze of the drone are utterly banalized even as they are effectuated through quantum distribution in the technical rationality of computers, national security, military protocols, and the scoops of networked news that together produce the required taxidermic effect on each day's requisite Other. The moaning of the victims of "Predators" and "Reapers"—names for two of the most widely utilized drones—are even less audible than those of critical theory.

Thus, the drone, as both financial exploit and paradigmatic mode of visualization in the era of mediatic finance capital, also represents the full automation of not just visuality but also subjectivity. It is the avatar of capital, of masculinity, of whiteness. Just as the victim is deconstituted and reconstituted as a fungible blur, killers are recruited as users of the machine. Though there are many points of entry from pilot to willing or even ignorant citizen, the drone is at once a prosthesis of computation and of the dominant form of subjectivity, it is an avatar of the digitized neo-liberal and or fascist-populist subject who is constituted through murder. This is an accurate statement except for the fact that the neo-liberal/fascist-populist subject is no longer really a subject in the sense that they are in sovereign possession of agency. Rather, their subjectivity (and yours) is an interface for informatic flows structured, in the last instance, by market forces of racial capitalism.

Medea Benjamin in *Drone Warfare: Killing By Remote Control*, shows clearly how drone warfare is an effort to emasculate the enemy.[19] The observation grafts the psychologistics of the drone directly in line with the cinematic gaze. She also cites a 2003 Department of Defense computer program designed to show the human cost of an attack." "The dead show up as blob-like images, resembling squashed insects, which is why the program was called 'Bugsplat.' Bugsplat also became the "in-house" slang referring to drone deaths."[20] The automation that renders targets castrated or as vermin as a means to annihilation and thus also as a means to corporate/imperial subjectivity damages, as Benjamin points out, not just the thousands or tens of thousands of specific targets—whether defined by "personality," "signature," or "collateral damage"—but millions of Palestinians, Syrians, Somalians, and others for whom the fabric of life and time is destroyed. This destruction feeds back in the public relations calculus as volatility, and is used to further legitimate and financialize the drone vector.

The cybernetics of machines, including industrial machines, photographic technologies, cinema, computation and drones has been in a feedback loop with the bios for centuries. The technical and logistical dimensions have been and remain inseparable from racial capitalism. In *Control*, Franklin says of Kittler's cold technological determinism:

> After all, Kittler, whose technological a priori is in this book [*Control*] deformed into a subjective point of view that is intelligible as a double of that attributable to capital itself [a deformation I, as the author of *Message*, am sympathetic with], equates the displacement of the subject by the computer with a conflation of targeting and programmability or self-steering: 'bees are projectiles, and humans, cruise missiles,' Kittler writes, because 'one is given objective data on angles and distances by a dance, the other a command of free will.' What is critical about this claim is that its ballistic conceptualization of sociality rests on

historical conditions under which '[e]lectronics … replaces discourse, and programmability replaces free will.' Sociality, from an epistemic position that grounds the control era, can be understood only as targeting under the continued impression of free will—a conceptual frame underscored by the fact that the terms *reticle* (gun sight) and network share a root in the Latin *reticulum*, 'net.'[21]

Franklin sums up, "Under the control episteme, targeting, the practice from which Weiner first developed the concepts of control and steering and which, for Kittler, equates to the conflation of free will and programmability—becomes the horizon for all possibility."[22] Because all systems (computation, financialization, visualization, militarization, national borders and migration, racialization, aestheticization, etc.) tend toward and are shaped by the logic of financialized digitization, subjectivity within these programs relies on the instantiation of targets (iconic or blurred as necessary). It is, as an experience, only to be found, or at least is primarily found, in the various positions organized by the logistics of an annihilating gaze. In this way subjectivity has itself become a program for murder; it renders a subject programmed for murder with all outsides configured as zones of noisy crisis populated by targets. This neo-liberal, cybernetic subjectification through active annihilation of the outsider is one real, if unconscious meaning of digital "convergence." Computational capital instantiates its fractal subjects or dividuals as cruise missiles and all externalities as targets: the first person shooter game become world.

Thus alongside the regular games or risk management, we have war games, war porn, food porn, fashion porn, news porn, reality porn, and regular porn. In fact, this *is* the regular fare, a sick tableau of degraded crap, and it is all part of the attention economy, where everything we look at is emptied of essence and stuffed with psychotic emphasis in an effort to help everyone keep reality at bay in the half-light of the digital imaginary that is simulation. This all-consuming production by mediated sensual labor organized by the dead labor of information is an always on expropriation of the libido and the sensual that might otherwise have been turned to other uses (love, sensuality, poetry, community, caring, erotic forms that redefine a relationship to violence by receding from it). The libidinal expropriation and reconfiguration characteristic of what is nothing short of fractal fascism in a network of dividualized nodes functions at a variety of levels, from the ratification of a particular screen image thorough to the game, blog, show, channel, platform or interface and all of their advertisers, shareholders, banks, militaries, and states. We man our dividualizing peepholes as best we can (for who among us is really a man, and given the terms, who would want to be?), cutting up worlds in accord with an algorithmic function beyond our ken, while the bodies pile up to a height equaled only by that of the profits.

The engineering of fractal fascism bundles modes of attention by means of computerized systems of content delivery, value extraction and metrics of account. Platform "users" become conscious and unconscious organs of this vast automaton. We have, in short, the programmatic simulation of reality, the virtual mise-en-scène of all looking, without the guarantee of any real event beyond that orchestrated by the inexorable logic of advertising and value extraction. The logistics and indeed pathologistics of these increasingly formalized algorithmic processes preserve the basic annihilation-function of the gaze as operationalized in relation to race, gender and would-be intersubjective formations, but adds a new layer of fungibility that allows for the targeting of potentially anyone, anytime, anywhere with the proviso that the likelihood of a person being targeted is subject to prior encodings of their profile, their digitized identity. That our thoughts and perceptions are programmed, accumulated, and capitalized in relation to these fundamentally weaponized programs for race, gender and financialization, testifies to the automation and expropriation of the general intellect by racial capitalism. The overwhelming of the intellect by means of the algorithmic discrete state machine is the situation, and the irony that it was "humans," who programmed the machines, does nothing to return sovereignty in any meaningful form. Racial capitalism achieves further autonomy and impunity by means of computational automation. To be meaningful, that is to say in radical sense "political," sovereignty would have to diverge from the programmatic leveraged accumulation of value and its corollary murder, but few seem capable of offering a new way of organizing things—the white sovereignty of what Benjamin Bratton and others refer to as "the stack" maintains its stranglehold.[23]

The general intellect, distributed across media platforms and automated in various apparatuses, is not just part of the means of production in the industrial sense, that is, in the sense understood by traditional capitalists; it is the means of production of sense perception and knowledge. Neither is it an ideal or an immaterial formation. It is itself distributed among the bodies and machines that constitute the socio-historical domain—the sociality of machines. The general intellect has been rendered as forms of sensuality that are themselves sites for value production that include modes of subjectivity at once fully automated and fully virtual. They are virtual in the sense that the referent that would anchor the subject in question—is strictly speaking a non-entity, that is, a computational entity, a simulation. Subjectivity is a contingent instantiation, a plug-in (and always was), but the mediatic matrix of its materialization, exceeds the pre-individual linguistic world detected by Freud, Lacan, structural linguistics and poststructuralism, as its local conditions of production and reproduction have been overtaken and absorbed computation. The unconscious is structured like a language: a computer language, and that language is built on racial violence.

Derivations and derivatives of computational racism

In some brilliant pages of Alex Galloway's book *The Interface Effect* is the following proposition: "The computer however, [which Galloway calls a metaphysical medium because it functions through simulation and instantiates its own objects] is not of an ontological condition [as cinema is purported to be], it is on that condition. It does not facilitate or make reference to an arrangement of being, it remediates the very conditions of being itself. If I may be so crude, the medium of the computer is being."[24] Galloway continues: "If the cinema is, in general, an ontology, the computer is, in general, an ethic."[25] The distinction, as Galloway tells us, is comparable to that between a language and a calculus: the profilmic event as "referent" versus the program that in object-oriented computing instantiates the very objects it will then manipulate. As evocative, lucid and arresting, as this formulation is in defining the flight from being as a metaphysical transformation ushered in by the digital computer, it is also partially incorrect, at least in regard to the profilmic if we are going to abide by Vilém Flusser's notion of the photographic apparatus as a machine that automates forms of thinking by executing concepts in a programmatic fashion.[26] For Flusser, "the technical image," produced by the apparatus known as the camera, is the first postindustrial image, inasmuch as the camera is *already* a computer—a programmed apparatus whose function is informed by concepts derived from the linearly written notations of the sciences of optics and chemistry. An apparatus, for Flusser, is something that automates an aspect of intelligence, and it no less consists of programs than does a digital computer. What appears in the photograph is not the "thing" but a simulation mediated by materially embedded concepts. Thus, Flusser claims, quite convincingly, that for nearly two centuries cameras have organized the world for the improvement and proliferation of cameras, such that today everything exists in relation to the black box that is photography, suggesting that this constellation of programs evolves as the photographic apparatus by subjugating humans to its functions, much as a Darwinian evolutionary vector might transform and then dominate a habitus.

With this in mind, one might say that if, as Galloway says, computation is an ethic—the imposition of strict rules upon the emergence and trajectories of instantiated entities—then cinema was a mode of computation whose ethos was ontological reality—at least for a time. This time was that of Bazin with his emphasis on realism and deep focus, and, as we saw in a previous chapter, the same was true for photography, although with different consequences even in the time of Roland Barthes. We already knew that this ontological assumption, the translation of the profilmic real onto celluloid, was only truly significant for a specific modality of cinema, deep focus, since montage with its production of attractions and concepts (rejected by Bazin as a lesser and incomplete realization of "total cinema") already involved a derealization of the "profilmic" content of the image. It is useful to say things thus not only because it suggests that "ontology" itself is a program creating a metaphysical mise en scène necessary for a certain order of representation, but because doing so provides a necessary corollary to W. J. T. Mitchell's notion that "there are no visual media." This corollary can be used to show that the computer, despite its invisible binary churn, is still fundamentally embroiled in the visual.[27] Mitchell argues that since even the most "purely visual" media rely on other mediatic modes to function—silent cinema, for example, had its musical score and intertitles, and abstract expressionism had its critical discourse— no medium is really visual. The corollary then, indeed anticipated by Mitchell himself, is that with regard to media in general, they are all visual media—at least today. Presently no mediation escapes some relation to visuality, Mitchell tells us, and goes back to Marshall McLuhan to emphasize that what is important is the sense ratios. Now that we understand computation as the financially driven decodification and digital recodification of prior media formations, we must add to the shift in sense ratios, the organizational and indeed metaphysical power of the program. For visuality is totally overrun with programs. These have been consolidated, abstracted, intensified, digitized, and algorithmically redeployed in feedback loops that have their own histories of overlap and emergence. Thus, we see that the digital computer is a break in the mode of informaticization, the way in which worlds are textualized and *then* treated as information. It must be remembered that, as demonstrated previously, nothing is ontologically information, and "information" is itself at once a technics and a practical conceptualization of what to do with being, and thus a strategy—a program for programming language. The camera was a computer and a device for programming the socius. Computation, its languages and its effects on language, remains under the sway of programs of visualization induced by the co-function and indeed convergence of visual media, which, now, emphatically, are all of them.

Making this argument regarding the relation of capital, film, photography, digitality and computation airtight, and furthermore, the argument that these media in their dominant forms at once recapitulate and revitalize an originary violence founded on and ongoing in racial capitalism, requires a long-term, sustained and multi-faceted investigation. Expressed in its most reduced form, the substrate of data-visualization is murder, unequally distributed and fractal, but murder nonetheless. In White cinema we can already see the waning of the real under the informatics of photography in Michelangelo Antonioni's *Blow-Up* (1966) in which the liquidation of the referent is cast as symptomatic of both the photographic universe and the nuclear age, and even as far back as Sergei Eisenstein's films in which the montage relation did not represent something extrinsic (profilmic) but the creation a new reality. At multiple points we might understand that the profilmic real was not real in any of the senses usually intended by "realism;" it was material, raw material organized by semiotic retentional systems, in which there was not an atom of reality in their visualizations.

This abstraction by means of material organization is even more pronounced with computation, which utilizes the rigorous organization of matter in the discrete state machine to produce abstraction that works on the world. Beyond even Trinh T. Minh-ha's brilliant critique of documentary objectivity (along with her equally brilliant critiques of anthropology, first world spectatorship, U.N. humanism, and Western post-colonial subjectivity) in which "reality is organized into an explanation of itself," the computer is an apparatus consisting of apparatuses, a program consisting of programs—a matrix of automatons and interoperative logistics. For all this, actually existing computing is no less keyed into the subject constituting visual and the pathologistical vectors I have identified in these chapters. These at once structure the parameters of data intelligibility and are introduced into programming in ways that have been recursively self-modifying, that is emergent. The alienation of "man" from "his" object is not alienation 2.0; it is alienation to the "google" (and now to the "alphabet"): programmed, weaponized, photographic-discursive-informatic, *intelligent* apparatuses evolving recursively with the socius in an extraordinary materialist complexity that runs on scales from the subatomic to the cosmic. "Evolving," we note, by mobilizing the logistics of racialization and sex/gender models to siphon off the sensuous activity of human life to the point in which this process has presided over a generalized liquidation of being. It being understood, of course, that being too, was an artifact of a prior regime—or, at least, it looks that way from here. The practical deconstruction of being and the de-ontologization of life-forms are directly proportional to the degree of distributed computation in a semiotic system. No one bothers with the analytic deconstruction of essentialisms any longer because fixed entities are deconstructed in practice faster than the speed of theory. Such is the world indexed by the post-factual world. If, speaking metaphysically, Simulation = ~~Nature~~, aesthetically the dominant genre is post-factual realism, a genre that represents on a slightly elevated abstraction from "reality-TV."

Emergent media, like the species' enlarging carbon footprint, do not cancel what has gone before but instead develop media-ecologically, that is, in relation to extant energetics, whether considered from the standpoint of thermodynamics, labor, or information. No doubt new media are marked by quantitative transformations that precipitate qualitative effects; however, we are considering a transformation that has taken place over seven centuries or more in the eco-system of racial capitalism. The ontological categories and ontology itself have been shifting toward a complete liquidation of being—as a category, as an experience, or (and here this word ceases to make sense) as a "reality." Reality was the artifact of an earlier media technics. It's disappearance, indeed, is the story of twentieth-century philosophy in the West—one that with post-structuralism led to its implosion and philosophy's rebirth as "theory." (As previously indicated, the effort to maintain the practice of Western philosophy past this break is akin to psychosis in the sense developed in this chapter.) Taken as a whole the implosion of philosophy and language's ability to signify being would turn out to be a theory (if only elliptically) of the image and information—which is why philosophy, crippled by its own incapacity to historicize its situation became theory to remain useful, and remained philosophy to offer comfort to white people. This historical superiority of theory during the second half of the twentieth century however does little for contemporary theory, which crippled by its own status as theory, (and even as postcolonial theory) presided over by an informatic regime that would render all discourse a computational subroutine, realizes next to nothing.

Nonetheless and against the odds, we find it necessary to embrace this "next to nothing"[28] and insist that race- and gender-based exploitation, systemic encampment, rape, enslavement, national wholesaling of populations, forced migration, incarceration, military, police action and murder continue apace with capitalism's evolving algorithms— that inequality and injustice and the murders they distribute are the mediological substrate of capitalist simulations. Thus, we can be sure that while the pathologistics of capitalism are our common lot, they function on a system of differences. These differences that make a difference are lived, and contradictorily perhaps, we will claim that these lived differences matter in a different way. For otherwise love is outmoded and indeed impossible, and there is nothing to noncapitalist values, except perhaps profound naïveté or extreme cynicism. Capitalism, the very image of nonbeing, the very life of nonlife, the spitting image of death, would remain our conceptual horizon, however; the world that haunts today's images persists and seeks its insurrectionary ground. And it is calling you through its own rebellion. The past, the non-capitalist ontologies, the outsides, the break-away voices, the fugitive poetry of objects ran and run other programs that still have resources to offer even if there can be no isolation or complete return. We do not need to argue for the persistence of alternatives on metaphysical ground, even if, as Feldman brilliantly demonstrates in *Archives of the Insensible*, metaphysics have become a medium of war. Jameson's "History is what hurts and requires no theoretical justification," still a zinger after thirty-odd years, provides one script for the instantiation of enough ground to stand on in the regime of simulation. Spillers' notion of "the flesh" offers another counter-historic foundation that exposes psychology, sociology, normativity, linguistic function and epistemology, to rest on an axiomatics of racial domination. And, of course, there is the world.

Paul Virilio, whose inflection of the term "logistics" I have relied upon in this volume, would I think agree that there is a crisis and that the intensifying rhythm of the pulverization and reformation of subjectivity is today endemic to the maintenance of power. In his recent book-length interview entitled *The Administration of Fear*, he speaks of the developmental sequence of three bombs: the atomic, the informational, and the ecological. "The second [bomb] is no longer atomic and not yet ecological but informational."[29] This bomb comes from instantaneous means of communication and in particular the transmission of information. For Virilio, the informational bomb plays a prominent role in establishing fear as a global environment because it allows the synchronization of emotion on a global scale. Because of the absolute speed of electromagnetic waves, the same feeling of terror can be felt in all corners of the world at the same time. It is not a localized bomb: it explodes each second. The informational bomb creates a "community of emotions," what Virilio only half-ironically calls "a communism of affects." "There is something in the [global] synchronization of emotion that surpasses the power of standardization of opinion that was typical of the mass media in the second half of the twentieth century." And a little later on he comments that "With the phenomena of instantaneous interaction that are now our lot, there has been a veritable reversal, destabilizing the relationship of human interaction, and the time reserved for reflection in favor of the conditioned responses produced by emotion."[30]

So rather than deep focus and the time of the long take, Virilio sees us in the thrall of a new order of montage (already dimly visible in the newsreel from *Citizen Kane*)— the cinematic mode of production, now rendered fully ambient and ballistic by computationally cut and mixed datavisualization.[31] Far more intensive than Eisenstein's programmatic montage or even the ambient but still cinematic montage of mid-twentieth-century mass media, this digital montage is produced by the continued and near continuous arrival of information and affect bombs all competing—in increasingly self-conscious ways that are feedback loops of the market— for the capture and expropriation of human attention and neurological function. Ours is an increasingly impoverished and militarized society, characterized by a total war on the body, on consciousness, and on the senses but also on equality, on solidarity, and on democracy. Today's attractions rely on sequence, certainly, but also on frequency, intensity, channel, repetition, and spectrum—an infinite scroll. New financialized avenues of absorption and therapy have emerged as apps, as pharmacology, as the many pornographies. Taken together, these attractions generate ideas, affects, panics, crises, and swarms along with massive caches of information: a global impulse network evolved (if that's the word) to manage and expropriate a world population (capable of knowing itself to be such) by revamping its sensory inputs in a thoroughgoing proletarianization that keeps so many on the razor's edge of fear and/or sublime abjection. The cultural ballistics, arguably akin to the sensory deprivation and oversaturation of interrogation techniques designed by torturers to force the ego into existential crisis, institute an establishment of abject fear as a so-called global media environment.

The cut and bundled expropriation of increasing quantities of subjectivity that might otherwise have been used for purposes different from the capitalist production of dispossession, abjection psychopathology and murder is today the condition of and for the intensification of the computational capitalist media environment—the obscene fragmentation and, fascistic fractalization induced by capitalized media machines capable of creating dividualized nodes through the expropriation of other people's attention and lifetime. The induction of fear and a prevailing if not entirely ubiquitous psychosis is at once a result and a strategy, a mise en scène and a modus operandi that everywhere instantiates racialized and gendered orders, that have a direct relation to the phallic order of the white supremacist capitalist value form. The psychotic bent that results in murderous eruptions from otherwise impotent subjects is not just a result of but a condition of production of the reigning administration, one that, it must be admitted, has succeeded in giving us many good reasons to be afraid. But the administration in question is also one that, as Pussy Riot recently wrote from prison in Russia in 2012, may fear nothing more than poetry and thus makes every effort to drive it out.[32] For it may be that the world-making and solidarity-making practice of poetics, in all its forms, is what remains to those crisis zones systemically configured as extrinsic: zones, peoples, parts of people, fugitives of all types, aware of their oppression and refusing to seek liberation through the oppression of others. Otherwise, awash in intentional signals, literally caught in myriad and all-pervasive gazes in which seeing and being seen have become one and the same act, everyone, à la Baudrillard,[33] à la Borges, is just sending messages that ratify and indeed "improve" the dominant codes.

This compression and indeed collapse into the machine is the logical outcome of computational capital. Today's tramp falls into their phone.

Threatened with the abjection of invisibility and non-existence, everyone is desperate to make words, to make images, to garner attention that will testify to their existence in an informatic environment of semio-war. But the situation functions as if each and all were suddenly in the position of Jorge Luis Borges's narrator Yu Tsun in "The Garden of Forking Paths," each person a nodal point of multiple inheritances operating under the weight of functioning as a sign yet seeking agency in a battle for the control of information. Warding off abjection for themselves and for their ancestors in an informatic war, they are forced to convert another or many others and even themselves into a sign, by murder if necessary, if only to momentarily flash a small testament of their own existence on some platform's program.[34]

Let us then at long last offer a definition of psychosis in the contemporary: The instrumental inscription of signs and images on the lives of others, at speeds and intensities that expropriate their potentials and foreclose their being in an effort to constitute oneself as the subject of archetypical desires purveyed in the informatic war waged by the global market. *"The author of an atrocious undertaking ought to imagine he has already accomplished it, ought to impose upon himself a future that is as irrevocable as the past."* This rejection of any prior integrity of the target-object by representational programs is a repudiation of the Name of the Father in the analogical realm of the symbolic undertaken in order to preserve it as the law of white capitalist patriarchy within the visuo-informatic. It is white supremacy in excess of the discourse of white supremacy; it is a program running through discourse and also machine-mediated beyond its comprehension. It poses a Batesonian double bind, that requires cutting up or out aspects of the socio-linguistic, in order to salvage a traumatized, and indeed schizoid sovereign ego by means of images and the imaginary. This schizoid psychosis is today, as a dominant formation, a sociopathic response to the blowback from historical racism, sexism, homophobia, colonialism, imperialism, now fractally distributed throughout the socius. Psychosis is the white-man's only answer to global resistance, if he is fool enough or sick enough to want to remain a white man or to emulate his/capital's mode of power through accumulation. White-identifying is symptom and result of attention economies built on the expropriating negation of those who look. It is a script available to all comers, however, as a virtual prosthetic white psychosis is cut statistically to favor those who can most easily identify with and conform to the affordances of whiteness. This psychotic program means that for capital, and therefore for capitalists, the human species *en toto* has become a means to profit that requires this very mode of world-mediated machinic representation and visualization accommodated by schizoid recuperation. This mode engages in the practical deconstruction of being itself through the fractal dissemination of celebrity and other factors previously discussed. The corollary instantiation of objects, targets and disappearances, as the vehicles for psychotic self-propulsion into micro-celebritydom must not be forgotten. These vehicles, fractionally or totally dispossessed are among the substrates of computational capital.

For capital the species as a whole has become the graduatedly enslaved substrate of a means of representation that as a programmed and programmable worksite is also a factory and a system of accounts. People and indeed the *bios* as a whole are functionalized by financialized media such that their sensuous capacities are monetized by means of capitalist informatic management and value extraction. This de-essentializing instrumentalization of the *bios* that grants it no integrity whatsoever, resonates with the dire pronoucement of Guy Debord: "in the spectacle all that once was directly lived has become mere representation."[35] But now representation is really an end in a double sense: first as the drive to which all human production accedes but second as a new program of alienated production that results for post-Fordist workers (and nearly everyone else) in what precisely Marx wrote 170 years ago resulted for the industrial worker alienated from his product, "the loss of reality."[36] Today, in the near total ramification of mental life by distributed capitalist media, representational programming titrates the denial, the rejection, the negation, and finally the foreclosure of reality. Representation's functioning is, in short, at once the process of dispossession and the mechanism of psychosis. No wonder that today, all the news is fake… it's post-factual realism.

This hollowing out and recoding of the world of images and signs, long directed at the colonized and enslaved as a strategy of occupation, dispossession and domination that functioned by volatizing the referent, today is applied even to white people. (The horror!) Though this should give us no special cause for concern, it does illustrate that, as Malcolm X said, the chickens come home to roost. Antonioni, though without any critique of whiteness in mind, illustrated this homecoming clearly in the mode of "Art" with the sudden disappearance of his main character from the field of grass in the final second of *Blow-Up*, after his having, while in pursuit of glamour, unwittingly undertaken an investigation into the vast universe of absence, denial and murder underpinning images. *Blow-Up* shows us that the reality is that, at least as far as computational capital is concerned, even white men are but a mirage, a placeholder, a function, and strictly speaking no longer exist. Well, that's the theory anyway. If, as McLuhan said with the onset of the market economy the chicken was an egg's idea to get more eggs, in the process (and the processing) since then, the caged chicken "himself" has become by turns neurotic, psychotic-abject, and schizoid.

I have tried to indicate some of the major (infra)structural positions available for subjectification/desubjectification in computational capital. The list is not exhaustive. Under the regime of computational capital, programmable representation effects a wholesale production of nonbeing. This nonbeing is no mere metaphor. Like the state and the banks that are themselves constituted in it, representation—visual and linguistic—is structured by a matrix of pathologistical processes in which desires are welded to mechanisms of account that if stopped, even for a moment, would reveal themselves as totally bankrupt. The world is run by sick chickens that, from their cages target any alien whoever in a psychotic hope to become roosters or eggs. This desperate warding off of bankruptcy through the frantic constitution of investment worthy targets unfolds catastrophically even as it mounts various exploits and derivatives— abstractions—to stave off a final accounting. This final accounting would be reparations, the payment of which would burn the entire computational-representational-psychotic infrastructure to the ground.

The white man not content to embrace the dissolution of his white privilege brought about by the very systems (and forms of resistance) he has endeavored to preside over, may only reconstitute himself as agent/ white through a psychotic embrace of reality denying negation and the instantiation of new targets. Racism mutates and "evolves." If it sounds to you like I am saying that any self-identifying white person is sick, then you heard right. It's time to end whiteness now. If psychosis, in service of the preservation of the historically and now evermore precariously constituted ego, entails the denial of reality, then speaking at all today in the mode of sovereignty risks being its number one symptom. Where representation is captured and foreclosed by computational capital, the only cure for psychosis is revolution. It almost goes without saying that such a revolution would require, along with the unmaking of whiteness, a thorough reimagining of sovereignty—and everything else.

9

The Capital of Information: Fractal Fascism, Informatic Labor, and M-I-M'

Image-Code-Financialization

With the undeniable rise of variants of fascism in the United States and around the world, an up to date account of the logistics of antidemocratic mediations is urgent. Here as everywhere I take it as axiomatic that capitalism and democracy are structurally contradictory—both "capitalist democracy" and "democratic capitalism" are oxymorons. The strategic management of that contradiction by a system dedicated to conserving class power leads to what Walter Benjamin famously identified as the aestheticization of politics ("the processing of data in a fascist sense"), or what Orwell understood as a short-circuiting of thought ("doublethink"), and what some are calling "the politics of affect," a term that among other things would indicate a schism—and thus a mediation—between individual experience and systemic rationale. To a degree, the pathologistical vectors outlined in the previous two chapters provide an architectonics of an array of affective dispensations. Affect, the general term for a panoply of unnameable micrological emotions and sentiments, is an aesthetic category emergent in subjectivities seeking adequation to a computer-mediated world. The affective field may not settle on paradigmatic structures iconic in the earlier psychoanalytic model; it is rather a distribution of possible emotive states. Everything discussed previously in terms of pathologistics with regard to the cinema can be generalized to the positioning of affect between a calculus of capital investment and capital return—most notably today by social-media. The logistics of affect, aesthetic and non-rational at the analogue level, can be ever more finally calculated, varied and calibrated when submitted to financializing digitization. The expansion of affect is in fact the expansion of sites of production.

By means of aestheticization and the preservation/re-invention of ritual (cult) values, Benjamin told us nearly a century ago now, the masses are granted "not their right but instead a chance to represent themselves."[1] Since the 1930s, the Führer cult and the celebrity, as both artifact and means of expropriation have obviously "evolved," even as they provided the shape of things to come in what now appears as a kind of fractalization of celebrity. Fractal variants would include the branded conversions of persons and objects into franchises on Instagram and Youtube; fundamentalisms from that of ISIS to the Alt Right, other racist nationalisms like Golden Dawn in Greece, Le Pen in France, and #45 or the NRA in the US; as well as many state nationalisms including (but unfortunately not limited to) those of France, China, Israel, and the US. Such opportunistic occasions for representation—in which individuals, icons, scapegoats, guns and flags serve at once to figure collective authority and as points of narcissistic subjectification and phallic compensation for dividuals who are separated from any ability to transform hierarchical property relations and thus the very conditions of their existence—exist necessarily, through the suppression, that is, the unrepresentation and unrepresentability of others. The non-representation of most of us in these racializing and gendering iconographies of disavowal that, in the last instance, are written on our bodies and indeed on every body, is a condition of possibility for both the leveraged accumulation of private property and the star-commodity and provides a lingua franca for political struggle enframed by a capitalist imaginary. One level down from the iconicity of classical fascism, these transactions take place as affective accumulation. Here, with the body as a signifying surface, writing then means also the practical subjugation of peoples to meet the exigencies of hierarchical structures of representation—Debord's spectacle in binary code. The accumulation of attention, cathexis and information are means to capture and sustain the hegemony of the universal form of value, capital. Thus, symptoms of such social suppression include not only the celebrity form (the authoritarian personality and its fractal multiplications on, for example, Instagram, who exist through the accumulation of our attention), but the various and dynamically evolving racisms, sexisms, and nationalisms, with their circulating, prejudices, hatreds and phobias.[2] The plurality of fascisms, its fractalization, represents, quite literally if not quite intelligibly, the mutual competition at multiple scales among the many capitals.

The cultural field, as Marxists, Feminists, Anti-colonialists, Anti-racists, Queer theorists, radical filmmakers, poets, activists, and many others have long recognized (despite our significant and often problematic differences) is also a battlefield. Since Benjamin, and with the passage through what was called "postmodernism"—a periodization that retrospectively can be understood to have marked the real subsumption of the cultural by the economic—we have learned to understand culture not merely as a medium of politics, but as a means of socio-economic production and reproduction as well as of potentially radical transformation. Here I have in mind a broad range of phenomenon informed by radical imaginaries, found nearly everywhere we people seek freedom in cultural pursuits: from its trace presences in fan detournement in places like "An Archive of Our Own" to its concerted concentrations in a socio-critical work like Feldman's *Archives of the Insensible* with its indefatigable critique of "dismediation," "apophatic blurring," and metaphysics as a medium of war.[3] The forms of counter-culture are, of course, myriad, and every sentence made for this book owes an unsettled (and unsettling) debt to an infinity of struggle—I mention the archive because it indicates a topos for this struggle in addition to the more familiar notions of literature, cinema, ideology, etc.

The new situation of culture as means of production (and here we should probably say "cultures," even though, given the situation, inclusivity is the last thing some of us want) is that "culture" has been largely functionalized by political economy. This historical repositioning of culture as on a continuum with the shop floor and the factory is an economic and technical result and extends the question of a technics of fascism to that of a technics of computation and racial computational capital. While it is usually understood that culture has a relation to economics and technology, what remains less well understood is the degree to which, from a hegemonic standpoint, culture has become a technical and economic relation.

Cultural practices are posited and presupposed as productive for a capitalism that was, as we have seen, itself already a computer (Digital Culture 1.0) and that today requires discrete state machines (Digital Culture 2.0) for its profitable and intensifying operations by which qualities are ever more intensively transformed into quantities. The rise of visual culture during the twentieth century, and the re-organization of the life world by that interface called the screen along with the calculus of the image, was a requisite step in the financialization of culture and its real subsumption by capital. The succeeding phase, for which DC2 serves as both consequence and pre-requisite, marks a heavy investment in the extension of quantitative logics into the micro- and nano-logical operations of the formerly analogue endeavors—all of which, including language, images, aesthetic form, philosophy, spirituality, the imagination and the like, fell under the auspices of the now defunct humanities and are today rigorously and almost inexorably submitted to background monetization.

This financialization of culture requires the informationialization of social practice, indeed, of the social metabolism. Managed by means of screens, information flows from users (and the used) to capital in a pattern that can be described by the sequence Image-Code-Financialization. In reality, this movement from image to code to financialization is recursive, reversible and continuous: … I-C-F-I-C-F-C-I-C-C-I-F, etc. Indeed, as we shall see in a moment it is the uptake of species metabolism through computational interfaces that drives the numbercrunching treadmill of informatics and thus capital accumulation.

Understanding the emergent relationships between image, code and discourse/culture/profit effectively exposes sites and possibly means by which to interrupt the expropriative valorization processes of capitalism—"valorizing information," to use the term that Romano Alquati presciently used to describe workers' contributions at Olivetti in the 1960s—that is today everywhere extracted.[4] It also suggests that despite the invisibility of an increasing proportion of machine operation in ultra-fast, ultra-small computation, in the internet of things and in what, as we saw, crypto-currency programmers call "the internet of value," the screen/image retains key functions and is, in fact a necessary moment in the valorization process of capitalist computing. "Valorizing information," was for Alquati, the workers' micro-contributions in the Olivetti factory that improved the early computers made in the plant. It was their innovation and know-how absorbed by the firm. The analysis of the screen/image that at once serves as interface, factory-floor and site for production and abosrption of both data and meta-data raises the question of what it might mean to seize the means of production, particularly when many if not most readers here (just like most readers and non-readers everywhere) are experiencing a crisis of control not just over the management of the (built) environment, the workplace and its infrastructure, but over their attention, interiority, self-image, imagination, social practices, relationships, and time. Survival among these forms of precarity, remunerated or not, mediated by the irreversible intermingling of life and its "devices," is at once bound up with the seeming impenetrability of informatics and algorithmic governance, and is also the very means of production for capital. As I hope will be apparent, the struggle over the means of production then, includes the domain of socio-cultural analysis and conceptualization, as well as of culture and interiority. It also includes the more familiar notions of fixed capital and, we must today add, programming. Such a critical analysis provides a necessary, even if by no means sufficient, component of struggle.

If it can be said that fractal fascism and/or other contemporary antidemocratic state-formations legitimating hierarchizing modes of production depend upon leveraged value extraction, and that much if not all of that value passes through/as data and its organized transmission (number of hours worked, links clicked, pages viewed, posts made, money banked), then data flow disruption or redistribution—though tremendously varied and relatively unexplored through the lens of a critique of political economy—presents key tactics and perhaps strategies in an anti-fascist praxis. Indeed, it may turn out that any interruption or intervention in data flow is in fact a financial endeavor in addition to whatever else it may be, and that such "re-financing" (refinancing an image?) may have unexplored radical political potentials. Capital cannot maintain a monopoly on creative destruction. The flow of information-value up the value chain does not ordinarily trickle back down in equal amount either to populism's mass participants or really to most content providers, but perhaps it could be made to do so. I would have liked to give a set of examples of partial or successful data-flow disruptions, and more pointedly to conceptualize forms of potential intervention through data disruption by analytically parsing the micro-dynamics of images and screens and the practices they organize, but that will have to wait for another time.

The programmable image, or, from M to M'

In an essay from 2016 entitled, "The Programmable Image of Capital: M-I-C-I'-M' and the World Computer," I argued that in order to correct the multiple misunderstandings in various "post-Marxist" analyses of capital that assume that value has become "immeasurable," it is necessary once again to bring the labor theory of value up to date.[5] Thinking about the programmable image I extended the earlier hypothesis of the attention theory of value offered in *The Cinematic Mode of Production* (in which "labor" was understood as a subset of the emergent yet more capacious category of "attention" and, conversely, attention reduces to what used to be called labor at the sub-light speeds of non-screen-mediated production), by rewriting the general formula for capital, M-C-M' (where M is money, C is the commodity, and M' is a greater quantity of money realized in the sale of the commodity C), as M-I-C-I'-M'.

In this new equation, we replace commodity C with I-C-I', where I is image, C is Code and I' is a modified image). Where paradigmatically, labor had once been sedimented in the commodity-object, I had argued in *The CMP* that attention was sedimented in the image, and furthermore that commodities and images converged as image-commodity.[6] In the cases of both labor and attention, sensuous activity produced surplus value for capital through dissymmetrical exchange. Here attention modifies image and code. With the wage, as Marx clearly showed, workers put more value into the creation of commodities than they receive in their wages, with spectatorship, spectators do more to valorize and legitimate images, media platforms and the *status quo* than they receive in pleasure or social currency (gesture, know-how, anesthetization, etc.). They also do work to transform themselves. In bringing the Industrial Revolution to the eye, the cinema opened up the mediational spaces of what would become known in autonomist Marxism as the social factory—albeit "known" in a manner that was, in that corpus at least, more or less blind to the technical and indeed techno-logical aspects of this very mediation. In my most recent work I demonstrate that forms of attention result in the modification of code on the pathway to market monetization. These modifications are themselves the absorption of attention as informatic labor. Whereas retrospectively the commodity can be grasped as a moment of data-visualization, with new media the relationship between image and code has become the paradigmatic form of leveraged mediation in the distributed production and consumption of post-Fordist capital. Value extraction, instead of taking place only during wage labor as it was purported to do under industrial capital, can take place anywhere in a network in which modifying oscillations between image and code occur. The embodied entity, formally known as the "laborer" or the "human" is still the source of all value for capitalism, but they/we have, to use a cutting term from Sean Cubitt, been structurally reduced to a "biochip" in an increasingly ubiquitous computational armature that extracts and abstracts their/its activity.[7] The absorption and abstraction of value is thus no longer, paradigmatically organized around a factory worker producing an object for a wage.

Rather it is organized around a dividually produced affect wrung from the "biochip" (and the rest is treated as externality).

In our era there has been an exponential intensification of the number, form, and distribution of sites of production as well as in the metrics of evaluation and remuneration. Production and valorization have become, "cellularized" as "'Bifo' aka Franco Berardi" puts it.[8] This cellularized production means, in short, that our neurological activity as interfaced with images and ambient computation, functions to shift the states of discrete state machines. Like the mule tethered to the mill, we biochips drive the processors that crunch the numbers. Who knew that computation could so multiply, disburse and miniaturize the affective power of a carrot?

While it is patently true that hundreds of millions of people still work in much the same way as in the industrial age (on assembly lines, in factories, for subsistence wages, without safety nets) and the feudal era, it is also true that any and nearly all commodities (the iPhone, say) today rely on the integration of various moments of valorization: commodities are no longer paradigmatically objects with singular points of sale, but rather arrays of materially mediated images (imaginaries) tethered to financial derivatives and other forms of computable information, and anchored to a distributed info-material system with multiple points of interface. The iPhone is a particularly good example (though in truth even the small Indian farmer must hedge market risk all year long) because even as the A-side of its screen is immersed in networks and clouds that deliver numerous images and apps that themselves have affective and material effects, the B-side depends on a network of labor practices that are effectively forms of enslavement.[9] Therefore, when considering informatic production in the world of the programmable image, think not just of Disney's organization of the imagination through franchises and product lines of *Frozen*, but also of the share pricing of Apple and of Google with its tendrils in rare-earth mines, factory servitude, national and geo-politics, social-media, incubators, start-ups, schools and a rentier model of the general intellect. Think also of the background monetization of all activity all the time related to using a smartphone.

With this in mind we can see that early capital's generalized quantification/digitization that increasingly renders nearly all human practices computable in industrialization but also, and emphatically, through colonialism, is the pre-history of the current moment. As Simone Browne's *tour d'force* recent book *Dark Matters: On the*

Surveillance of Blackness, brilliantly demonstrates, the technologies of racialization and enslavement were at once horrific technologies of capitalist production, bent as they were on the violent conversion of people into objectified beings and processes, and also the precursors to current technologies. The histories and practices of racial violence are embedded within technologies of, for example, shipping and branding, and they are perpetuated by their contemporary development into logistics of surveillance and transmission. Like the metrics utilized in the construction of slave ships, the ledgers of the East India Company, plantation management and monopoly cartels, the (bio-) metrics of data-veillance too are precisely the modern metrics of valuation. They measure the very metabolism of a society organized by screens in a way that shows that computational capital and its biometrics of risk management is also computational colonialism: the informatic organization of life for profitable value extraction along vectors of social difference. Neither the racializing components nor the racial violence has disappeared. Postmodern screens interface the dynamic data-visualizations of computational capital and differentially convert the general population into content providers. They are also worksites—points where attention is required to valorize capital through the production of new information and new discrete states. Types of work and forms of payment in social currency are structured according to a complex calculus of valuation that is, in effect, the real-time summation of computational function. Meanwhile the entire infrastructure produces and reproduces radical dispossession.

There is more to this formula and its functionality in the post-fordist milieu defined by computational capital, but I do not want to repeat all of the main points of the M-I-C-I'-M' essay. I'll just add here that fractal celebrity on social-media (and the currencies of "likes" and the like, are one of the salient features of the ways in which we (as individuals, dividuals, cellularized intensities, whatever) are enjoined to wager in the programmable image to get ahead in the thoroughly financialized market of daily life that has become inseparable from sociality itself. We are programmed by images and we program with images, all the while generating data, that is, modifying code. Significantly different from but less different than one might think from the plantation if one follows out the pre-conditions and consequences of this economy, this sense-/attention-/cognitive-/neural-/location-mediated modification of code is the paradigmatic mechanism of value extraction today; it is the unhappy evolution of labor and the new expansive and all-encompassing form of work in what Matteo Pasquinelli terms "the society of metadata."[10] As with the regime of labor and cinematic attention, there are some pleasures involved both in the processes and as the results of computational capital, but their distribution is profoundly unequal. And as with prior regimes the majority of suffering that results from and is disavowed in the name of progress is at once unaccounted for and unrepresentable—a systemic externality. The 2 billion-person planet of the dispossessed (population Earth, 1929), for example, that are nonetheless living upon this planet, are both the condition and result of the computational regime. The colonies were the first content providers. The Instagram porn star in Moscow or LA and the Syrian refugee struggling for survival, are each overdetermined if not almost fully absorbed in the ambient semiosis that is part of the precarity of informatic financialization, but the benefits of this (partial) self-empowerment via a struggle with info-servitude, computer mediated abstraction, and corporealized signification accrue unequally along the lines of a hierarchy of historically negotiated codes and codifications—including those of race, gender, nation, class, citizenship, etc.—that are among the vectors of what is increasingly statistically imposed algorithmic governance.

As it turns out, given that, as shown in the chapter on Marx, information emerges in the footprint of the value form, the formula for capital in information society (the society of meta-data) can be written even more concisely as M-I-M', where I is now the more abstract category information. Rather than mediating leveraged value extraction through the specific case of wage labor and the commodity, the mediations between image and code produce new information, and it is this passage of species metabolism through informatic processing and conversely, informatics processing through species metabolism that best characterizes capital accumulation today. This is the general case of leveraged value extraction for which wage-labor/commodity production was the first, specific, widely instituted case of the digitization of qualitative processes by capital logic, but is no longer the most advanced. Currently, with ubiquitous computation, the species metabolism runs (and runs on) the treadmill of the world computer. In other words, the shifts in discrete machine states are driven by life activities (labor) or the absorptive extraction by fixed capital of what Neferti Tadiar calls life-time.[11] Thus we have in principle a formula for the capitalization of all difference that makes a difference—a fundamental law of the known universe and also a simple yet clear description of the current limits imposed upon our knowing. This imposition of the framework of capital upon informatics labor and knowledge prevails because the machinic infrastructure that makes possible the acquisition, processing and storage of information is an integrated system, the exact antithesis of a commons. The communications infrastructure is fixed capital, and even pure theory, even pure information theory, along with everyday dreaming, feeds that regime. The differences that make a difference are social differences after all, but society as a whole does not benefit from informatic differentiation.

Capital is thus in effect an extended informatics-machine-mediated calculus of social difference, an algorithmic management of rights that differentially severs producers from the value they create. Its managerial infrastructure casts its networked epistemology, its means of production, to posit the cosmos as information and sets everyone to work generating more information in the name of sorting it out and oftentimes in the name of survival. Thus a book like Steven G. Marks' *The Information Nexus*,[12] which argues that capital, long misunderstood, was always characterized not by the "cash-nexus," but by what Marks calls the "information nexus" is on the mark, but for one important detail: Information, as we have seen, did not always exist. Marks' discovery of the management of information at the center of capitalist "advancement" is in many ways elucidating and on point in as much as it insists that capitalism and its development of communications systems was key to increasing efficiency and to risk management. Marks suggests that what here we would call a mediological account provides a more compelling analysis of capital emergence. With this I agree, yet it is anachronistic to say that capital was organizing information all along. Information as such is an historical achievement of capital, a higher order (real) abstraction of the perceptual logic endemic to capital that, once instantiated, retroactively makes new sense of the history of capital. To not understand the historical emergence and the historical production of the concept of information from the value form itself is thus still to endeavor to comprehend capital by utilizing the instruments of its own self-idealization. One can no more understand capital by presupposing the existence of information than one can understand capital by pre-supposing the existence of private property. Such a lack of a historico-materialist analysis of the categories of account is precisely why it becomes as difficult as it seems undesirable for the apologists and legitimators of capitalism to see that the history of their concepts, like the history of capital itself, is bathed in blood. Too often, the digital ideology, like the "German ideology" takes the effects of political economy as cause. Information, as we have shown, does not merely exist; it is not a Platonic form, an ontolotical condition, or a glimmering and transcendent divinity. Like private property, its history of formation is as violent as the history of capital itself, because its history is the history of capital itself.

Working for the blockchain

Given the everywhere present mediation of social processes by the computation of information, the list of new pathways from M-M' capable of capturing socio-subjective activity might be extended infinitely, but I will not attempt to extend it here. Elsewhere I will try to provide multiple instances where breaking the script/program leading from M-M' yields unexpected results and surfaces new forms of community. In closing this volume, however, it is worth gesturing once again toward bitcoin and cryptocurrency in general as a significant development of the relationship between computation, mediation and the socius.

Bitcoin is a directly monetizing social medium; it is an abstraction and crystallization of contemporary financial logic, of the computational mode of production. As has been said, it signals the emergence of the internet of money—or as some say, the internet of value. Arguably (we have argued this here), money has always been social-media—an encoding and indeed an encryption of social relations. Money was and remains a platform that sheared off ungainly and difficult-to-abstract stuff like qualities and history in the practice of its own increasingly digital rationale, while simultaneously creating its own mechanisms of storage, retrieval, circulation and account.[13] Historically, subjective activity was encrypted in commodities that were themselves encrypted by the value-form—this encryption was in fact the very condition of wage-labor and capital whereby exchange values could be represented in use-values and vice-versa. Money in its various determinations, as store of value, as medium of exchange and as capital, is currently being abstracted as user interface, platform and operating system.

Cryptocurrencies avail of the fact that money is inexorably a social and a computational relationship, and emphasize the possibility of developing a distributed proprietary relation to the encryption process itself, rather than leaving that surplus to banks, nations and states as they mint fiat currencies. With bitcoin, this proprietary relation to encryption is engineered by mathematically formalizing every transaction and inscribing it into a permanent distributed public record known as the blockchain. All owners of bitcoin own a piece of its distributed computational platform and thus of the sedimented computational history of the platform. The functioning of the platform generates coins and fees for "miners," those whose computers work to solve a cryptographic hash puzzle. Whichever computer solves the problem (and the chance of solving it is random so it could be any computer running the code) becomes the leader and sets the order of the transactions as the next block in the blockchain. What is less well understood, and in fact almost completely unexplored is that each block is effectively a hash of the sociality percolating around the bitcoin blockchain in as much as it takes the transaction records (what was spent) of any given block as a summation of that sociality. The blockchain is the permanent, unforgeable public ledger of those interactions. Thus it directly monetizes social participation by abstracting it out from the social, and by creating a permanent record or ledger of a set of agreements regarding value transactions, agreements that are cryptographically verified and then computationally distributed without the need of banks or states.

One great advantage of the distributed blockchain is that it serves as a distributed and un-falsifiable public ledger, taking monetary issuance and accounting out of the hands of banks and states or "trusted" third parties, and putting it into mathematically verifiable computational protocol. The interest in this process alone (the collectively perceived socio-historical need) then sets people to work supporting the machines. Everyone who owns bitcoin is also a shareholder in the bitcoin blockchain, which is to say, the entire bitcoin system. This system now composes the largest computer in the world. The encryption process, which requires both subjective and fixed capital investment, includes the program-controlled issuance of monetary units (coins, asymptotically approaching 21 million) by mining, as well as organizing their circulation, storage, and sites of exchange for other commodities. As the seven-year history of bitcoin attests, this cryptographic endeavor, which solves the double spend problem seemingly inherent in the easy copy-ability of digital files by creating a permanent ledger of each computation mediated transaction that cannot be duplicated or reversed without controlling more than half the computational power in the entire bitcoin system, is also an exploit of the monetary practices and sensibilities of the current conjuncture. First only visionaries, fanatics, libertarians, those who had to send overseas remittances, and citizens of failing states were interested, but now, sensing the power of institutional dis-intermediation and instantaneous incontrovertible trade settlement, banks and states are also expressing interest—which is to say investing their own capital—in blockchain technology and, over the last couple of years, hundreds of new cryptocurrencies. This year the industry is valued at over 100 billion USD and that amount will only increase.

Admittedly, the absorption of already computational capital by a globally distributed discrete state virtual machine potentially has increased utility, higher resolution, and greater stability than earlier forms of money. For example, a distributed world computer could be far more stable than any existing nation-state. Here the stability and inexorability of distributed, machine-mediated computation will very likely take over the function of the state in securing currency and will eliminate the third party guarantor/beneficiary of the bank through the operation of its own "trustless" algorithm. But in spite of the real possibility of a Benjaminian work-of-art type of reading (Walter, not Franklin)—utopian with regard to the democratizing potentials of the distributed, immutable public ledger and the re-engineering of the social contract that is blockchain—bitcoin, though fundamentally anti-state, is not demonstrably anti-capitalist and given its mode of dissemination which disproportionately rewards early adopters with the funds of latecomers can likely be no more democratic than its predecessor monetary systems. This discussion could prove to be a long one opening as it does questions on the future of money and the political meanings of financialization, so I will simply state that, much as I would like to be proved wrong here, bitcoin appears to be a new type of anti-social social-media. As participants speculate on the increasing value (M-M') of a system that converts speculation, human zeal and computational energy (in March 2017 the bitcoin system directly used more than US $471,694 of energy per day), into a monetary platform in which the monetary units are themselves shares in the overall value of the platform, they accrue profits. Risk is rewarded by value extraction from others. We should note that this share in the platform represented by a bitcoin, is also true with other currencies (though few remark on this fact) with the important difference being that the platforms of fiat currencies are capitalist states—national economies characterized by all the opacity, militarism, and anti-democratic centralization that is implied by that term. With the state, values are sustained by economic prowess, military might and PR, and profits are reaped (for states) by buttressing their economies, collecting taxes and printing money. Bitcoin is anti-state because its value is not "guaranteed" by a government, as in fiat currencies, but by the collective (machine-mediated) perception of and participation in its computer mediated utility as money and as capital. As it is not backed by gold or a state but is rather, mathematically secured proprietary access to a publicly encrypted quantity of a social relation, it suggests an increasing convergence of capitalization and computational sovereignty. The often vague perception of this convergence, in which government by the many (computers) will take over state functions, and agency will be enacted from the margins of distributed platform sovereignty, constitutes a large part of the discursive excitement and therefore of the general development surrounding this technology: as investors and enthusiasts say, buying bitcoin (limited to 21 million coins each divisible into 100 million units) is like getting in on the ground floor of the internet.

At this writing, the most recent notable development in crypto-currency is Ethereum. Ether, the unit of value, is programmable money. It is different from bitcoin in that while it is blockchain based, it is fully programmable or, as its inventors and adherents say, Turing complete.[14] It offers the possibility of "trust-free smart contracts" that according to proponents will "disintermediate" the banks (destroy them) by making transactions and settlements one and the same—different from securities, for example, where the trade and the settlement are separate acts. Ethereum also allows for the creation of autonomous entities that could own themselves: to give a favorite example, a driverless car that services passengers and sees to its own fuel and repairs with the money it makes. More than likely though, rather than one car doing well and purchasing millions of other cars to become king of the road, the result will be that the car will yield "its" profits to its programmers/owners via an organization that is currently being called a DAO (Distributed Autonomous Organization)—unless, of course, someone figures out how to program the car to return its profits to the socius by purchasing carbon offsets and the like. Here again though, we see how even the need to get from point A to point B (in a car) modifies code and is converted by screen-mediated ubiquitous computation into value-productive activity by spurring programmers and investors to create automatons that will serve/harvest such needs in perpetuity: the very acting on a socially produced need is slated for informatic capture and monetization. We see also that a technocratic transformation, even one that erodes state power, will by itself be inadequate to political revolution.

Both program and archive, as money, commodity, screen-image, interface, derivative, data visualization and capital, cryptocurrency is thus far an exploit that churns and swarms in, through and as our money, our code, our images, our words. In this respect it is paradigmatic—shifting the computational ecology and infiltrating it by introducing new levels of programmed functionality and absorption to the already existing world-historical program of computational capital. As exhibit A of "the programmable economy," bitcoin, and the blockchain technology on which it is built, was perhaps the paradigmatic incarnation of computational capital. Ethereum, which is developing partnerships with Microsoft and numerous banks, as well as spurring a whole new spate of start-ups, takes computational capital to the next level with "programmable money." As the cryptocurrency exploits intimate, we inhabit a media-environment where capital circulation is grasped and abstracted as encryption and data visualization, and can therefore be consciously developed as production via the extraction of informatic labor (all the sociality organized around crypto) from people acting on historically produced needs.

But as it turns out, on a planet that has been completely transformed by computational finance, computational colonialism and the programmable image, everything else in circulation may have its informatic vectors, its media, its enumeration, including history's dispossessions, enslavements, genocides, and massive accumulations of violence, violation and presently innumerable sufferings. Just as the mind and the senses may rebel against capital, so too perhaps might computation and informatic sensors. Where the plantation and the factory were once the paradigmatic sites of struggle, today, the sites are semiotics, visuality, information processing and perhaps finance—though they may still very well be the semiotics, visuality, information processing and as it pertains to the still extant colonial plantation and/or the proletarian factory. Despite the hostile, rampant practices of dismediation, perhaps everything that ever was leaves its informatic trace. Today we must ask: What are the anti-capitalist data-visualizations to which we might affix our energies? What non- and anti-capitalist resources remain ambient?

In a forthcoming book I will endeavor to lay out a possibility I see on the horizon. What if it were possible to use cryptocurrency and computational metrics to create value abstraction without value extraction? What if the expressivity of financial media could be made to express an anti-capitalist message and create cooperative platforms? Despite brutal and relentless colonization, consciousness as a world-historical product has its counter-hegemonic possibilities, its contingent pathways—so too does computation. What if it were becoming possible, through a democratization of financial tools and a decolonization of finance to create new economic spaces and within these spaces utilize subaltern and revolutionary cultural forms and practices to redefine what is valued? And what if it were also possible to create these spaces in such a way that they became interoperable, meaning that different radical enclaves could effectively trade with one another and indeed with society at large by means of currencies that abstracted value without extracting it from its producers. Today the surplus value extracted through wage-labor, attention and cognition is accumulated by capital, and the information and meta-data extracted in post-Fordism is likewise alienated and accumulated. This accumulation is alienated subjectivity, power, value—we know the story of this all too well. What if innovations in financial tools could take such tools out of the exclusive hands of banks and states and put them in the hands of migrants, activists, artists, radicals and poets such that we could keep the value that we produce for ourselves? I am suggesting that if the internet of value were in fact collectively owned, a commons, then M-I-M' might be accomplished without exploitation and that we might enter a transitional period in which the metrics of valuation could be deployed to work against the gradients of exploitation. This would mean a hollowing out of capital from within by creating financial tools in accord with the needs not of capitalists but with all the rest. The design of such an eco-system, were it possible, would be as far reaching as prison abolition or the radical notion of an increasingly borderless world that still created spaces of dignity for all people and peoples—both necessary conditions of world peace. It would require the scale of social participation and change that is implicit in either of these or in other revolutionary movements. Indeed it is fair to say that it would require these other movements. While it may be a safer bet for media theory and even critical race media theory to stay cynical and say that oppression will intensify until the end of the world, it suddenly seems that many of the suppressed revolutionary histories might find a way to enter into computation not as amortized aspirations for life subsumed and erased in programs and infrastructure dominated by the capitalist value form, but as guiding spirits that may remake that infrastructure. We might at last build machines that heed both the cries of the past and the calls for liberation from a more just future.

The fact that the message is murder has caused and continues to cause unfathomable pain; it has made genocidal dispossession the price of everyday communication. A re-conceptualization of financial tools that democratized them and enfranchised marginalized cultural practices and peoples in pursuit of equality and peace, would be a cultural, economic and computational undertaking that, if it would scale, could change the world. Make no mistake, bitcoin is not this solution, nor is Ethereum, but the publicly auditable, anti-state nature of programmable monetary platforms, opens the door to transnational currencies and controls that could limit or perhaps eliminate many exploitative relationships. There is a possibility that people no matter their situation could selectively participate in economies of their own choosing. Programming such new currencies and economic spaces might allow people to decide for themselves what and how they value what they do. A valorization of life that left its qualities intact, while also abstracting it without passing through extractive accumulation, would constitute an economic and cultural movement that might make critical, anti-racist, anti-sexist, social-justice values interoperable both culturally and monetarily. If so, it would finally bring the era characterized by the message as murder to a close.

What new programs might we engender? And how? Down and off the grid as we may be, we cannot do without some programs. Or without computers—they too are "our" history and "our" history is complex. Though we seek openness and liberated spaces, the revolution cannot leave everything to chance. The possible answers here are myriad and indeed already in the making. In a Gramscian mode we might predict that we will link the programmatic with the poetic in wagers of shared sensibility and historical (re-)affiliation ventured against the multiple forms of deferred justice and counter to the widespread, ongoing violence.

Appendix
From the Cinematic Mode of Production to Computational Capital: An Interview conducted by Ante Jeric and Diana Meheik for *Kulturpunk*

KP: The cinematic mode of production was the term by which you seemed to be introducing a new order of intelligibility into the historical experience of looking and, more broadly, living under capitalism. What is the relationship between the capitalist mode of production and cinematic mode production?

J.B.: The original title of *The Cinematic Mode of Production* was *Towards the Political Economy of the Postmodern*. In the late eighties I thought that I could try to build on Fredric Jameson's insights, which powerfully elucidate a sea change that the intensification of capitalism brought about in our then current reality. In the Postmodernism essay, Jameson posed a challenge that called for a rethinking of political economy in the context of a transformed cultural logic—what he famously denominated "the cultural logic of late capitalism." My work actually sought a method to undertake that project through trying to understand what appeared to me as the newest strategy of capitalist accumulation—though it had been nascent for some time—one that utilized culture itself as an economic engine of sorts. It seemed to me what was really going on now, with the flattening of language, the disappearance of the real and the crisis in representation brought about by the rise of simulation and virtuality, was a shift in not just the metaphysics but the physics of production. If I learned anything at Duke (and I did) it was that social production and reproduction were not merely the unthought of the object world, but of the cultural world as well—and these relations were inflected by exigencies of temporality, scale, presence and spectacle (as well as oppression), that had everything to do with the systemic requirements of capitalist expansion. The way I understood the transformed cultural-material world gelled for me in a recognition that the assembly line was no longer the paradigm of capitalist accumulation and the fact that the whole mechanical process of assembly line labor was being translated into a new paradigm that was directly addressed to the senses and furthermore that the paramount sensory input was now—or perhaps had long been—visual. Cinema, as I argued in that book, is not an incidental technology, but brings the Industrial Revolution to the eye and transforms looking by positing it as value-productive sensual labor. This all sort of takes place in the unconscious operations of the cinema as an industry. But, as I worked through the book, through revolutionary cinema, and simultaneously on another book about Philippine visual culture, I began to see that there were a lot of resistance practices in the visual which signaled a kind of corrective attempt to outflank capitalist accumulation strategies. Cinema was actually entering into the visual space in a revolutionary mode and it had to be reformatted by capitalism as a way of absorbing revolutionary energies and converting them into productive labor. I called these changes in which machine-mediated mass sensibility/expression was commandeered by capital "the cinematic mode of production" because it's a way of recognizing the dialectics of a whole industry of the senses, of the visual, and of the imaginary that was historically necessary to develop new mental processes while forestalling revolution such that capital was allowed to preserve its accumulation and the necessary correlate of capital accumulation: hierarchical society.

KP: In your assessment of revolutionary cinema you have singled out Vertov and Eisenstein as major figures whose film practices did not fulfill their theoretical ambitions, but who recognized the visual sphere as a sight of revolutionary praxis and shaped our understanding of that which constitutes cinematic critique of capital and the revolutionary praxis. In which way do their respective approaches differ from one another?

J.B.: One of the things I was trying to do with the idea of cinema was to de-fetishize the platform by raising questions about the materiality and social embeddedness of cinema through apparatus theory. All these machines built for doing things with sight! I tend to understand that cinema is actually embedded deeply in myriad social practices— mechanical, cultural, economic, psychological, aesthetic. Its ontology, if you will, is political and social and it can only be understood as a change in the way that representation functions. Part of that change is that practices of representation were being mechanized (and later electrified, and rendered computational) while also being turned towards value accumulation for capitalism. The way I came to understand that was, strangely, through Eisenstein and Vertov. Their turn towards the visual as a sight of revolutionary praxis made me think about the necessity of moving into the space that was not yet necessarily foreclosed by the domination of capitalism. It was actually the alternative to extant production regimes that the visual provided that also provided an opportunity for revolution because the visual was still open in some ways—incompletely coded and colonized, at least from the standpoint of today. Eisenstein and Vertov pursued this opening, which was sensual, affective, epistemological and utopian, according to their own, very different, visions of revolutionary struggle. Vertov says that the film is "a factory of facts." By being what Deleuze calls *an eye in matter* cinema can be everywhere (in places, times and things) and can bind itself cybernetically to human perception, allowing people to perceive the totality of the *socius* as well as its processes of production. You can see all the perspectives of production while sitting in the theater and understand that not only is each person working in the part of city on a part of this or that, but also that the very consciousness that you are having in the cinema is a result of the collective industrial formation. In Vertov's work you are actually seeing through the totality and seeing through the collective when you are in the cinema—and you know it. It was a very beautiful and extraordinary thing which didn't work out, but it was an amazing achievement on Vertov's part to understand that cinema had this potential. The fact is that he failed and the fact is that the whole dialectics of cinema was foreclosed—even by Eisenstein who had a very different practice, also incredible, but in some ways more conventional. Hollywood was the one who was victorious. This Vertovian possibility was foreclosed precisely by the visual logic that became necessary, not as a supplement but as a central stage in the organization of the psyche and the social through visual understanding and the visual ordination of discourse and social practice. Vertov's film and his revolutionary insights show us the opening of the visual and his failure allows us to mark its foreclosure. In the chapter of the book called "Dziga Vertov and The Film of Money" I argue how for Vertov cinema had the ability to become an alternative kind of currency. By taking the imprint of a commodity that would function very much like a price that allowed for the object's circulation, cinema, rather than repressing the object's history as does the market, would allow the object to carry it's history along with it, thus enabling one to see the social relations in each moment in their interdependent, networked totality. It was actually the first attempt to transform perception in a way which would enable people to see dialectically. This attempt was intended to become a template for film practice and eventually for a mode of perception that would be adequate to industrial production by allowing all of the social relations to become visible by passing through those things (commodities) that we now perceive as objects. Reification and fetishism kind of won the day. Vertovian opening was foreclosed and, when you think of it, it had to be foreclosed visually. That's why I said earlier that all these innovations in perception that were a result of industrial progress and had revolutionary, democratizing possibilities, capitalism simply had to address in order to contain them. Cinema as we know it was the revolutionizing of the productive forces that gave bourgeois society its new life and current form. The whole advertising industry and "theater of the mind" was an attempt to use images to tap into human hopes and aspirations and convert them into precisely the thing that would foreclose the possibility of realizing these hopes and aspirations. People are being introduced to the regime of commodity consumption and educated to desire only commodities—items that are presented as an answer to their problems but in fact they only create more problems.

For Eisenstein film was "a tractor ploughing over the audience's psyche in a particular class context" which is to say that he recognized very directly that the filmmaker was an engineer of the soul as Stalin had said. He was in fact trained as an engineer and worked very self-consciously as an engineer dedicated to reprogramming and reformatting workers' and spectators' conditioned reflexes so that they could actually make the revolution. This was an avant-gardist practice, which without a doubt was radical in its way, but also quickly became kind of a reflexological Pavlovian paradigm for the emerging advertising industry. "The Spectatorship of the Proletariat," another chapter in The CMP, was really about the double-edged sword of organizing the revolutionary class through an avant-gardist perspective that fundamentally neither could nor can be democratic. It could have democratic sensibilities but it had come from above in some ways and stood as an appropriation of technology by subjective agents that, to some extent, foreclosed other kinds of subjectivity. The people are represented but did they create their own representation? Of course, that was always a problem with revolutions:

how do you constitute a form of agency in which a collective can express itself socially and practically? It's still a problem.

KP: Marx in *Capital* does not determine labor in the immediate form as a source of wealth. The social substance of wealth or value in capitalism is abstract labor. It does not matter whether this abstract labor can be traced back to labor-power expended in the process of production, or to the transfer of value of used means of production. So, if we continue to treat abstract labor as the substance of value, then it is not clear why labor time can no longer be its intrinsic measure nor why production based on exchange value should necessarily collapse. I am lifting this already known objection addressed to the theorists of immaterial labor because in the course of your lecture you had pointed out that many of them hold the opinion that value has become immeasurable after which you expressed your disagreement with them on this matter. Can you clarify your position vis-a-vis the problem of value?

J.B.: What I used in my talk yesterday and what I find important to think about is what Marx said about the price-form. The Price-form posits an abstract labor content; it posits value, to pretty much anything it can be assigned to regardless of the way in which that thing was actually produced. The value may be real or imaginary but it can be treated as if it had abstract universal labor time. To me (and I may not answer this as well as I would like to in the given space and time) the fact that price still continues to measure something implies that abstract universal labor time has not disappeared as a standard. It only disappears as a standard if you forget that underneath the global capitalist production, underneath that which I call the World Media-System, is radical dispossession and that dispossession is integrated from the bottom-up in relationship to the production of value. The value-form is the dialectical antithesis of human exploitation. From the most abject, and from the rest, wealth is taken by profiteers of the derivative. What is not well understood is that—and this is why I used the logic of the derivative in what I was talking about yesterday regarding the nature of the commodity-form— is that multitasking and the interface of the screen become the means of separating or chunking people's temporal capacities and bundling them according to the requisites of the specific derivative. It's a misunderstanding to think that the commodity form is necessarily or even fundamentally an object, and that misunderstanding, I think, is what leads people astray. Theorists who treat commodity-form as an object, and observe that more and more people are no longer making objects, conclude that labor must be immaterial and that there must be no temporal standard, no abstract universal labor time, constituting what are now, admittedly, very-difficult-to-identify commodities. But if you think of commodity as an integrated product—made across a network rather than across an assembly line—that is made of chunks of subjective time that are re-bundled through a computational process—and capital is fundamentally such a process—you can see that human time, that is, sensual labor, or we could say attention, still underlines this system. It's a question of metrics, which is precisely what is implied when the business folks talk about monetization. There is a need for the political project which would aim to articulate and track that process of separation and recombination. In this sense my commitment to abstract universal labor time is actually a political one. It makes it impossible to disavow exploitation, immiseration, and the Global South.

KP: Another distinguishing feature of your work in respect to aforementioned theorists is your emphasis on the role which the so-called Third World plays within the what you call World-Media System. You don't seem to think that existence of slum dwellers or the informal proletariat is outside of and external to capital's productive base. In which ways are the subalterns constitutive for the reproduction of capital?

J.B.: I want to register my complete disagreement that there is a fundamental disconnection between colonialism, imperialism, and the contemporary system of global apartheid and the accumulation of wealth in the Global North. As I said earlier, this is an integrated process. What is not well researched is the way this integration functions and also that this functioning depends upon the continual disappearance and resignifying of what used to be called "The Third World" by systems of account, which today no doubt include what Debord called "the spectacle" and, I would wager, every other system of representation that is materially linked to globalized production. What I argued in the short essay called *Paying Attention* that was published in *Cabinet* a couple of years ago is that the bodies of the dispossessed have become signifying surfaces for world media's representational practices (politics), which is to say the lives of the dispossessed have become the material substrate for the spin practices that the media captains require in order to deliver the commodity that they are trafficking, that is basically value-productive human attention. Our leaders would like to be able to signify on the surface of the global population in a way which would make legitimate, meaning to say *produce* legitimacy for requirements imposed by the sovereign banks and their states. Often it comes down to securing the expansion of business practices for associates who have huge investments behind them and necessitate a kind of market (for weapons, for example) or development (for fossil fuels, say). These exploitative vectors of desiring practice are injected through the psychology and the intelligence of the globe. People, the masses, in my understanding are forced to labor in the image that are in fact the machines that organize social relations and sociality itself, or, they are forced to live beneath these images (as refugees, terrorists, peasants, migrants, slum dwellers, non-entities) as a support network or signifying stratum, sometimes both. One has to labor to survive in the World Media-System which means s/he could easily end up being signified on or signifying on someone else's back. In another essay I critique Agamben because of the disappearance (repression) of his own signifying practice from the concept of 'bare life'. 'Bare life' should always be written in quotation marks in order to, at the very least, mark the fact that you are signifying on the body which has been historically dispossessed and that you are engaging that body in a kind of representational politics. This may be an unavoidable practice to a certain extent because anyone who is enfranchised by the Global North is by definition beneficiary of the history of dispossession. Nevertheless, it is, I would say, only responsible (responsive) and also politically astute to recognize this relationship and try to transcend it by engaging it in a way which allows the creative agency of survival, that endures in the Global South, to be at once legible and resonant. There is one additional dimension of this relationship which complicates things further: Every discursive instance has a politics to it. There are no isolated spaces that are somehow separated from global production—for us, at least. The whole Virno idea of capital capturing our cognitive-linguistic capacities, brilliantly articulated in *A Grammar of the Multitude,* shows that the discursive ground itself has been captured by capitalist production, that we have become very good speakers for capital and that, no matter what else we do, our very negotiation of our own survival is in part complicit with the system of accumulation that perpetuates hierarchical society. To me an awareness, an abiding awareness, of this condition mandates a kind of politics that I call "the politics of the utterance." It is a kind of haunting by the unrepresented and, under current conditions, perhaps unrepresentable which (who) demand/s something from us. These agents are not only extrinsic (as in beyond "our" borders) but also intrinsic (part of the very constitution of consciousness). I would say that one thing that is demanded is a recognition that our own signifying practice at the most fundamental level depends upon the history of dispossession and the logic of it and that whatever we say, will say or might say owes something to the invisibility and the foreclosure of the representation of the exploited global poor past and present.

KP: Your account of capitalist capturing devices clearly affirms the position that our thoughts, imagination and bodily practices are being increasingly governed by an ever-developing matrix of control. Nevertheless, as you hinted earlier in the course of the interview, throughout your work you have traced the emergence of all sorts of oppositional practices within cinematography. Since they are given special emphasis in your analysis of the Philippine cinema, it would be interesting to know more about the ways in which it helped you to refine your theoretical framework and informed your subsequent work.

J.B.: I went to the Philippines in the mid-nineties for a variety of reasons, but I saw my first two years there as an occasion to really test out ideas developed in the dissertation (the first draft of *The CMP*) and see how they stood up to what I felt as a kind of postcolonial critique of the things I was saying. My own dialectical practice had maybe just a little too much Eisenstein in it in some ways. The theory first appeared through the set of abstractions which were sort of burbling up in the Global Northish space of Duke's Program in Literature in Durham, North Carolina, and not arrived at through the immersion in the mass. In the Philippines I was faced on a daily basis with what for me was a new reality and I needed to change in order to understand things from there. For the Philippines to become the place of understanding for me, it actually required a lot of changes in the way I thought, in the way my body works, the way in which I spoke to people on a daily basis, and many other things that I won't go into here. The thing I really wanted to test in relation to the analytical intervention that I was trying to bring into focus was the idea that visuality was transformed by "the people" at least as much as by "capitalism," and that capitalism really was one step behind the innovation of the collective. If the proletariat *really* is the subject of history, or a subject in the sphere of visual or cinematic culture, then it would be a terrible mistake to think that creativity resides primarily on the side of domination and on the side of power. I wanted to see if my ideas could in some ways redefine themselves in relation to that. My analysis started from my interest in the work of the preeminent Philippine modernist painter H.R. Ocampo. He started out as a fiction writer and wrote a little known, serially-published novel called *Scenes and Spaces* in which his young main character ends up feeling humiliated and indeed unmanned by his experience in the English language classroom presided over by a female American teacher with whom he also fell in love. Ocampo's character couldn't construct himself as the agential subject in language, in large part because English was being used to erase Tagolog in accord with the U.S. imperial project begun there in the moments before the Philippine-American War, and the young man begins to cultivate hallucinations as a kind of compensatory practice. These hallucinations, rising up (sometime right out of the ground) in the face of subjective and discursive failure, always provided some kind of revelation and transformation as well as sensual and intellectual pleasure. Years later, following Ocampo's imprisonment during WWII for being a collaborator with the Japanese in the war against the Americans, H.R. Ocampo, the writer, stopped writing and became an abstract painter—he painted the hallucinations cultivated by the young protagonist of *Scenes and Spaces*. I've gotten from this episode that he actually saw the visual as a space of possibility for the redemption of a Philippine nationalist struggle that was historically and therefore discursively foreclosed. The inability to realize himself narratively and discursively—the blockage of historical becoming—pushed him to the space of the visual where the possibility of pleasure, creativity, community and understanding became actual through creation of the biomorphic abstract forms that didn't really have any specific figurations but were very mobile and capable of taking on many different possible configurations depending on the observer and this observer's concentration or perspective. That extraordinary formal innovation, which depended in part on being able to shift foreground into background and vice versa, kept people from being locked into the set of discursive meanings that any way you sliced it could only mean colonization, and therefore inferiority and secondary. With Ocampo's paintings the painter and the observer were engaged in a kind of open play where agency and pleasure were shared and combined.

In the subsequent creation of a national abstract art by numerous Filipino Modernists, the visual was opened up as a new space of freedom which was then contested radically on the one hand by the unbelievable movement revolutionary social realist cinema represented, spurred by the people like Lino Brocka, Ishmael Bernal, Mike de Leon and others and fascistically on the other by the Marcos spectacle. The social-realist filmmakers (and with them a new group of social-realist painters) launched an attempt to show that there was an abstract logic functioning within the concrete of visibility of social life, and that one had to go beyond the surface of mere appearances in order to understand the organizing force of the social in an intersubjective manner. Simply put, that means that none of the characters in some of Brocka's films were able to realize their individual dreams or find in their own lives or even to perceive the solutions to the problems they were confronted with. Abstract forces were not merely at work in the picture plane of high art, but in the most banal and quotidian challenges faced by the masses. For the poor working-class protagonist, there was simply no answer on how to make more money in order to pay for the hospital care your lover needs without killing somebody else. At the level of what was socially given or perhaps "thrown," that compulsion to violence was the only thing that was there. Narratively, however, in the films at least, stealing from a friend or killing somebody else in order to get the money you needed to survive led to your own destruction in the end, and often to the destruction of everything you loved. All too often the central characters were destroyed in Brocka's films, so an audience, looking for answers—Brocka always said he was committed not to the great Filipino film but to the great Filipino audience—had to think beyond the concrete situations and beyond the world of appearances in order to begin to posit solutions to the problems these films so eloquently presented. Thinking a few steps further than given reality ordinarily allowed and envisioning social alternatives beyond the confines of formal narrative conventions lodged a radical change inside of the visually concrete problems that were being presented. Brocka's films showed that an abstract logic that foreclosed people's possibilities held sway, and that it would take a radical change in multiple circumstances, let us call them those circumstances that constitute the totality of the situation, in order to generate a space where the population of Philippines might receive some relief from the immanent tragedies of colonialism, imperialism and fascism, and at the same time achieve some kind of genuine autonomy.

KP: The opening and widening the space of possibilities for some different way of living you described accords well and is in fact grounded by your insistence that the real subsumption of life under capital can never be complete if the talk of changing the existing state of affairs is to have any meaning at all. The concept you use to elucidate your point on this matter is wager. What does the wager mean to you?

J.B.: If everything that we are talking about is even close to being correct, metaphysical ground, meaning to say ontological "reality," is not really an option. As we might learn from Ariella Azoulay's brilliant treatment of photography (since many it seems did not properly learn it from Nietzsche or Derrida), all so-called ontology is political. As soon as you say that, then you are in a situation that requires movement and then the question becomes where, when and how? To me that's a wager. It's a bet that certain directions are more productive in struggle for transformation than others. The wager is also—and this is another part of the concept that is equally important—what you do to survive. Gayatri Spivak used the term strategic essentialism to finesse that question of ground for would-be metaphysicians making their way in a post-colonial, post-structuralist milieu, but often the whole modality of metaphysics is an appurtenance that smacks of luxury. Brillante Mendoza has a really extraordinary film called *Lola* that is about two grandmothers who have grandsons. One grandson murders the other grandson and the murderer ends up in jail. The film is about a way in which two grandmothers have to seek some kind of justice, some kind of resolution, in a society that is completely indifferent to them, a society whose law and social relations are so overcoded by the logic of wealth, power and structural indifference to the poor that they don't matter at all. These ordinarily invisible and most often unremarked personages are the subjects of the film. What happens is that they make wagers of their life energy and power in accord with their own aspirations towards achieving a life worth living. To me the wager comes from the existential question of whether or not there is a life worth living and, if there is one, what concrete form could it take? Here there are no ontological guarantees. Because we cannot know the answer, and because we as individuals will never solve the problem of capitalism by ourselves, we have to call on our collective knowledge and singular capacities to address the question and problem of life—and I mean that in a very complicated way. The collective knowledge is in each of us, because we are the repository of practices for which there really is no complete archaeology, there are so many historical forces operating between and within us, so many voices, that we selectively have to discover from which ones we can draw on in order to connect with everybody else through cultural network, through socialization, through aesthetics, through our political practices, through who and how we love, through many, many things. The resources of the collectivity inhere in each of us to varying degrees, and the less obscured the collective in each of us is, by bourgeois forms of individuality, morality or the State, the more access we might have—and the more solidarity we might find. To me this question of the collectivity, of consciousness, of representation and the wager goes back to what I call the politics of the utterance. It's a wager that some ways, some statements, some ideas, some connections and concerns are better than others. I know that sounds quite unsatisfying because there are no fast rules there that say 'this way to the revolution', but if we ourselves draw on progressive forces of our time and align ourselves with the people, and movements, and histories which have proven successes in a movement towards democratization, people's autonomy and social justice, then we are in a good company: and that is something I would bet on.

KP: Does the vote today constitute one form of wager?

J.B.: To say that would be to make voting far more responsive and complex than it seems to be in current state practices. In a way the vote in most states functions as the most artificial of all choices. In the United States for example the vote may have some significance somewhere but the deeper meaning of it is the legitimation of the American system. Even Obama who brought so much promise—and was a genuine manifestation of marginalized historical experiences making claims on the social and the state—has really become just another leader of Empire: his record on immigration is abysmal, he supports imperialistic modes of governance including incarceration, settler colonialism, and the ramping up of surveillance and drone warfare. The thing in question is a micrological process in which, with the refinement of thinking, discourse and even bodily practice, one can make choices which as much as possible forestall the practice of capital's capturing of one's productive capacities. Capital has become so vast an apparatus of enclosure and capture that is almost impossible to elide it, and of course computation has been central in increasing the granularity of its resolution and thus it's co-ordination of expropriative value-production. But if you don't think that it is possible to elide capital in some way or another then there's no point to this conversation. If this conversation, as you reminded me earlier, is actually to be different from every other conversation in *The Economist* or in *Business Today*, it has to posit a practice or practices that have a kind of negative capability in relationship to capitalist agendas. If one were to think of voting like *that*, as a metric of anti-capitalist contestation that might be applicable at a variety of scales, then voting would become much more interesting, then we would really have a model for agency, a kind of micrological agency of choice which can in some ways defy the way in which capital is capturing our senses and discourses. This is what flashed for a moment in Greece and is visible in petition forums like Avaaz, and even to a certain extent in entrepreneurial platforms such as Kickstarter, although there, the political vision is subsumed by corporatism. Capitalism operates ubiquitously and micrologically. We need to recognize that and we need to seek every opportunity, every moment, every nanosecond, as having an opportunity for transformation. Back to the politics of the utterance, we need to be voting against capitalism, against exploitation, against inequality, not just every four years, but all the time. And we need to build these ideas into the infrastructure and the hardware, the very materials and machines of our society. It's what used to be called a program and could be again, but now in a new sense.

KP: While delivering your lecture on computational capital you touched an idea of communist computing. Being curious where your future work may be headed, we are eager to discover more about what you mean by that phrase. Is there a concept behind it?

J.B.: I alluded to the couple of works published recently. One of them is Nick Dyer-Witheford's *Red Plenty Platforms* and the other is Joss Hands' *Platform Communism,* both published in Volume 14 of *Culture Machine.* One idea brilliantly laid out in *Red Plenty Platforms* is that planned economy was not able to outflank the market because the Party's computational capacity was not adequate to the situation of production and distribution in the field. As Hayek claimed, it was not possible to figure out who needed what, when, where and how to distribute it in the way that matched the speed and the efficiency with which the market at that stage of technical development functioned. The idea that I am developing in *Computational Capital*, is that capitalism today functions like a computer, is, in fact, a computer. Early capitalism was really Digital Culture 1.0 and represented the imposition of large-scale quantification upon the life-world. Famously, capitalism turns qualities into quantities. Digital Culture 2.0 with the advent of the Universal Turing

Machine becomes an intensification of that process of working on the world by means of numbers, in part through the ability to represent and manipulate any element whatever to the point at which both markets and galaxy formation can today be simulated by big digital computers. Seeing computation as emerging out of capital-logic marks the discrete state machine as another evolutionary moment, a kind of sea change, that I am tempted to say definitively confirms the need to change the way in which one thinks about the history of the screen and of cinema in accord with what I attempted in *The CMP*, and also places so-called digital culture (the pundits leave off the 2.0) where it belongs, that is to say at the very center of financialization. The fact is that computation has advanced to the point where it can and does track capitalist practices. For example, as Dyer-Witherford shows by citing Jameson's characteristically unforgettable analysis of Wal-Mart, Wal-Mart handles and tracks more than 680 million items per week and 20 million customer transactions per day; that's an unbelievable amount of information and it is used to increase both the efficiency of Wal-Mart's distribution of use-values and the vast fortune of Waltons. Wouldn't it be possible, Dyer-Witherford asks, to create communist agents or communist algorithms? I think that it is possible and necessary. If capitalism is actually organizing time in increasingly small fragments and discourse in increasingly small pieces, then it is functioning to program sight, sound and time; and if it is programming sight, sound and time, these can also be deprogrammed or reprogrammed—at the speed of life and in ways in which collective social knowledge organizes production and distribution. I don't want this to sound like a cliché, but to a certain extent this intensification of communication is something that we want, this is, the collectivization of life is the other side of the real subsumption. Significant aspects of the processes of communication and interconnection which have been developed are actually, like visual culture before, consequences of the desire of people to talk to one another, to know one another, to be among each other: the desire for solidarity, mutual recognition, autonomy, peace. The problem has been that these technologies of exchange have been captured through the logic of private property. As "Bifo" might say, the general intellect is alienated—it is in search of a body. You have users of Facebook or Google left out of what could be the far more profound benefits of a Facebook or a Google, platforms that though collectively built are privatized and geared towards making profits to be shared only among shareholders. All that work of attention, all that infrastructure provided by bodies and minds and their practical activities, new habits and desires, are stolen and then sold on the market. We need to understand and to rethink those practices. Communist computing would mean rethinking from the ground up the interface and the bios within the digital domain. I don't know if that is a concept, but it is certainly an aspiration.

Notes

Contents

1. A section of Chapter 4, "Another Method for the Letters," was published in *Social Text* 26.3—it has been revised. Two chapters of Part II have been published in different venues: Chapter 6, "Camera Obscura After All," in *Scholar and Feminist* (2012); Chapter 7, "Pathologistics of Attention," in *Discourse* (2013)—also revised. Sections of Chapter 9 were published as "Informatic Labor in the Age of Computational Capital" in *Lateral*, 5.1 (2016)—these have been thoroughly revised. The last few pages of this chapter owe a tremendous debt to my work with the Economic Space Agency (ECSA) collective.

Introduction

1. Cedric Robinson, *Black Marxism* (Chapel Hill & London: The University of North Carolina Press, 2000).
2. Ruth Wilson Gilmore, *Golden Gulag: Prisons, Surplus, Crisis, and Opposition in Globalizing California* (Berkeley, Los Angeles, London: University of California Press, 2007) 28.
3. Norbert Weiner, *Cybernetics: or Control and Communication in the Animal and the Machine*, 2nd edition (New York: MIT Press, 1961).
4. Robin Kelley, "Thug Nation: On State Violence and Disposability," in Jordan Camp and Christina Heatherton, eds., *Policing the Planet*, London: Verso, 2017. See Simone Browne, *Dark Matters: On the Surveillance of Blackness*. Duke University Press. 2015. See also Katherine McKittrick, "Mathematics Black Life," *The Black Scholar: Journal of Black Studies and Research*, 44:2, 16–28.
5. Benjamin H. Bratton, *The Stack: On Software and Sovereignty* (Cambridge, MA: MIT Press, 2016).
6. Mary Keeler and Christian Kloesel, "Communication, Semiotic Continuity, and the Margins of the Peircean Text," in (ed) David Greetham, *Margins of the Text* (Ann Arbor: University of Michigan Press, 1997), 5.

Chapter 1

1. Antonio Gramsci, "State and Civil Society," in *Selections from the Prison Notebooks*, translated by Quintin Hoare and Geoffrey Nowell Smith (New York: International Publishers, 1971) 171.

2. Hortense Spillers, Mama's Baby, Papa's Maybe: An American Grammar Book," *Diacritics*, vol. 17, No. 2 (Summer 1987), pp. 64–81.

3. Wiener, *Cybernetics*, 160.

4. Karl Marx, *A contribution to the critique of political economy*, in (ed) R. C. Tucker, *The Marx-Engels Reader* (New York and London: Norton, 1859/1978).

5. Weiner, *Cybernetics*, 180.

6. Antonio Gramsci, "The Modern Prince," in *Selections from the Prison Notebooks*, translated by Quintin Hoare and Geoffrey Nowell Smith (New York: International Publishers, 1971), 388.

7. Max Horkheimer and Theodor W. Adorno, *Dialectic of Enlightenment*, (ed) Gunzelin Schmid Noerr, translated by Edmund Jephcott (Stanford: Stanford University Press, 2002) 23.

8. And the non-subject of OOO. Conference idea: ooo>OOO or vice versa?

9. Vilém Flusser, *Towards a Philosophy of Photograpy* (London: Reaktion Books, 2007).

10. Alan Turing, "On Computable Numbers. With an Application to the Entscheidungsproblem," *Proceedings of the London Mathematical Society*, 2nd series, vol. 42 (1936), pp. 230–65.

11. Horkheimer/Adorno, DE, 12–13.

12. Marshall McLuhan, *The Gutenberg Galaxy* (Toronto: University of Toronto Press, 2011), 312–13.

13. Marshall McLuhan, *Understanding Media: The Extensions of Man* (New York: McGraw-Hill, 1964), 205.

14. Nick Dyer-Witheford, "Red Plenty Platforms," *Culture Machine*, vol 14 (2013), pp. 1–27.

Chapter 2

1. Jorge Luis Borges, "The Garden of the Forking Paths," in *Ficciones*, translated by Anthony Kerrigan (New York: Grove, 1962), 34.

2. Ibid., 30.

3. Ibid., 31.

4. Ibid., 32.

5. Here I borrow theoretical vocabulary from Neferti Tadiar, whose terms life-time and remainder, offer precise dialectical advances with respect to the development of labor and the codification of subjectivity. See Neferti Tadiar, "City Everywhere," *Theory, Culture and Society*, vol. 33 (7–8) (2016), pp. 57–83.

6. I will address some of the aspects of non-Western, namely Soviet and Chilean, cybernetics in a forthcoming essay, "Digital Specters of Communism," *Social Identities* (forthcoming).

7. Guy Debord, *Society of the Spectacle*, translated by Black & Red (Detroit: Black & Red, 1977), no. 80.

8. See Jonathan Beller, "The Programmable Image," *Postmodern Culture*, vol. 26, no.2 (January 2016).

9. There is also an urgent question haunting whatever it is that Marxism is becoming, that of the concept of totality vs. the registration and mobilization of forms of social difference. Does a totalizing concept of the world system—itself a theoretical wager, an (essentially violent) abstraction, and not necessarily a given—have anything to contribute to the struggles that have been of late, both more urgently waged and indeed more successfully waged when staged on the basis of the experience of antagonism: the ostensibly analogue categories and fault lines of sexuality, race, nation and even class. These domains, are of course (and as we have seen), not without their codes, and the enemy, found everywhere, "knows" that or at least acts in ways that speak the systems language of racialization and social differentiation—giving what is necessary with one hand while taking with the other. The imperative is to come to terms with computational capitalism as racial capitalism, with computational capitalism as sex/gender capitalism. The point is to understand racialized violence and sex/gender violence as part of a program in all senses of that term.

10. Roberto Fernández Retamar, *Caliban and Other Essays*, translated by Edward Baker (Minneapolis: University of Minnesota Press, 1989), 29.

11. Retamar, 28.

12. Ibid., 45.

13. Ibid.

14. Diane M. Nelson, *Who Counts: The Mathematics of Death and Life after Genocide*, Durham and London: Duke University Press, 2015.

Chapter 3

1. Alan Turing, "Computing Machinery and Intelligence," *Mind*, vol. 59 no. 236 (October 1950) in *The New Media Reader*, (ed) Waldrip Fuin and Nick Montfort (Cambridge, MA: MIT Press, 2003), 50–64.

2. Turing, "Computing Machinery and Intelligence," 60.

3. Turing, "Computing, Machinery and Intelligence."

4. Katherine Hayles, *How We Became Posthuman: Virtual Bodies in Cybernetics, Literature, and Informatics* (Stanford: Stanford University Press, 1999).

5. Turing, "Computing Machinery and Intelligence," 50.

6. In friendly disagreement with Jacob Gaboury, I would here want to suggest that Turing's theory of computing was queer not only in relation to "uncomputable numbers," but to the core.

7. Emma Goss, "The Artificially Intelligent Woman: Talking Down to the Female Machine," Senior thesis submitted to Department of American Studies, Barnard College, Columbia University (unpublished manuscript); 2015.

8. Emma Goss, 13.

9. Ibid., 6.

10. Ibid.

11. Turing, "Computing Machinery and Intelligence," 58.

12. Turing, "Computing Machinery and Intelligence," 63.

13. Friedrich A. Kittler, *Gramophone, Film, Typewriter*, translated by Geoffrey Winthrop Young and Michael Wutz (Stanford: Stanford University Press, 1999), 18.

14. Turing, "Computing Machinery and Intelligence," 55.

15. Ibid.

16. Turing, "Computing Machinery and Intelligence," 56.

17. Ibid.

18. Ibid.

19. Ibid.

20. Fredric Jameson, *The Political Unconscious: Narrative as a Socially Symbolic Act*, (Cornell, Cornell University Press, 2014), 35.

Chapter 4

1. With thanks to Tavia Nyong'o for insightful commentary.

2. Kittler, *Gramophone, Film, Typewriter*, 4.

3. Claude E. Shannon. "A Mathematical Theory of Communication," in *Bell Labs Innovations,* 1998, with corrections from *Bell System Technical Journal* 27 (1948), pp. 1, 379–423, 623–56.

4. Shannon, "Mathematical Theory of Communication," 1.

5. Shannon, "Mathematical Theory of Communication," 2–3.

6. Jorge Luis Borges. "The Library of Babel," in *Collected Fictions*, translated by Andrew Hurley (New York: Penguin, 1999). I am grateful to Lucinda Warchol for reminding me of this passage.

7. Shannon, "Mathematical Theory of Communication," 6–7.

8. Ibid.

9. Jacques Lacan, "The Agency of the Letter in the Unconscious, or Reason since Freud," in Écrits: A Selection, translated by Alan Sheridan (London: Tavistock, 1977), 146–78.

10. Freud writes, "An ego thus educated has become 'reasonable'; it no longer lets itself be governed by the pleasure principle, but obeys the reality principle, which also, at bottom, seeks to obtain pleasure, but pleasure which is assured through taking account of reality, even though it is pleasure postponed and diminished." Sigmund Freud, *Introductory Lectures on Psychoanalysis. Vol. 1* (Harmondsworth, UK: Penguin, 1974), 402–3.

11. This invocation of Borges refers to another section in *The Message Is Murder*.

12. Michel Foucault, *The History of Sexuality: Vol.1 An Introduction*, translated by Robert Hurley (New York: Pantheon Books, 1978), 49; Eva Illouz, "Suffering, Emotional Fields, and Emotional Capital," in *Cold Intimacies* (London: Polity, 2007), 40–73.

13. For a similar reading of this film albeit in a different key, see my article "Pathologistics of Attention."

14. Laurence A. Rickles, *The Psycho Records* (London and New York: Wallflower Press, 2016), 152–68. Great title for a great book. For variety peppered with revelation try putting the emphasis on the last word of the title.

15. Lydia H. Liu, *The Freudian Robot: Digital Media and the Future of the Unconscious* (Chicago: University of Chicago Press, 2010).

16. Shannon, "Mathematical Theory of Communication," 7–8.

17. "If the language is translated into binary digits (0 or 1) in the most efficient way, the entropy is the average number of binary digits required per letter of the original language. The redundancy, on the other hand, measures the amount of constraint imposed on a text in the language due to its statistical structure—for example, in English the high frequency of the letter ε, the strong tendency of H to follow T or of V to follow Q. It was estimated that when statistical effects extending over not more than eight letters are considered, the entropy is roughly 2.3 bits per letter, the redundancy about 50 percent." Claude Shannon, "Prediction and Entropy of Printed English," *The Bell System Technical Journal*, (January 1951), p. 50.

18. See Shannon, "Prediction and Entropy of Printed English," *The Bell System Technical Journal*, (January 1951), p. 57.

19. Marshall McLuhan, *Understanding Media: The Extensions of Man* (New York: McGraw-Hill, 1964).

20. Wikipedia, "Dumas Malone," en.wikipedia.org/wiki/Dumas_Malone (Accessed April 14, 2017).

21. Hortense Spillers, "Mama's Baby, Papa's Maybe: An American Grammar Book," *diacritics* 17, no. 2 Spillers (1987), p. 67.

22. Wikipedia, "Dumas Malone."

23. Annette Gordon-Reed, *Thomas Jefferson and Sally Hemings: An American Controversy* (Charlottesville: University of Virginia Press, 1998), 80–83.

24. Shannon, "Mathematical Theory of Communication," 53.

25. Shannon, "Prediction and Entropy of Printed English," 54.

26. See for example the works of Julia Kristeva, Hélène Cixous, and Luce Irigaray.

Chapter 5

1. Karl Marx, "Economic and Philosophic Manuscripts of 1844," in *The Marx-Engels Reader*, (ed) R. C. Tucker, (New York and London: Norton, 1978), 79.

2. Marx, *MER*, 114.

3. Sean Cubitt, "Decolonizing Ecomedia," *Cultural Politics*, vol. 10, issue 3; 275–86 (2014) see also Cubitt, "Integral Waste," *Theory, Culture, Society* (June 2014) p. 1–13.

4. Donna Haraway, "Anthropocene, Capitalocene, Plantationocene, Chthulucene: Making Kin," *Environmental Humanities*, vol. 6 (2015) pp. 159–65.

5. The plasiticity of the environment is then dramatically affected by the emergence of the dynamics of the value-form, an emergence which is itself a computational process. Thus we see that the organization of matter, though extrinsic to value is nonetheless subject to its permutations. Catherine Malabou, who identifies neuro-plasticity as at once "the capacity to receive

form" and "the capacity to give form" well understands the social history, that is, the dialectics of the brain as a structure. She writes, "How could we not note a similarity of functioning between this economic organization and the neuronal organization? How could we not interrogate the parallelism between the transformation of the spirit of capitalism between the sixties and the nineties) and the modification, brought about in approximately the same period, of our view of the cerebral structures? I have underlined the effect of the naturalization of the social attached to neuronal functioning. Boltanski and Chiapello confirm this: 'This is how the forms of capitalist production accede to representation in each epoch, by mobilizing concepts and tools that were initially developed largely autonomously in the theoretical sphere or in the domain of basic scientific research. This is the case with neurology and computer science today. In the past it was true of such notions as system, structure, technostructure, energy entropy, evolution, dynamics and exponential growth' (). Like neuronal cohesion, contemporary corporate economic and social organization is not of a central or centralizing type but rests on a plurality of mobile and atomistic centers, deployed according to a connectionist model. In this sense, it appears that neuronal functioning has become the nature of the social even more than its naturalizing tool. Catherine Malabou, *What Should We Do with Our Brain?* (New York: Fordham University Press, 2008), 5, 41–2.

6. Karl Marx, *Capital Vol.1*, cited in (ed) R. C. Tucker, *The Marx-Engels Reader* (New York and London: Norton, 1978), 201.

7. Sebastian Franklin, *Control: Digitality as Cultural Logic* (Cambridge, MA: MIT Press), 24. Italics in original.

8. Marx, *Capital: A Critique of Political Economy*, vol. 1, translated by Samuel Moore and Edward Aveling, (London: Lawrence & Wishart, 1996), 55.

9. Franklin, *Control*, 24.

10. Norbert Weiner, *Cybernetics*, cited in N. Katherine Hayles, *How We Became Post-Human* (Chicago and London: The University of Chicago Press, 1999), 14.

11. Weiner, *Cybernetics*, 125.

12. Alan Turing, "On Computable Numbers. With an Application to the Entscheidungsproblem," *Proceedings of the London Mathematical Society*, 2nd series, vol. 42 (1936), pp. 230–65. For an amazing text on this text, see Charles Petzold, *The Annotated Turing* (Indianapolis: Wiley Publishing Inc., 2008).

13. Neferti Tadiar, "City Everywhere," *Theory, Culture and Society*, vol. 33 (7–8) (2016): 57–83.

14. Karl Marx, *Karl Marx, Frederick Engels: Collected Works, Volume 28* (London: Lawrence & Wishart, 1986), 125.

15. Marx, *V28*, 129.

16. The distinction between the price of a particular "commodity x" and value inherent in a particular "commodity x" amounts to the distinction between a proprietary contract (as price) and a specific derivative of the social totality at point "commodity x"—an exchange value as a measure of

abstract universal labor time. The market is a space of adequation where in one and the same process value can realize its price and capital can valorize itself. The expansion of the market meant the proliferation of both exchange values and prices. These quantitative transformations lead to qualitative shifts, as, for example the shift from the commodity as object to the commodity as integrated components distributed across a network. In the CMP I argued that price was a proto-image, that the fetish character of the commodity was already a becoming-image of the commodity-form. Leaving aside the fascinating discussion of photography as a "civil contract" (Azoulay), let me just say here that with the expansion of prices into images comes the development of exchange value into information. This is another way of saying that new orders of pricing were being born that required both the generalization of exchange value as information and the movement of commodification away from objects per se toward sociality itself. Returning to Borges we note the requirement for new methods of measurement and accounting necessary for the increasing complexity of social relations materially affecting every spatio-temporal movement. The "information age" follows upon the Industrial Revolution as a transformation in the modality of capitalist exploitation, as the first blush of computational capital.

17. Marx, $V28$, 131–2.
18. Ibid., 154.
19. Ibid., 155.
20. Ibid.
21. Marx, $V28$, 157.
22. See Brian Rotman, *Signifying Nothing: The Semiotics of Zero* (New York: St. Martin's Press, 1987).
23. I can think of no better example of this practice than Diane Nelson's book *Who Counts*. Diane M. Nelson, *Who Counts: The Mathematics of Death and Life after Genocide*, Durham and London: Duke University Press, 2015.
24. Cited in Benjamin Peters, *How Not to Network a Nation: The Uneasy History of the Soviet Internet* (Cambridge, MA and London: MIT, 2016), p. 15.
25. MIT Physicist Max Tegmark claims that consciousness is a state of matter. And "how the particular properties of consciousness might arise from the physical laws that govern our universe. Interestingly, the new approach to consciousness has come from outside the physics community, principally from neuroscientists such as Giulio Tononi at the University of Wisconsin in Madison. In 2008, Tononi proposed that a system demonstrating consciousness must have two specific traits. First, the system must be able to store and process large amounts of information. In other words consciousness is essentially a phenomenon of information. And second, this information must be integrated in a unified whole so that it is impossible to divide into independent parts. That reflects the experience that each instance of consciousness is a unified whole that cannot be decomposed into separate components. Both of these traits can be specified, mathematically allowing physicists like Tegmark to reason about them for the first time. He begins by outlining the basic properties that a conscious system must have. Given

that it is a phenomenon of information, a conscious system must be able to store in a memory and retrieve it efficiently. It must also be able to process this data, like a computer but one that is much more flexible and powerful than the silicon-based devices we are familiar with. Tegmark borrows the term computronium to describe matter that can do this and cites other work showing that today's computers underperform the theoretical limits of computing by some 38 orders of magnitude. (https://medium.com/the-physics-arxiv-blog/why-physicists-are-saying-consciousness-is-a-state-of-matter-like-a-solid-a-liquid-or-a-gas-5e7ed624986d)

Chapter 6

1. Paul Virilio, *Speed and Politics*, trans. Mark Polizzotti (New York: Semiotext(e), 2006).
2. Jacqueline Goldsby, *A Spectacular Secret: Lynching in American Life and Literature* (Chicago: University of Chicago Press, 2006), p. 237.
3. Ibid., 238.
4. Stephen Heath, "Questions of Cinema" in *Narrative, Apparatus, Ideology: A Film Theory Reader*, ed. Philip Rosen (New York: Columbia University Press, 1986).
5. Martin Jay, "Scopic Regimes of Modernity," *Vision and Visuality*, (ed) Hal Foster (New York: New Press, 1988).
6. Gilles Deleuze and Claire Parnet, *Dialogues*, trans. Hugh Tomlinson and Barbara Habberjam (New York: Columbia University Press, 1987).
7. Jacques Lacan, *The Four Fundamental Concepts of Psychoanalysis*, translated by Alan Sheridan (New York: W. W. Norton, 1977), 106.
8. See Chela Sandoval, *Methodology of the Oppressed* (Minneapolis: University of Minnesota Press, 2000) and Fred Moten, *In the Break: The Aesthetics of the Black Radical Tradition* (Minneapolis: University of Minnesota Press, 2003).
9. Roland Barthes, *Camera Lucida: Reflections on Photography*, trans. Richard Howard (New York: Hill and Wang, 1982), 10.
10. Ibid., 11.
11. Frantz Fanon, *Black Skin, White Masks*, trans. Richard Philcox (New York: Grove, 2008), 113.
12. Barthes, *Camera Lucida*, 13.
13. Barthes, *Camera Lucida*, 81.
14. Saidiya V. Hartman, *Scenes of Subjection: Terror, Slavery, and Self-Making in Nineteenth-Century America* (Oxford: Oxford University Press, 1997).
15. See Vicente Rafael, *White Love and Other Events in Filipino History* (Durham: Duke UP, 2000); Malek Alloula, *The Colonial Harem*, trans. Myrna Godzich and Wlad Godzich (Minneapolis: University of Minnesota Press, 1986); Jane Gaines, *Contested Culture: the Image, the Voice and the Law* (Chapel Hill: University of North Carolina Press, 1991).
16. Franklin, Control, 30.
17. Barthes, *Camera Lucida*, 34.

18. Richard Avedon, *William Casby, Born a Slave*, in Barthes, *Camera Lucida*, 35.

19. Barthes, *Camera Lucida*, 36.

20. Barthes, *Camera Lucida*, 80. Italics in the original.

21. Regis Debray, *Media Manifestos: On the Technological Transmission of Cultural Forms* (London: Verso, 1996), 31.

22. Jacqueline Goldsby, *A Spectacular Secret: Lynching in American Life and Literature* (Chicago: University of Chicago Press, 2006), 249.

23. Gwendolyn Audrey Foster, *Captive Bodies: Postcolonial Subjectivity in Cinema* (Albany: State University of New York Press, 1999); Hortense Spillers, "Mama's Baby, Papa's Maybe: An American Grammar Book," *Diacritics* vol.17, no.2 (1987).

24. Vilém Flusser, *Towards a Philosophy of Photography*, trans. Anthony Matthews (London: Reaktion, 2000).

Chapter 7

1. George Lukacs, "The Ideology of Modernism" in (ed) Arpad Kadarkay, *The Lukacs Reader* (Oxford: Blackwell, 1962/1995).

2. Regis Debray, *Media Manifestos: On the Technological Transmission of Cultural Forms* (London: Verso, 1996), 13.

3. Benjamin H. Bratton, *The Stack: On Software and Sovereignty* (Cambridge, MA: MIT Press, 2016).

4. Karl Marx, "Economic and Philosophic Manuscripts of 1844," in The Marx-Engels Reader, edited by Robert Taylor (New York and London: Norton, 1978), 89.

5. Lawrence Rickels, *The Psycho Records* (London and New York: Wallflower Press, 2016).

6. Allen Feldman, *Archives of the Insensible: War, Photopolitics, and Dead Memory* (Chicago: University of Chicago Press, 2016).

7. While the shattering of historically and biopolitically established continuities (of the sensory-motor schema, of the temporality of contemplation, of the grammar of sense) through the fragmentation and fractalization of attention by and as media technologies indicate the objective matrix of events that capital-logic has imposed upon the numerous members of our species, the psycho-subjective results of post-Fordist digital labor are aphasia, abjection, autism, dyslexia, fear, panic, exhaustion, and collapse. In this context of expropriation distributed over the whole social field and of its resultant physical, psychic, and metaphysical collapses, it is difficult to identify the real source of our problems. For an excellent account on the emergence and formation of attentional practices, see Bernard Stiegler, "Relational Ecology and the Digital Pharmakon," Culture Machine 3 (2012), www.culture machine.net/index.php/cm/article/view/464/501 [Accessed April 14, 2017].

8. Owen Hatherley, *The Chaplin Machine: Slapstick, Fordism and the Communist Avant-garde* (London: Pluto Press, 2016), 42.

9. Walter Benjamin, "Chaplin," in Michael W Jennings, Howard Eiland and Gary Smith (eds), *Walter Benjamin: Selected Writings Volume 2: Part 1 1927–1930* (Cambridge, MA: Harvard University Press, 1929/2005), 94; cited in Owen Hatherley, *The Chaplin Machine: Slaptstick, Fordism, and the Communist Avant-Garde* (London: Pluto Press, 2016), 43.

10. Nor, I think, does the fact that the scene was created with what was known as a glass shot: "The deep drop-off to the department store's lower floors was actually painted on a pane of glass, placed in front of the camera and perfectly aligned with the real setting, creating a seamless illusion." For the full text, see Bill Demain, "6 Dangerous Stunts of the Silent Movie Era," *Mental Floss* (August 4, 2011) http://mentalfloss.com/article/28422/6-dangerous-stunts-silent-movie-era#ixzz2WDaJv8RG.

11. Second version in *Walter Benjamin: Selected Writing Volume 3: 1935-38*, Howard Eiland and Michael W Jennings (eds) (Cambridge: Harvard University Press, 2002), 118.

12. Andre Bazin, *What Is Cinema?, Vol. 1*, translated by Hugh Gray (Berkeley and Los Angeles: University of California Press, 1973).

13. Gilles Deleuze, *Cinema 2: The Time-Image* (London: Continuum, 1989), 98ff.

14. Sigmund Freud, "Fetishism," in *The Standard Edition of the Complete Psychological Works of Freud*, vol. 21, (ed) James Strachey (London: Hogarth, 1927/1961), 154.

15. Antonio Gramsci, "State and Civil Society," in *Selections from the Prison Notebooks*, translated by Quintin Hoare and Geoffrey Nowell Smith (New York: International Publishers, 1971), 206–76.

16. Walter Benjamin, "The Work of Art in the Age of Mechanical Reproduction," in *Illuminations* (New York: Schocken, 1968), 218.

17. Julia Kristeva, *The Kristeva Reader*, (ed) Toril Moi (New York: Columbia University Press, 1986), 7. Italics in original.

18. Laura Mulvey, "Visual Pleasure and Narrative Cinema," in Visual and Other Pleasures (Bloomington and Indianapolis: Indiana University Press, 1989), 14.

19. Ibid.

20. François Truffaut, *Hitchcock/Truffaut* (New York: Simon and Schuster, 1967). Accessed in excerpted form at http://somecamerunning.typepad.com/some_came_running/2012/11/literary-interlude.html. [Accessed April 17, 2017].

21. Mulvey, "Visual Pleasure and Narrative Cinema," 19.

22. Sylvi Federici, *Revolution at Point Zero: Housework, Reproduction, and Feminist Struggle* (Oakland, CA: PM Press, 2012).

23. Mulvey, "Visual Pleasure and Narrative Cinema," 20–21.

Chapter 8

1. The numbers vary, of course. See, for example, John Thomas Didymus, "Pornography, 'Everybody' Is Watching It, Statistics Say," *Digital Journal*

(April 9, 2012) http://digitaljournal.com/article/322668 [Accessed April 16, 2017].

2. Bernard Stiegler, *For a New Critique of Political Economy*, translated by Daniel Ross, 45–56 (Cambridge, UK: Polity, 2010). See also Herbert Marcuse, *One-Dimensional Man* (New York: Beacon, 1964).

3. Frantz Fanon, *Black Skin, White Masks* (New York: Grove, 1967).

4. Anne Anlin Cheng, *The Melancholy of Race: Psychoanalysis, Assimilation, and Hidden Grief* (New York: Oxford University Press, 2001).

5. Ibid., 11.

6. Ibid., 14.

7. bell hooks, "The Oppositional Gaze: Black Female Spectators," in *The Feminism and Visual Culture Reader*, (ed) Amelia Jones (London: Routledge, 2003), 94–105.

8. Frank B. Wilderson III, *Red, White & Black: Cinema and the Structure of U.S. Antagonisms* (Durham & London: Duke University Press, 2010), 304.

9. Wilderson, 265.

10. Wilderson, 263.

11. Wilderson, 281.

12. Raoul Peck, *I Am Not Your Negro: A Major Motion Picture By Raoul Peck* (New York: Vintage Books, 2017), 87.

13. Cheng, *The Melancholy of Race*, 9.

14. Cheng, *The Melancholy of Race*, 334.

15. Robert Silva, "Flashback Five—The Best Dirty Harry Movies," *AMC Blog* (September 10, 2010), http://blogs.amctv.com/movie-blog/2010/09/the-best-dirtyharry-movies.php.

16. Nicole Fleetwood, *Troubling Vision* (Chicago: University of Chicago Press, 2011).

17. Grégoire Chamayou, *A Theory of the Drone* (New York: New Press, 2015).

18. See Allen Feldman, "The Structuring Enemy and Archival War," *PMLA* 124, no. 5 (2009), pp. 1704–13, and "Securocratic Wars of Public Safety: Globalized Policing as Scopic Regime," *Interventions* 6, no. 3 (2004), pp. 330–50. See also Allen Feldman, *Archives of the Insensible: War, Photopolitics and Dead Memory*, University of Chicago Press, 2016.

19. Medea Benjamin in *Drone Warfare: Killing By Remote Control* (New York & London: Verso Books, 2013), 158.

20. Benjamin, *Drone Warfare*, 157.

21. Franklin, *Control*, 166.

22. Ibid.

23. Benjamin H. Bratton, *The Stack: On Software and Sovereignty* (Cambridge, MA: MIT Press, 2016).

24. Alexander Galloway, *The Interface Effect* (Cambridge, UK: Polity, 2012), 21.

25. Ibid., 22, emphasis in original.

26. Vilém Flusser, *Towards a Philosophy of Photography* (London: Reaktion Books, 2007).

27. W. J. T. Mitchell, "There Are No Visual Media," *Journal of Visual Culture* 4, no. 2 (2005), pp. 257–66.

28. Tadiar, "City Everywhere."

29. Paul Virilio, *The Administration of Fear* (New York: Semiotext(e), 2012), 30.

30. Ibid., 30, 31.

31. Jonathan Beller, *The Cinematic Mode of Production: Attention Economy and the Society of the Spectacle* (Lebanon, NH: Dartmouth College Press/ University Press of New England, 2006).

32. Maria Alyokhina, Nadezhda Tolokonnikova, and Yekaterina Samutsevich, "Pussy Riot Closing Statements," *n+1* (August 13, 2012), http://nplusonemag. com/pussy-riot-closing-statements. [Accessed April 17, 2017]

33. Jean Baudrillard, "Requiem for the Media," in *The New Media Reader* (ed) Waldrip Fuin and Nick Montfort (Cambridge, MA: MIT Press, 2003), 277–88.

34. Jorge Luis Borges, "The Garden of the Forking Paths," in *Ficciones*, translated by Anthony Kerrigan (New York: Grove, 1962), 89–104.

35. Guy Debord, *The Society of the Spectacle* (New York: Zone Books, 1994), 12.

36. Marx, "Economic and Philosophic Manuscripts of 1844," 133. Flusser makes a similar argument in *Towards a Philosophy of Photography*. Vilém Flusser, *Towards a Philosophy of Photography*, translated by Anthony Matthews (London: Reaktion, 2000).

Chapter 9

1. Walter Benjamin, "The Work of Art in the Age of Mechanical Reproduction," in *Illuminations*, translated by Hannah Arendt (New York: Schocken, 1969), 241.

2. Sara Ahmed, "Affective Economies," *Social Text*, 22.2 (2004), pp. 117–39.

3. See anarchiveofourown.org, "a fan-created, fan-run, non-profit, non-commercial archive for transformative fanworks, like fanfiction, fanart, fan videos, and podfic." See also, Allen Feldman, *Archives of the Insensible: Of War, Photopolitics and Dead Memory* (Chicago: University of Chicago Press, 2016).

4. Romano Alquati, see Matteo Pasquinelli, "Italian Operaismo and the Information Machine," *Theory, Culture & Society*, 32(3) (February 2, 2014).

5. Jonathan Beller, "The Programmable Image of Capital: M-I-C-I'-M' and the World Computer," *Postmodern Culture*, vol. 26, no. 2 (January 2016).

6. Beller, *The Cinematic Mode of Production*.

7. As we saw earlier, Cubitt brilliantly argues that "the environment" as an idea is itself the result of the economic "externalities" of the accounting systems of capitalism and colonialism—it is the supposedly extrinsic space of capital (the colonies, "nature") where it can freely dump its waste, including the energetic and toxic waste of computational processes. See Sean Cubitt, "Decolononizing Ecomedia," *Cultural Politics*, vol.10, no.3 (2014), pp. 275–86; and "Integral Waste," *Theory, Culture and Society* (July 27, 2014).

8. Franco "Bifo" Berardi, *After the Future* (Edinburgh, Oakland, Baltimore: AK Press, 2011), 35.

9. The working conditions at Foxconn factories are fairly well known, but mining conditions for tin and coltan in Congo are less well documented, as is the emergence of this brutal rare-earth industry in the footprint of rubber plantations. For more see Kevin Bales, "Your Phone Was Made By Slaves: A Primer on the Secret Economy" from Bales, *Blood and Earth: Modern Slavery, Ecocide, and the Secret to Saving the World* (New York: Spiegel and Grau, 2016) excerpted at blog.longreads.com.

10. In the article sighted above, Pasquinelli outlines three determinations of metadata *1. Metadata as the measure of the value of social relations. 2. Metadata as implementation of machinic intelligence. 3. Metadata as new form of biopolitical control (dataveillance),* Pasquinelli, "The Labor of Abstraction," 64.

11. Tadiar, "City Everywhere," 57–83.

12. *The Information Nexus: Global Capitalism from the Renaissance to the Present* (Cambridge: Cambridge University Press, 2016).

13. For an excellent analysis see, Max Haiven, *Cultures of Financialization: Fictitious Capital in Popular Culture and Everyday Life* (Palgrave Macmillan, 2014).

14. See ethereum.org for the details.

Index

Made in United States
North Haven, CT
08 February 2023

32194025R00136